Rail-Trails
New Jersey
& New York

The definitive guide to the region's top multiuse trails

T0151124

WILDERNESS PRESS ... *on the trail since 1967*

Rail-Trails: New Jersey & New York
1st Edition, 6th printing 2024
Copyright © 2019 by Rails-to-Trails Conservancy
Cover and interior photographs copyright © 2019 by Rails-to-Trails Conservancy

Maps: Lohnes+Wright; map data © OpenStreetMap contributors
Cover design: Scott McGrew
Book design and layout: Annie Long

Library of Congress Cataloging-in-Publication Data

Names: Rails-to-Trails Conservancy, author.
Title: Rail-trails : New Jersey & New York : the definitive guide to the region's top
    multiuse trails / Rails-to-Trails Conservancy.
Other titles: Rail trails New Jersey and New York | Rail trails New Jersey | Rail trails
    New York
Description: First Edition. | Birmingham, Alabama : Wilderness Press, an imprint
    of AdventureKEEN, [2019] | Series: Rails-to-Trails Conservancy guidebook |
    "Distributed by Publishers Group West"—T.p. verso. | Includes index.
Identifiers: LCCN 2018061564| ISBN 9780899979656 (paperback) |
    ISBN 9780899979663 (ebook)
Classification: LCC GV199.42.N5 R35 2019 | DDC 796.50974—dc23
LC record available at https://lccn.loc.gov/2018061564

Manufactured in China

Published by: 🐸 **WILDERNESS PRESS**
              An imprint of AdventureKEEN
              2204 First Ave. S, Ste. 102
              Birmingham, AL 35233
              800-678-7006; fax 877-374-9016

Visit wildernesspress.com for a complete listing of our books and for ordering information. Contact us at our website, at facebook.com/wildernesspress1967, or at twitter.com
/wilderness1967 with questions or comments. To find out more about who we are and what
we're doing, visit blog.wildernesspress.com.

Distributed by Publishers Group West

Front and back cover: New York's Albany County Helderberg–Hudson Rail Trail (see page
74); front photographed by Kimberly Tate-Brown; back photographed by Brian Housh

SAFETY NOTICE: Although Wilderness Press and Rails-to-Trails Conservancy have
made every attempt to ensure that the information in this book is accurate at press time,
they are not responsible for any loss, damage, injury, or inconvenience that may occur to
anyone while using this book. You are responsible for your own safety and health while in
the wilderness. The fact that a trail is described in this book does not mean that it will be
safe for you. Be aware that trail conditions can change from day to day. Always check local
conditions, know your own limitations, and consult a map.

About Rails-to-Trails Conservancy

Headquartered in Washington, D.C., Rails-to-Trails Conservancy (RTC) is a nonprofit organization dedicated to creating a nationwide network of trails from former rail lines and connecting corridors to build healthier places for healthier people.

Railways helped build America. Spanning from coast to coast, these ribbons of steel linked people, communities, and enterprises, spurring commerce and forging a single nation that bridges a continent. But in recent decades, many of these routes have fallen into disuse, severing communal ties that helped bind Americans together.

When RTC opened its doors in 1986, the rail-trail movement was in its infancy. Most projects focused on single, linear routes in rural areas, created for recreation and conservation. RTC sought broader protection for the unused corridors, incorporating rural, suburban, and urban routes.

Year after year, RTC's efforts to protect and align public funding with trail building created an environment that allowed trail advocates in communities across the country to initiate trail projects. These ever-growing ranks of trail professionals, volunteers, and RTC supporters have built momentum for the national rail-trails movement. As the number of supporters multiplied, so did the rail-trails.

Americans now enjoy more than 23,000 miles of open rail-trails, and as they flock to the trails to connect with family members and friends, enjoy nature, and get to places in their local neighborhoods and beyond, their economic prosperity, health, and overall well-being continue to flourish.

A signature endeavor of RTC is **TrailLink.com,** America's portal to these rail-trails as well as other multiuse trails. When RTC launched TrailLink.com in 2000, our organization was one of the first to compile such detailed trail information on a national scale. Today, the website continues to play a critical role in both encouraging and satisfying the country's growing need for opportunities to ride, walk, skate, or run for recreation or transportation. This free trail-finder database—which includes detailed descriptions, interactive maps, photo galleries, and firsthand ratings and reviews—can be used as a companion resource to the trails in this guidebook.

With a grassroots community more than 1 million strong, RTC is committed to ensuring a better future for America made possible by trails and the connections they inspire. Learn more at **railstotrails.org.**

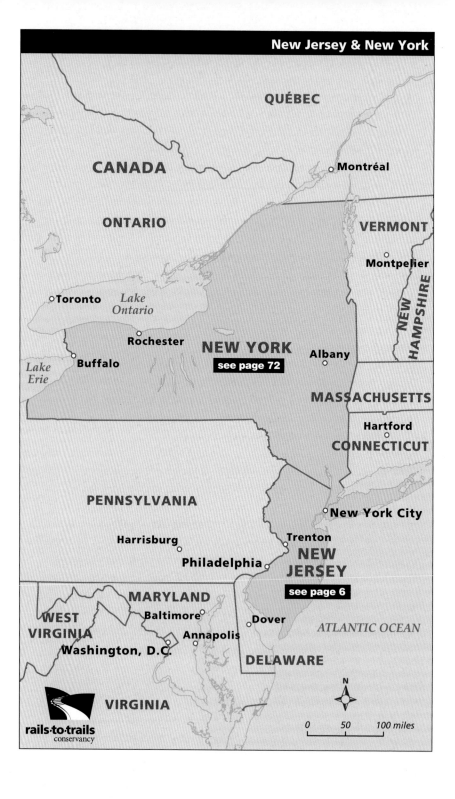

QUÉBEC

○ Montréal

CANADA

ONTARIO

VERMONT

○ Montpelier

NEW HAMPSHIRE

○ Toronto

Lake Ontario

Rochester ○

NEW YORK
see page 72

Albany ○

Lake Erie

Buffalo ○

MASSACHUSETTS

Hartford ○
CONNECTICUT

PENNSYLVANIA

○ New York City

Harrisburg ○

Trenton ○

Philadelphia ○

NEW JERSEY
see page 6

MARYLAND

Baltimore ○

Dover ○

ATLANTIC OCEAN

WEST VIRGINIA

Annapolis ○

Washington, D.C.

DELAWARE

rails·to·trails
conservancy

VIRGINIA

N

0   50   100 miles

Table of Contents

Nine miles of paved asphalt create an enjoyable riding experience on New York's Albany County Helderberg–Hudson Rail Trail (see page 74).

Welcome to *Rail-Trails: New Jersey & New York,* a comprehensive companion for discovering the region's top rail-trails and multiuse pathways. This guidebook will help you uncover fantastic opportunities to get outdoors on the region's trails—whether for exercise, transportation, or just pure fun.

Rails-to-Trails Conservancy's mission is to create a nationwide network of trails, just like these, to build healthier places for healthier people. We hope this book will inspire you to experience firsthand how trails can connect people to one another and to the places they love, while also creating connections to nature, history, and culture.

Since its founding in 1986, RTC has witnessed a massive growth in the rail-trail and active transportation movement. Today, more than 23,000 miles of completed rail-trails provide invaluable benefits for people and communities across the country. We hope you find this book to be a delightful and informative resource for discovering the many unique trail destinations throughout New Jersey and New York.

I'll be out on the trails, too, experiencing the thrill of the ride right alongside you. Be sure to say hello and share your experience with us on social media! We want to hear how you #GoByTrail. You can find us @railstotrails on Facebook, Instagram, and Twitter.

See you on the trail!

Ryan Chao, President
Rails-to-Trails Conservancy

Special acknowledgment goes to Laura Stark, editor of this guidebook, and to Derek Strout for his work on the creation of the trail maps included in the book. Rails-to-Trails Conservancy also thanks Gene Bisbee and Amy Ahn for their assistance in editing content. We are also appreciative of the following contributors, editors, and trail managers we called on for assistance to ensure the maps, photographs, and trail descriptions are as accurate as possible.

Kevin Belanger   Torsha Bhattacharya

Ryan Cree   Andrew Dupuy

Leah Gerber   Eli Griffen

Katie Guerin   Avery Harmon

Brandi Horton   Brian Housh

Alan Ibarra   Willie Karidis

Joe LaCroix   Anthony Le

Suzanne Matyas   Kevin Mills

Yvonne Mwangi   Liz Sewell

Leeann Sinpatanasakul   Patrick Wojahn

The 212-foot-high bridge that comprises New York's Walkway Over the Hudson (see page 193) affords views in all directions.

In *Rail-Trails: New Jersey & New York*, we highlight nearly 60 of the region's top rail-trails and other multiuse pathways. These trails offer a broad range of experiences to suit nearly every taste, from vibrant cities to quiet forests, from vacation hot spots like Niagara Falls to hidden gems in small rural towns, and from challenging mountain-biking adventures to relaxing beach boardwalks.

Four exemplary rail-trails in this book have been inducted into RTC's Hall of Fame, including New York City's High Line, a celebrated urban park and aerial greenway towering 30 feet over Manhattan's West Side. North of the Big Apple, a trio of connected Hall of Fame rail-trails—the Hudson Valley Rail Trail, Walkway Over the Hudson, and William R. Steinhaus Dutchess Rail Trail—form a seamless 20-mile paved pathway capturing the beauty of New York's Hudson Valley.

New York is also home to the Empire State Trail, a developing 750-mile trail network that will tie together hundreds of communities across 27 counties. Included in the expansive project is the Erie Canalway Trail, which will span 360 miles across the state from Albany to Buffalo. Along the way, travelers will see many tangible connections to history, including original canal locks, lift bridges, a century-old aqueduct, and a Colonial fort.

New Jersey also has an impressive growing trail network: the Circuit Trails, which will encompass 800 miles of trail in the Camden and Greater Philadelphia region. A crown jewel in this network is the incredibly scenic Delaware and Raritan Canal State Park Trail, which spans more than 70 miles in the shape of a V, with the New Jersey capital of Trenton at its center.

Within these pages, you'll find trails offering views of some of America's most iconic natural treasures, such as the Great Lakes, the Atlantic Ocean coastline, the Adirondacks, the Finger Lakes, and the Catskill Mountains. But no matter which routes in *Rail-Trails: New Jersey & New York* you choose, you'll experience the unique history, culture, and geography of each, as well as the communities that have built and embraced them.

What Is a Rail-Trail?

Rail-trails are multiuse public paths built along former railroad corridors. Most often flat or following a gentle grade, they are suited to walking, running, cycling, mountain biking, in-line skating, cross-country skiing, horseback riding, and wheelchair use. Since the 1960s, Americans have created more than 23,000 miles of rail-trails throughout the country.

OPPOSITE: *New York's Allegheny River Valley Trail (see page 77) provides recreational opportunities in all seasons.*

These extremely popular recreation and transportation corridors traverse urban, suburban, and rural landscapes. Many preserve historical landmarks, while others serve as wildlife conservation corridors, linking isolated parks and establishing greenways in developed areas. Rail-trails also stimulate local economies by boosting tourism and promoting trailside businesses.

What Is a Rail-with-Trail?

A rail-with-trail is a public path that parallels a still-active rail line. Some run adjacent to high-speed, scheduled trains, often linking public transportation stations, while others follow tourist routes and slow-moving excursion trains. Many share an easement, separated from the rails by extensive fencing. More than 350 rails-with-trails exist in the United States.

What Is the Rail-Trail Hall of Fame?

In 2007 RTC began recognizing exemplary rail-trails around the country through its Rail-Trail Hall of Fame. Inductees are selected based on such merits as scenic value, high use, trail and trailside amenities, historical significance, excellence in management and maintenance of facility, community connections, and geographic distribution. These iconic rail-trails, which have been singled out from more than 2,000 in the United States, have earned RTC's highest honor and represent tangible realizations of our vision to create a more walkable, bikeable, healthier America. Hall of Fame rail-trails are indicated in this book with a special blue icon; for the full list of Hall of Fame rail-trails, visit **railstotrails.org/halloffame.**

What Is TrailNation™?

At RTC, we believe that communities are healthier and happier when trails are central to their design. Everything we love about trails gets better when we connect them, creating seamless trail networks that link neighborhoods, towns, cities, and entire regions together. That's why we're committed to connecting trails and building comprehensive trail systems that bring people together and get them where they want to go.

We've invested in eight TrailNation™ projects across the country—found in places that are diverse in their geography, culture, size, and scope—to prove what is possible when trail networks are central to our lives. One of those TrailNation projects can be found in Pennsylvania and New Jersey—the Circuit Trails, with an ambitious goal to create a vibrant trail system across the region. Look for the Trail-Nation project logo throughout the book to find trails that are part of this network. Learn more about RTC's vision to connect the country by trail at **trailnation.org.**

About the Circuit Trails

Led by a coalition of dozens of nonprofit organizations, foundations, and agencies, the Circuit Trails are part of a vast trail network that will ultimately include 800 miles of multiuse trails across nine counties in the Greater Philadelphia–Camden, New Jersey, region. More than 350 miles of the network are already complete, and the coalition is working to have 500 miles built by 2025. Learn more at **thecircuittrails.org.**

THE
CIRCUIT
TRAILS

How to Use This Book

Rail-Trails: *New Jersey & New York* provides the information you'll need to plan a rewarding trek. With words to inspire you and maps to chart your path, it makes choosing the best route a breeze. Following are some of the highlights.

Maps

You'll find three levels of maps in this book: an **overall regional map, state locator maps,** and **detailed trail maps.**

The trails in this book are located in New Jersey and New York. Each chapter details a particular state's network of trails, marked on a locator map at the beginning of the chapter. Use these maps to find the trails nearest you, or select several neighboring trails and plan a weekend hiking or biking excursion. Once you find a trail on a state locator map, simply flip to the corresponding number for a full description. Accompanying trail maps mark each route's access roads, trailheads, parking areas, restrooms, and other defining features.

Key to Map Icons

parking

drinking water

restrooms

featured trail

connecting trail

active railroad

Trail Descriptions

Trails are listed in alphabetical order within each chapter. Each description leads off with a set of summary information, including trail endpoints and mileage, a roughness index, the trail surface, and possible uses.

The map and summary information list the trail endpoints (either a city, street, or more specific location), with suggested points from which to start and finish. Additional access points are marked on the maps and mentioned in the trail descriptions. The maps and descriptions also highlight available amenities, including parking and restrooms, as well as such area attractions as shops, services, museums, parks, and stadiums. Trail length is listed in miles.

Each trail bears a **roughness index rating** from 1 to 3. A rating of 1 indicates a smooth, level surface that is accessible to users of all ages and abilities. A 2 rating means the surface may be loose and/or uneven and could pose a problem for road bikes and wheelchairs. A 3 rating suggests a rough surface that is only recommended for mountain bikers and hikers. Surfaces can range from asphalt or concrete to ballast, boardwalk, cinder, crushed stone, gravel, grass, dirt, sand, and/or wood chips. Where relevant, trail descriptions address alternating surface conditions.

All trails are open to pedestrians, and most allow bicycles, except where noted in the trail summary or description. The summary also indicates wheelchair access. Other possible uses include in-line skating, mountain biking, horseback riding, fishing, and cross-country skiing. While most trails are off-limits to motor vehicles, some local trail organizations do allow all-terrain vehicles (ATVs) and snowmobiles.

Trail descriptions themselves suggest an ideal itinerary for each route, including the best parking areas and access points, where to begin, your direction of travel, and any highlights along the way. Following each description are directions to the recommended trailheads.

Each trail description also lists a local website for further information. Be sure to visit these websites in advance for updates and current conditions. **TrailLink .com** is another great resource for updated content on the trails in this guidebook.

Trail Use

R ail-trails are popular destinations for a range of users, often making them busy places to enjoy the outdoors. Following basic trail etiquette and safety guidelines will make your experience more pleasant.

➤ **Keep to the right,** except when passing.

➤ **Pass on the left,** and give a clear audible warning: "Passing on your left."

➤ **Be aware** of other trail users, particularly around corners and blind spots, and be especially careful when entering a trail, changing direction, or passing, so that you don't collide with traffic.

➤ **Respect wildlife** and public and private property; leave no trace and take out litter.

➤ **Control your speed,** especially near pedestrians, playgrounds, and heavily congested areas.

➤ **Travel single file.** Cyclists and pedestrians should ride or walk single file in congested areas or areas with reduced visibility.

➤ **Cross carefully** at intersections; always look both ways and yield to through traffic. Pedestrians have the right-of-way.

➤ **Keep one ear open and volume low** on portable listening devices to increase your awareness of your surroundings.

➤ **Wear a helmet** and other safety gear if you're cycling or in-line skating.

➤ **Consider visibility.** Wear reflective clothing, use bicycle lights, or bring flashlights or helmet-mounted lights for tunnel passages or twilight excursions.

➤ **Keep moving,** and don't block the trail. When taking a rest, turn off the trail to the right. Groups should avoid congregating on or blocking the trails. If you have an accident on the trail, move to the right as soon as possible.

➤ **Bicyclists yield** to all other trail users. Pedestrians yield to horses. If in doubt, yield to all other trail users.

➤ **Check the trail's pet policy.** Dogs are permitted on most trails, but some trails through parks, wildlife refuges, or other sensitive areas may not allow pets; it's best to check the trail website before your visit. If pets are permitted, keep your dog on a short leash and under your control at all times. Discard dog waste in a designated trash receptacle.

➤ **Teach your children** these trail essentials, and be especially diligent to keep them out of faster-moving trail traffic.

➤ **Be prepared,** especially on long-distance rural trails. Bring water, snacks, maps, a light source, matches, and other equipment you may need. Because some areas may not have good reception for mobile phones, know where you're going, and tell someone else your plan.

Key to Trail Use

| walking | cycling | wheelchair access | in-line skating | mountain biking |

| fishing | horseback riding | cross-country skiing | snowmobiling |

Learn More

To learn about additional multiuse trails in your area or to plan a trip to an area beyond the scope of this book, visit Rails-to-Trails Conservancy's trail-finder website **TrailLink.com,** a free resource with more than 34,000 miles of mapped rail-trails and multiuse trails nationwide.

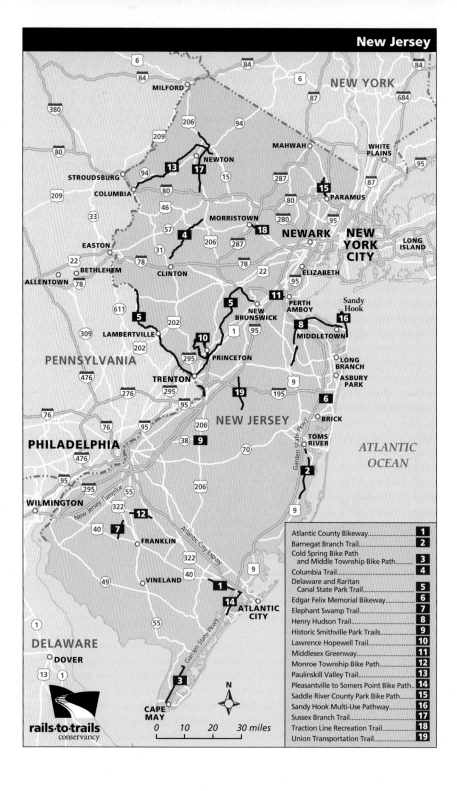

NEW YORK

MILFORD

MAHWAH

WHITE
PLAINS

STROUDSBURG

NEWTON

13   17

COLUMBIA

PARAMUS

15

MORRISTOWN

4   18

NEWARK

NEW
YORK
CITY

LONG
ISLAND

EASTON

BETHLEHEM

ALLENTOWN

CLINTON

ELIZABETH

5

NEW
BRUNSWICK

11

PERTH
AMBOY

Sandy
Hook

16

8

MIDDLETOWN

PENNSYLVANIA

LAMBERTVILLE

5

10

PRINCETON

LONG
BRANCH

ASBURY
PARK

TRENTON

19

6

NEW JERSEY

BRICK

PHILADELPHIA

9

TOMS
RIVER

2

ATLANTIC
OCEAN

WILMINGTON

12

7

FRANKLIN

9

VINELAND

1

14   ATLANTIC
CITY

DELAWARE

DOVER

3

CAPE
MAY

N

0   10   20   30 miles

rails·to·trails
conservancy

A deer grazes on the ground cover beside the Saddle River County Park Bike Path (see page 56).

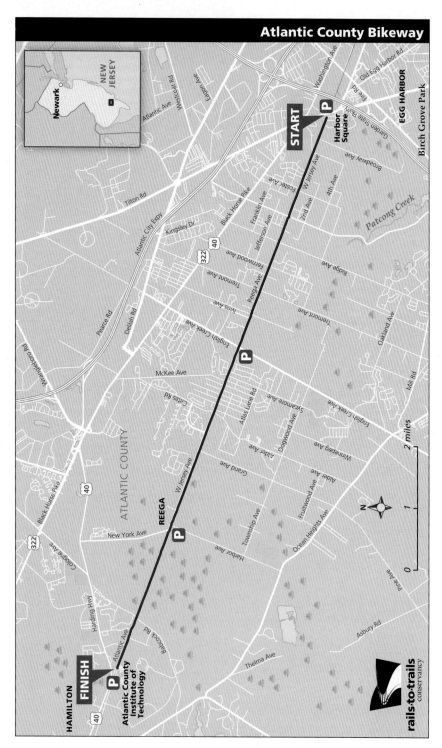

Atlantic County Bikeway

If you're looking for a change of luck on your gambling getaway to Atlantic City, try visiting the 7.6-mile Atlantic County Bikeway. The paved trail runs straight and flat as it offers a relaxing escape from the crush of traffic around the beachfront gaming and resort town located about 10 miles away.

The bikeway got its start as the West Jersey and Atlantic Railroad, a 40-mile subsidiary of the West Jersey Railroad's parent Pennsylvania Railroad. Completed in 1880, the tracks ran from Newfield to near Atlantic City. It later became known as the Newfield Branch of the West Jersey & Seashore Railroad, another subsidiary of the Pennsylvania Railroad, and eventually became part of the Pennsylvania-Reading Seashore Lines. The railroad stopped using the western half of the line between Newfield and Mays Landing in 1958 and the remainder in 1966. A section between Shore Mall (now Harbor Square) and the Atlantic County Institute of Technology reopened as the bikeway in 2003.

Trees buffer much of the trail, providing a peaceful respite from the surrounding Atlantic City area.

County
Atlantic

Endpoints
W. Jersey Ave. near E. Black Horse Pike (Egg Harbor Township) to Atlantic Ave. and 19th St. (Hamilton Township)

Mileage
7.6

Type
Rail-Trail

Roughness Index
1

Surface
Asphalt

The trail connects shopping and residential areas as it runs between the nexus of the heavily traveled Atlantic City Expressway and Garden State Parkway in the east through a dense forest to a government complex in the west. Numerous at-grade road intersections are well marked for pedestrians and motorists. Two-lane side roads parallel long sections.

Start at the eastern trailhead across West Jersey Avenue from Harbor Square, where trees screen the trail from adjacent streets and residential subdivisions as it heads northwest beneath power lines. The trail occasionally curves around utility poles in its path.

There are frequent benches for taking a breather, as well as informational signs about railroad history and the flora and fauna of the New Jersey Pinelands.

After 4.7 miles, the trail enters undeveloped woodland for about 2 miles to the outskirts of Mays Landing, the county seat of Atlantic County. The path ends at a vocational school on 58 acres that serves high school students and adults in the county. Although the trail ends here, historic downtown Mays Landing is about 2 miles ahead on Atlantic Avenue. Mays Landing sits on the eastern border of the 1.1-million-acre New Jersey Pinelands National Reserve, the largest open space in the Mid-Atlantic Seaboard between Boston and Richmond, Virginia.

CONTACT: atlantic-county.org/parks/bikeway.asp

DIRECTIONS

To reach the eastern trailhead at Harbor Square in Egg Harbor Township from Atlantic City, take US 322/US 40/N. Albany Ave. west from O'Donnell Memorial Park on Ventnor Ave. Go 6.9 miles, and turn left onto Tilton Road. Go about 300 feet, and then turn at the first right into the parking lot for Harbor Square. Go 0.1 mile, and look for marked trail parking on the right as the parking lot street becomes W. Jersey Ave.

To reach the western trailhead from the Atlantic City Expy., take Exit 17, and then turn right onto NJ 50/Egg Harbor–Green Bank Road. Go 4.7 miles (the road becomes NJ 50/Cape May Road), and then turn left onto US 40/Main St. Go 1.7 miles (the road becomes US 40/Harding Hwy.), and turn right onto Atlantic Ave. Go 180 feet, and then turn left to stay on Atlantic Ave. Go 0.2 mile, and then turn right onto 19th St. Look for parking on the left.

Eventually, the Barnegat Branch Trail will travel nearly 16 miles from Barnegat Township north to Toms River along a branch of the former Central Railroad of New Jersey. As of 2019, three disconnected segments of trail have been completed through the sandy soils of the Pine Barrens. From the 17th to the 20th century, people harvested and burned trees in this region to produce household goods, make charcoal, and control wildlife. Fire ecology is central to this region's ecosystem and continues to shape the landscape into the 21st century.

Barnegat Township to Forked River: 7.6 miles

The 7.6-mile southernmost segment runs from Barnegat Township to Forked River. It features a stone-dust surface, though the path is paved where it crosses roads. From the southern trailhead parking lot at Railroad Avenue in Barnegat Township, head north 3.1 miles to this

County
Ocean

Endpoints
Railroad Ave. and W. Bay Ave. (Barnegat Township) to Musket Road, 320 feet east of Lake Barnegat Dr. N (Forked River); William Hebrew Park at Railroad Ave. and South St. (Lacey Township) to E. Railroad Ave. and Hickory Lane (Berkeley Township); Mizzen Ave. and Railroad Ave. to NJ 166/Atlantic City Blvd. and Admiral Ave. (Beachwood)

Mileage
11.7

Type
Rail-Trail

Roughness Index
2

Surface
Asphalt, Crushed Stone, Dirt

The trail traverses New Jersey's heavily forested Pine Barrens region.

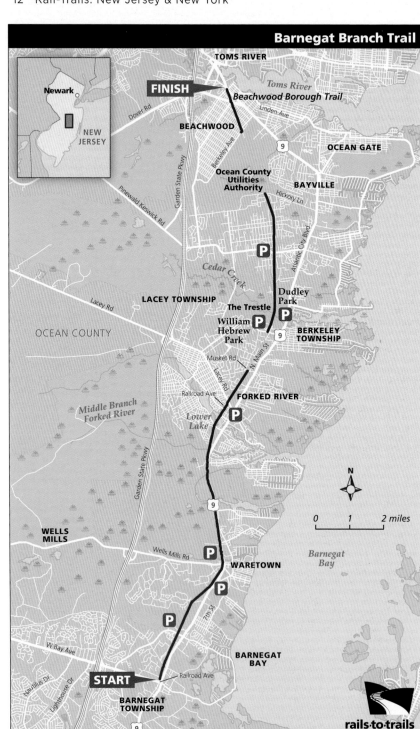

section's midpoint in Waretown. This small town offers a convenience store and drug store for refreshments.

Continuing north 4.5 more miles toward the community of Forked River, the trail crosses the Middle Branch Forked River on a converted railroad trestle. After crossing Lower Lake, the trail parallels Railroad Avenue to this segment's end, at Musket Road.

William Hebrew Park to Hickory Lane: 3.1 miles

A short section of trail, primarily stone dust, starts at William Hebrew Park in Lacey Township. As you head north, Dudley Park, at the southern edge of Berkeley Township, offers picnic tables, a covered pavilion, a playground, and a roller-skating rink. The park also includes an old railway relic called The Trestle, situated above Cedar Creek. Recently, a 150-foot bridge was installed to provide safe crossing over the creek for trail users, but some features of The Trestle were left in place as a reminder of the railroad's important place in the area's history. A popular spot for visitors and locals alike, The Trestle makes the perfect setting for everything from family cookouts to kayak excursions. This segment of trail spans just over 3 miles to the Ocean County Utilities Authority, also in Berkeley Township.

Beachwood Borough Trail: 1.0 mile

The oldest trail segment runs through the borough of Beachwood. Also known as the Beachwood Borough Trail, this 1-mile-long paved trail starts at Berkeley Avenue and spans the Beachwood community. It ends to the north near the border of the township of Toms River. Construction on an extension of the trail to NJ 166/Herflicker Boulevard in Toms River is expected to begin in 2019.

CONTACT: www.planning.co.ocean.nj.us/frmtpbarnegatbranch

DIRECTIONS

Parking access at the southernmost trailhead can be found just off of US 9/Main St. in Barnegat. From Garden State Pkwy., take Exit 67 (if heading north) or 67A (if heading south). If heading north, turn right onto W. Bay Ave. If heading south, turn right onto Lighthouse Dr., go 0.2 mile, and turn right onto W. Bay Ave. Go approximately 1.5 miles, and turn left onto Railroad Ave., an unmarked road that runs parallel to Memorial Dr. The southern trailhead can be found at the end of the parking lot on Railroad Ave.

Parking and trail access at William Hebrew Park can be found just off of US 9/Atlantic City Blvd. Turn onto South St. in Lacey Township, between Laurel Blvd. and Warren Ave. Follow South St. 0.3 mile to the park's entrance and parking lot on your right.

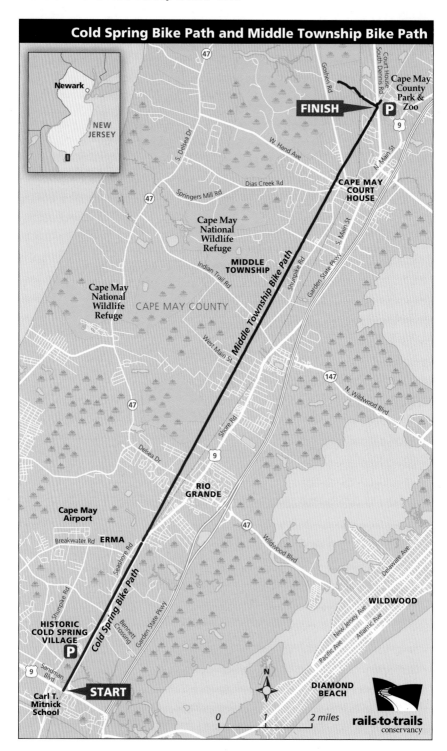

Cold Spring Bike Path and Middle Township Bike Path

NEW JERSEY

Newark

47

Court House
South Dennis Rd

Goshen Rd

Cape May
County
Park &
Zoo

FINISH

P

9

W. Hand Ave

S. Delsea Dr

Dias Creek Rd

**CAPE MAY
COURT
HOUSE**

47

Springers Mill Rd

N. Main St

Cape May
National
Wildlife
Refuge

**MIDDLE
TOWNSHIP**

S. Main St

Indian Trail Rd

Middle Township Bike Path

Shunpike Rd

Garden State Pkwy

Cape May
National
Wildlife
Refuge

CAPE MAY COUNTY

West Main St

147

47

N. Wildwood Blvd

Shore Rd

Delsea Dr

9

**RIO
GRANDE**

47

Wildwood Blvd

Delaware Ave

**Cape May
Airport**

Breakwater Rd   **ERMA**

Seashore Rd

Garden State Pkwy

Bennett Crossing

WILDWOOD

Shunpike Rd

Cold Spring Bike Path

New Jersey Ave
Atlantic Ave

**HISTORIC
COLD SPRING
VILLAGE**

P

Pacific Ave

9

Sandman Blvd

START

**Carl T.
Mitnick
School**

N

**DIAMOND
BEACH**

0   1   2 miles

rails·to·trails
conservancy

Cape May's 2.7-mile Cold Spring Bike Path and 8.9-mile Middle Township Bike Path were fully connected in summer 2017. Riders can now pick up the trail at US 9/ Sandman Boulevard in Lower Township across the street from the local elementary school and ride it just over 11 miles north to the Cape May County Park & Zoo. The trail acts as a backbone for the 16 municipalities that surround it, and future spur trails will connect even more communities and local attractions.

The Jersey shore was a major vacation destination for residents of the Delaware Valley region throughout the early 20th century. From the 1890s to 1930s, two parallel railroad lines—the Atlantic City Railroad and West Jersey & Seashore Railroad—shuttled passengers to the coast for a seashore break. The competing trains, visible to each other along the parallel tracks, used to race to see which company could reach Cape May the fastest. As private automobiles grew more popular and people began to turn their interest toward more exotic destinations, the railroads merged and service was eventually discontinued.

The wooded northern end of the Middle Township Bike Path runs adjacent to the Cape May County Park & Zoo.

County
Cape May

Endpoints
US 9/Sandman Blvd. at Seashore Road (Lower Township) to County Park Road, 345 feet east of Court House South Dennis Road in the Cape May County Park & Zoo (Cape May)

Mileage
11.6

Type
Rail-Trail

Roughness Index
1

Surface
Asphalt

This rail-trail journey will take you along a segment of the former West Jersey & Seashore Railroad railbed. Starting at the southern endpoint of the Cold Spring Bike Path (sometimes called the Historic Cold Spring Village Bike Path) at US 9/Sandman Boulevard, head north 1 mile to the Historic Cold Spring Village. At this nonprofit open-air living history museum, you can view life as it was in the early to mid-19th century and also enjoy a restored rail station. Just south of where US 9 meets the Historic Cold Spring Village, the path crosses an intermittent stream on an 8-foot wide, 40-foot-long trestle bridge for bike and pedestrian traffic.

The trail parallels Seashore Road as you travel under a canopy of trees, passing a high school and golf course to the right. Just past the suburban community of Erma, at 2.7 miles, the Cold Spring Bike Path transitions into the Middle Township Bike Path. You'll notice many idyllic camping areas and wineries to the east and west as you enter Erma and then pass through the Rio Grande community in 4.1 miles.

The homes begin to grow scarce as you enter the woods through Middle Township. You may even run across a bunny or deer as you continue to the northern endpoint at the Cape May County Park & Zoo at 11.6 miles. If you are here in the spring or summer, you'll enjoy a beautiful display of wildflowers and butterflies along the trail. Zoo admission is free, as is parking for cars.

CONTACT: capemaycountynj.gov/1026/Fitness-Trails

Near the southern end of the Cold Spring Bike Path, travelers will have a view of a passenger train station built in 1894.

DIRECTIONS

To reach parking near the southern endpoint, follow Garden State Pkwy. south to its end. Take Exit 0 for NJ 109, and turn right. In 0.6 mile, turn left onto US 9. A few parking spaces are available on your right in 700 feet, or continue 0.5 mile, and turn right onto Seashore Road. Parking for the trail's southern endpoint can be found at the Historic Cold Spring Village Museum, which appears on your left in 0.7 mile. If heading north on US 9 from Delaware, consider taking the US 9 N/Cape May–Lewes Ferry. Information on ferry vehicle fares can be found at **cmlf .com/schedules-fares.** From the Cape May Terminal, drive 2.4 miles on US 9 N/Lincoln Blvd./Sandman Blvd. Turn left onto Seashore Road, and go 0.7 mile to reach the Historic Cold Spring Village Museum on your right. Once you park, the southernmost endpoint can be found 0.7 mile south at the intersection with US 9/Sandman Blvd. Alternatively, you can pick up the trail from the museum and continue north from there.

To reach parking at the trail's northern endpoint from Garden State Pkwy., take Exit 11 for Crest Haven Road. Head west on County Road 609/Crest Haven Road, and travel 0.2 mile until it becomes County Park Road and enters the zoo, where parking is available. From the Cape May Terminal, drive 2.8 miles on US 9 N/Lincoln Blvd./Sandman Blvd. to NJ 109 S. Turn right onto NJ 109 S, and go 1 mile. Merge onto Garden State Pkwy., and continue 10.6 miles to Exit 11. Turn left onto CR 609/Crest Haven Road, and follow it 0.2 mile until it becomes County Park Road and enters the zoo, where parking is available.

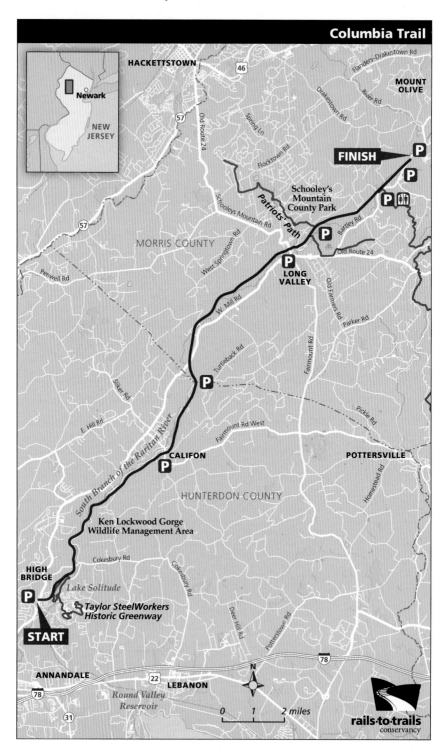

Columbia Trail

HACKETTSTOWN

MOUNT OLIVE

Newark

NEW JERSEY

FINISH

Schooley's Mountain County Park

Patriots' Path

MORRIS COUNTY

LONG VALLEY

Penwell Rd

Flanders-Drakestown Rd

River Rd

Drakestown Rd

Spring Ln

Flocktown Rd

Schooleys Mountain Rd

West Springtown Rd

W. Mill Rd

Old Route 24

Old Route 24

Bartley Rd

Old Farmers Rd

Parker Rd

Turtleback Rd

Fairmount Rd

Pickle Rd

POTTERSVILLE

Fairmount Rd West

CALIFON

HUNTERDON COUNTY

Ken Lockwood Gorge Wildlife Management Area

E. Hill Rd

Silker Rd

South Branch of the Raritan River

Cokesbury Rd

Cokesbury Rd

Deer Hill Rd

Pottersville Rd

Homestead Rd

HIGH BRIDGE

Lake Solitude

Taylor SteelWorkers Historic Greenway

START

ANNANDALE

LEBANON

Round Valley Reservoir

0   1   2 miles

rails·to·trails conservancy

The Columbia Trail has the distinction of being named for a natural gas pipeline that runs beneath it for 15 miles in rural northern New Jersey. The crushed-stone trail rolls along the South Branch of the Raritan River, passing through historical communities such as High Bridge and Califon, as well as a steep, natural gorge.

The Columbia Gas Transmission Corporation buried the gas pipeline beneath the old railbed of the High Bridge Branch of the Central Railroad of New Jersey in the 1990s. The railroad dates to 1876, when it started hauling iron ore from local mines. Passenger service ended in 1935, followed by cancellation of freight in 1976. After installing the pipeline, the company donated a trail easement to Hunterdon and Morris Counties to develop and maintain a recreational trail.

The Columbia Trail travels through mature deciduous and evergreen forests that create a canopy from the summer sun. White-tailed deer, raccoons, and coyotes, as well as the occasional black bear, make their home here. Heading north, the trail passes farm- and pastureland. There are several towns in which to stop for snacks along the way.

Nearly the entire length of the Columbia Trail is lushly forested.

Counties
Hunterdon, Morris

Endpoints
Main St. between Church St. and Center St. (High Bridge) to Bartley Road/County Road 625 between Bartley-Chester Road and S4 Bridges Road (Long Valley)

Mileage
15.0

Type
Rail-Trail

Roughness Index
2

Surface
Crushed Stone

Starting in High Bridge, you'll have a slight uphill grade all the way to Long Valley in the north. High Bridge gets its name from a former 112-foot-high bridge across the South Branch of the Raritan River on the main line of the Central Railroad. The bridge was replaced by an earthen embankment in the 1860s.

On the way out of town, you'll pass a connection at 0.4 mile to the Taylor SteelWorkers Historic Greenway. The 6.5-mile trail passes ruins of a historical ironworks complex that dates to the American Revolution. Back on the main trail, you'll soon pass the falls at the Lake Solitude dam and begin following the South Branch, one of the state's best fly-fishing rivers.

Not far upstream, the trail passes through the Ken Lockwood Gorge Wildlife Management Area for 2.5 miles. The steep slopes and boulders create a whitewater paradise for kayakers. The trail crosses a bridge here that was the scene of a tragic train wreck in 1885 when an engine and 45 cars plunged off a wooden trestle, which was later replaced.

Two-and-a-half miles past the bridge you'll arrive in the Victorian-style town of Califon, which has more than 240 structures on the National Register of Historic Places. Local legend says the town was originally called California, but a sign painter ran out of room and abbreviated the name.

Another 6 miles up the trail is Long Valley, where you'll find diners south of the trail on NJ 24. Leaving the community, you'll cross three junctions with the Patriots' Path, a 35-mile-long multiuse trail. The second heads north a short distance to Schooley's Mountain County Park.

Columbia Trail ends about 3 miles past Long Valley on Bartley Road, just shy of the Mount Olive community.

CONTACT: co.hunterdon.nj.us/depts/parks/guides/parkareas.htm and m66.siteground.biz/~morrispa/index.php/parks/columbia-trail

DIRECTIONS

To reach the northeast trailhead from I-80, take Exit 27A to US 206 S toward Somerville. Go 4 miles, and turn right onto Bartley Flanders Road. Then go 0.9 mile, and bear left onto Bartley Road. Go 0.3 mile, and turn right to stay on Bartley Road/County Road 625. Go 0.5 mile, and look for parking on the right.

To reach the southwest trailhead from I-78 W, take Exit 17 toward NJ 31. Merge onto NJ 31 N, go 1.9 miles, and turn right onto W. Main St. Go 1.1 miles, and turn right onto Bridge St. Then go 400 feet, and turn left onto Main St. Go 0.2 mile, and look for parking on the left.

To reach the southwest trailhead from I-78 E, take Exit 16. Merge onto NJ 173/Old Hwy. 22, and go 0.3 mile. Turn left onto CR 626. Go 0.1 mile and merge onto NJ 31 N. Go 1.5 miles, and turn right onto W. Main St. Go 1.1 miles, and turn right onto Bridge St. Then go 400 feet, and turn left onto Main St. Go 0.2 mile, and look for parking on the left.

Spanning more than 70 miles, the Delaware and Raritan Canal State Park Trail is the longest completed multiuse trail in the state and is described by many as the crown jewel of New Jersey trails. A portion follows the towpath of the Delaware & Raritan Canal, built in the early 1830s as a transportation corridor between Philadelphia and New York, while another portion tracks the route of the former Belvidere Delaware Railroad. It is part of both the Circuit Trails, an 800-mile trail network throughout the Philadelphia and Camden region, and the East Coast Greenway, an expansive trail system being developed between Maine and Florida.

The trail is shaped like a V, with Trenton at its center, and is paved within the capital city. Most of the trail runs along the canal, where it is a well-maintained surface of

Nature lovers will enjoy exploring the tree-lined waterway.

Counties
Hunterdon, Mercer, Somerset

Endpoints
County Road 619/ Milford Frenchtown Road between Stamets Road and Kappus Road (Frenchtown) and Landing Lane, just north of George St. (New Brunswick)

Mileage
72.8

Type
Canal/Rail-Trail/ Rail-with-Trail

Roughness Index
2

Surfaces
Asphalt, Crushed Stone, Dirt

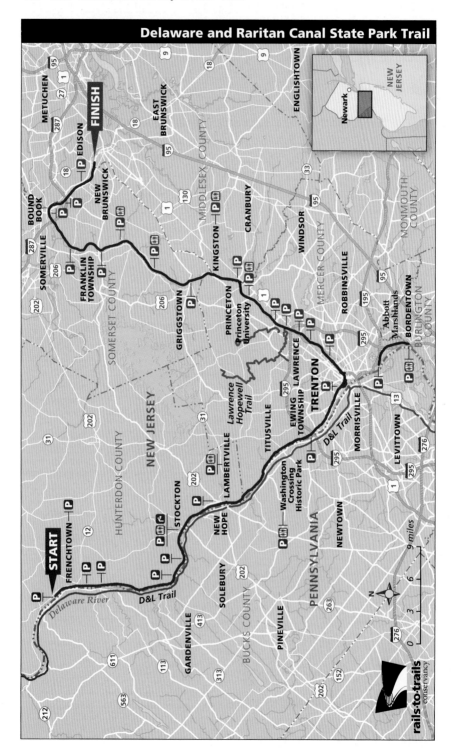

finely crushed stone over hard-packed dirt; travelers will be most comfortable riding it on a hybrid or mountain bike.

Two types of mileage markers are used along the canal. The concrete mile markers with two numbers etched on them are historical, indicating the number of miles between the terminus points at Bordentown and New Brunswick. The other type marks every 0.5 mile starting from the Battle Monument in Trenton.

Northwest of Trenton, the trail starts near Frenchtown, a pedestrian-friendly village, and connects many towns along the way, including Stockton, Lambert-ville, Titusville, and Ewing Township. Heading northeast out of Trenton, the trail runs through Lawrence, where a connection to the Lawrence Hopewell Trail (see page 40) can be made. Continuing farther, the trail skirts near the Princeton University campus and passes through Kingston and Franklin Township, ending in New Brunswick.

The trail offers something for almost everyone. Along the route, history buffs will appreciate the 19th-century bridges and bridge-tender houses, remnants of locks, cobblestone spillways, hand-built stone-arch culverts, rail depots, and historical railroad markers, as well as an early 18th-century gristmill near Stockton and a 19th-century one in Kingston. Hungry trail users can choose between periodic trailside picnic tables or trailside cafés in towns along the way, including Frenchtown, Stockton, and Lambertville. Nature lovers can

History buffs will appreciate seeing the remnants of the early-19th-century canal the trail parallels.

enjoy occasional wildlife sightings and river views. You can even rent canoes in Griggstown or Princeton if you prefer the water route.

Between Frenchtown and Trenton, there are six bridges that travelers can use to cross the Delaware River and explore the 141-mile D&L Trail, which follows the river on the Pennsylvania side. The combination of the two paralleling trails and multiple bridges means that travelers have the option to go on several looped routes. A noteworthy attraction just on the other side of the river is Washington Crossing Historic Park, commemorating the turning point in the American Revolution when, on that fateful Christmas night in 1776, George Washington's surprise attack and subsequent victory over opposing forces provided a much-needed boost to the Continental Army's dwindling morale.

South of Trenton, a relatively short, disconnected section of the trail spans 3.5 miles, beginning at Canal Boulevard and running through a wooded tract of the Abbott Marshlands. It ends at the historical outlet lock into Crosswick Creek at Bordentown. The trail here is dirt, with some narrow sections, mostly running next to a canal and an active rail line.

CONTACT: state.nj.us/dep/parksandforests/parks/drcanal.html and fodc.org/visit-the-canal/towpath-trail

DIRECTIONS

You can access the Delaware and Raritan Canal State Park Trail from dozens of places along the way. Below, we list directions to parking lots closest to the endpoints of the trail, but more options can be found on the trail website or **TrailLink.com.**

The northwesternmost parking lot for the trail is available at Old Frenchtown Field in Frenchtown. From the intersection of US 1 and NJ 29 in Trenton, take NJ 29 N, and go 32 miles to reach Frenchtown (NJ 29 makes a few turns, so make sure to follow the signs for NJ 29). Arriving in Frenchtown, you'll come to a T-junction; take a left onto Bridge St., then make your first right turn onto Harrison St. Take Harrison north 0.7 mile to 12th St. Take a left onto 12th St. and follow it a short distance to the parking lot at the northwest corner of Old Frenchtown Field.

The northeasternmost parking lot for the trail is available at Demott Lane in the unincorporated community of Somerset. To reach it from I-287, take Exit 10 for Easton Ave. Head southeast on Easton Ave., following the signs for Easton Ave./County Road 527 S to New Brunswick. Follow Easton Ave. 1.5 miles to Demott Lane. Make a left onto Demott Lane (it will look like a small driveway); you'll see a brown sign at the entrance that notes access to the historical Van Wickle House (owned by The Meadows Foundation) and the towpath. You'll travel a short distance to the parking lot; from there, a footbridge will take you across the canal to the trail.

Prepare to be whisked into the past when you take the Edgar Felix Memorial Bikeway. The paved trail follows a short-line railroad corridor from the coastal city of Manasquan to a village at Allaire State Park that features living-history exhibits, a museum, and rides on the vintage Pine Creek Railroad.

The trail gets its name from Manasquan cyclist Edgar Felix, who lobbied the town to convert to trail a section of the former Freehold and Jamesburg Agricultural Railroad, originally created as the Farmingdale and Squan Village Railroad in 1867. The first 2 miles of bikeway opened in 1971 and later became the first completed segment of the future 55-mile Capital to the Coast Trail, which will span the state from Trenton to Manasquan.

The rail-trail starts at North Main Street in Manasquan and follows the old railroad corridor northwest 3.4 miles to the Allaire State Park boundary on Hospital Road. Here, a spur of the Capital to the Coast Trail continues through the park 1.9 miles along the railroad right-of-way to a historical village and tourist railroad site.

Starting at the trailhead in Manasquan, you can take an on-street bike route through the town for 2 miles to the beach. Traveling in the other direction, the trail passes residential neighborhoods and a recreational complex on the way out of town. At 1.2 miles, you come to the Wall Township Bike Path, which heads north 1.7 miles to a government complex.

As you proceed along the trail, the surroundings become more rural with woods mixed with fields. You'll reach Allenwood about 2.7 miles from the start, where you'll find a general store with refreshments and trailside tables. Returning to rural countryside, you'll cross two pedestrian bridges that leapfrog trail users over the eight-lane Garden State Parkway.

Crossing Hospital Road, the trail continues as a spur route of the future Capital to the Coast Trail into Allaire State Park. (A left turn onto another trail adjacent to Hospital Road heads south 0.4 mile to a parking lot and

County
Monmouth

Endpoints
Main St. between Atlantic Ave. and Central Ave. (Manasquan) to Hospital Road, 0.25 mile south of Atlantic Ave./County Road 524 (Allenwood)

Mileage
3.4

Type
Rail-Trail

Roughness Index
1–2

Surface
Asphalt

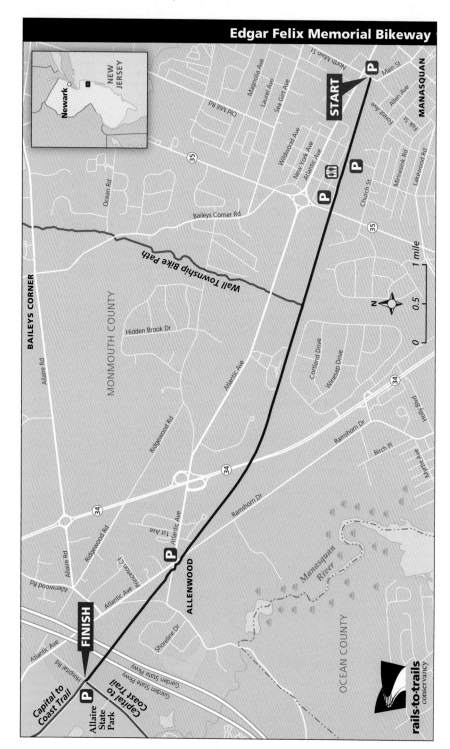

As you proceed west, the trail's backdrop becomes more rural.

fishing on the Manasquan River.) You'll pass old farm fields, forests, and ponds with waterfowl as you learn about the area from interpretive signs.

At the trail terminus in the state park, you can tour historical Allaire Village to experience a 19th-century iron-making community, or hop a ride on the vintage cars of the steam-powered Pine Creek Railroad. You'll also find hiking and mountain biking trails in the park, including a short dirt path along the old railroad corridor that dead-ends at I-195.

CONTACT: capitaltocoasttrail.org

DIRECTIONS

To reach the eastern trailhead in Manasquan from I-195, take Exit 35A onto NJ 34 S. Head south 2.3 miles on NJ 34, and exit onto County Road 524 Spur E/Atlantic Ave. toward Manasquan. Turn right, go 1.5 miles, and take the second exit off the traffic circle to stay on Atlantic Ave. Go 0.9 mile, and turn right onto Main St. Then go about 200 feet, and look for parking on the left.

To reach the western trailhead at Allaire State Park from I-195, take Exit 31B onto Lakewood Farmingdale Road. Head north 0.5 mile, and turn right onto CR 524; then go 1.2 miles, and turn right into Allaire State Park (entry fee charged Memorial Day–Labor Day). Follow the entrance road 0.3 mile to the parking lot, park, and then retrace your way to the entrance to find the trail on the right.

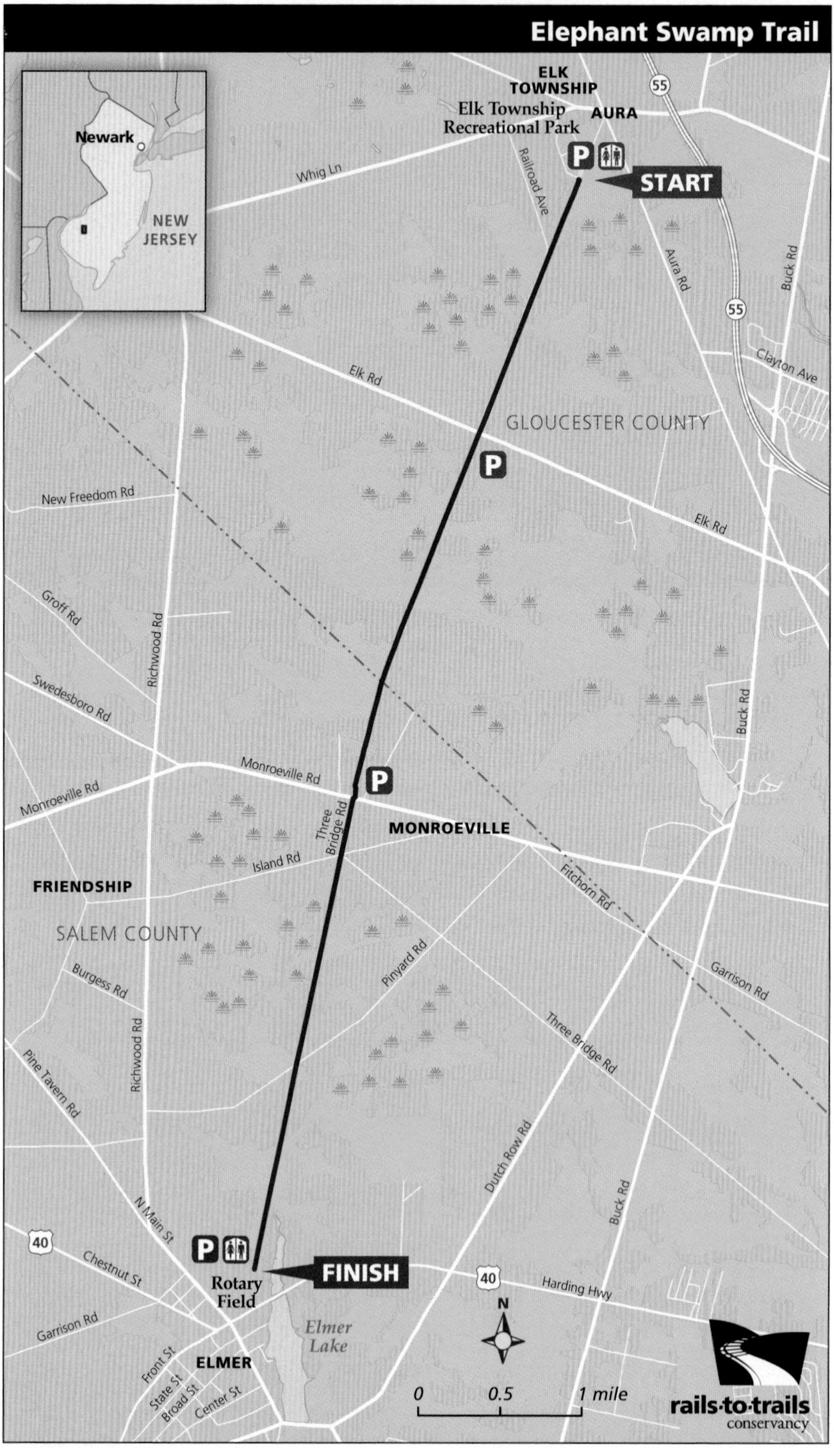

Elephant Swamp Trail

ELK TOWNSHIP

Elk Township Recreational Park

AURA

START

GLOUCESTER COUNTY

Whig Ln

Railroad Ave

Aura Rd

Buck Rd

Clayton Ave

55

55

Elk Rd

Elk Rd

New Freedom Rd

Groff Rd

Richwood Rd

Swedesboro Rd

Monroeville Rd

Monroeville Rd

Three Bridge Rd

Island Rd

MONROEVILLE

Fitchorn Rd

Buck Rd

FRIENDSHIP

SALEM COUNTY

Burgess Rd

Richwood Rd

Pinyard Rd

Three Bridge Rd

Garrison Rd

Pine Tavern Rd

Dutch Row Rd

Buck Rd

N Main St

Chestnut St

40

FINISH

Rotary Field

Garrison Rd

40

Harding Hwy

Front St

State St

Broad St

Center St

ELMER

Elmer Lake

N

0   0.5   1 mile

rails·to·trails
conservancy

NEW JERSEY

Newark

As you walk along the Elephant Swamp Trail, it's easy to see where it picked up the *swamp* part of its name. As for the rest, legend has it that in the late 1800s, an elephant got loose in the swamp when a traveling circus passed through Elk Township by railroad.

In 1878 the former Pennsylvania–Reading Railroad built the tracks as part of a route from Camden to Bridgeton. The tracks were removed a century later, and the Elephant Swamp Trail now stands in their place. To this day, the trail guide bids visitors to "listen closely for the footsteps of a wandering elephant." The pathway is part of the Circuit Trails, an expansive regional trail network across nine counties, including Gloucester County, which will eventually encompass 800 miles of trails.

The 5.1-mile community trail is unpaved, consisting mostly of large stones and wood chips that make it too bumpy for an enjoyable road or hybrid bike trip, though mountain bikes fare better. The natural flora and fauna of the trail (sometimes called the Elephant Swamp Nature Trail) make it ideal for a leisurely walk. From the path's northern endpoint, the western terminus of the Monroe Township Bike Path (see page 46) is only 3.4 miles northeast.

The trail offers a pleasant mix of rural fields and woodlands.

Counties
Gloucester, Salem

Endpoints
Elk Township Recreational Park at Recreation Dr. and Whig Lane (Elk Township) to Rotary Field at US 40/Chestnut St., 460 feet east of N. Main St. (Elmer)

Mileage
5.1

Type
Rail-Trail

Roughness Index
3

Surface
Crushed Stone, Dirt, Gravel, Wood Chips

Starting at Elk Township Recreational Park, follow the wide, trail-like sidewalks through the park past baseball fields and a soccer complex, where the wooded area becomes heavier and the trail begins. The recreational complex falls behind as greenery flanks you on both sides. Civilization is never too far, with the parallel Railroad Avenue—a nod to the trail's history—just barely peeking through the trees to the right. This section attracts many hikers and dog walkers.

After 1.2 miles, you'll arrive at the trailhead at Elk Road, with a parking lot on the left. Equestrians may enjoy the trail from this point on. Along this portion, you'll find burbling brooks, bunnies hopping across the path, butterflies crowning your head, and a farm to the left completing this nature scene. Elk Township has provided nine interpretive signage stations detailing natural features, such as the pitch pine trees that define the Pine Barrens of southern New Jersey. No need to memorize what you read—if you have a smartphone, you can take this information with you thanks to the town's Elephant Swamp Guide app, or you can download the brochure from the trail's website.

The trail opens up around mile 2.9, when you'll pass through the parking lot of a volunteer fire department and cross Monroeville Road. The pathway parallels Three Bridge Road before crossing Island Road and continuing into a wooded area. Not long after, you'll encounter the verdant swamp itself. With sunlight peeking through trees, the swamp is more picturesque than it is spooky.

Around mile 4.25, the canopy gives way to open sky as you pass the low fields of a farm. The stillness and quiet here are punctured only by the low buzzing of nearby transmission lines that run through the farmland. The trail continues another 0.9 mile before reaching the southern terminus at Rotary Field in Elmer.

CONTACT: elktownshipnj.gov/events-recreation/elephant-swamp

DIRECTIONS

To reach parking at Elk Township Recreational Park from the intersection of the New Jersey Turnpike and the North–South Fwy./NJ 42 in Bellmawr, head south on the North–South Fwy., and take Exit 13. Drive 11.1 miles on NJ 55 S, and take Exit 48. Turn right onto Ellis Mill Road, and then immediately turn left onto Aura Road. Go 1.7 miles, and turn right onto Whig Lane. The park, which offers ample visitor parking, is on the left in 0.2 mile. Once parked, turn left onto Recreation Dr. to pick up the trail heading south.

To reach parking at the southern terminus from the intersection of the New Jersey Turnpike and the North–South Fwy./NJ 42 in Bellmawr, head south on the North–South Fwy., and take Exit 13. Drive 14.7 miles on NJ 55 S, and take Exit 45. Turn right onto Buck Road, and go 3.8 miles. Turn right onto US 40, and go 1.6 miles. Just after crossing Elmer Lake, turn right into Rotary Field. Look for a parking lot across from the baseball fields. Head north through the parking lot to the start of the trail.

The tree-lined 22.5-mile Henry Hudson Trail is the definition of scenic variety. Traversing both urban and natural environments, the route passes wetlands, streams, fields, and the Garden State Parkway. Though the parkway divides the trail into northern and southern sections, an on-road route connects the two. Along this relatively flat path, users can expect to pass a backdrop varying from lush grassy meadows to utility corridors and suburban communities.

Monmouth Heritage Trail: 5.9 miles

The southernmost section, referred to locally as the Monmouth Heritage Trail, runs from Freehold up to Big Brook Park in Marlboro. Starting on East Main Street in Freehold,

County
Monmouth

Endpoints
E. Main St. between Zlotkin Cir. and Jackson St. (Freehold) to Big Brook Park near Newman Springs Road and Dunn Dr. (Marlboro Township); NJ 79 and Wyncrest Road (Morganville) to Clinton Street Park at Water St., 350 feet east of Orchard St. (Matawan); Gerard Ave. and Broadway (Aberdeen Township) to Ave. D between Kennedy Ct. and NJ 36 (Atlantic Highlands); Bay Ave. and Hennessey Blvd. (Atlantic Highlands) to Shore Dr. at Popamora Point, 0.15 mile north of Willow St. (Highlands)

Mileage
22.5

Type
Rail-Trail

Roughness Index
1

Surfaces
Asphalt, Gravel, Sand

The trail navigates through a number of natural environments, including wetlands, fields, grassy meadows, and woodlands.

Henry Hudson Trail

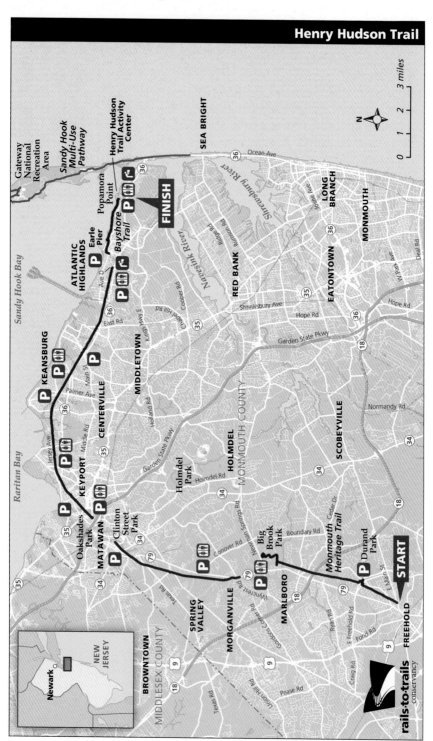

Gateway National Recreation Area

Sandy Hook Multi-Use Pathway

Henry Hudson Trail Activity Center

SEA BRIGHT

Ocean Ave

Popamora Point

Earle Pier

FINISH

ATLANTIC HIGHLANDS

Bayshore Trail

Shrewsbury River

LONG BRANCH

MONMOUTH

Sandy Hook Bay

Ave D

East Rd

Navesink River

RED BANK

EATONTOWN

Jones Ave

Hudson Rd

Hubbard Rd

Chapel Hill Rd

Cooper Rd

W Park Ave

Deal Rd

KEANSBURG

Main St

Palmer Ave

Kings Hwy E

Shrewsbury Ave

Hope Rd

Hope Rd

Garden State Pkwy

Raritan Bay

Jersey Ave

Middle Rd

CENTERVILLE

MIDDLETOWN

Holland Rd

SCOBEYVILLE

Normandy Rd

KEYPORT

Garden State Pkwy

HOLMDEL

Holmdel Park

Holmdel Rd

Cedar Dr

Oakshades Park

Clinton Street Park

MATAWAN

MONMOUTH COUNTY

Conover Rd

Newman Springs Rd

Big Brook Park

Boundary Rd

Monmouth Heritage Trail

Durand Park

START

Texas Rd

SPRING VALLEY

MORGANVILLE

Wyncrest Rd

MARLBORO

Ryan Rd

E Freehold Rd

E Main St

FREEHOLD

BROWNTOWN

Gordons Corner Rd

Pease Rd

Pond Rd

Craig Rd

MIDDLESEX COUNTY

Union Hill Rd

Newark

NEW JERSEY

rails-to-trails conservancy

N

0   1   2   3 miles

this portion of trail is primarily residential, transitioning between forest and suburban backyards. Approaching the end of this segment, trail users emerge into the scenic hills and meadows of Big Brook Park. Formerly farmland, this area is now maintained as part of the Monmouth County Park System. To reach the next segment of trail, exit the north side of Big Brook Park and take a left onto Newman Springs Road. In 1.5 miles, take a right to travel north alongside NJ 79. In 0.9 mile, the trail picks up at NJ 79 and Wyncrest Road.

Morganville to Matawan: 4.8 miles

The middle section of the trail from Wyncrest Road in Morganville up to Clinton Street Park in Matawan is an ideal rail-trail. Surrounding forests shield riders from the sounds of nearby NJ 79, providing a serene trail experience. This portion of trail contains several low-stress street crossings separated by long stretches of forested rail-trail. It also includes a utility corridor.

Aberdeen Township to Atlantic Highlands: 9.7 miles

The northernmost section begins south of Raritan Bay and roughly parallels NJ 36 to the north. Plans are underway to develop an on-street bicycle route that would connect Popamora Point to the Highlands–Sea Bright Bridge at Sandy Hook.

The Monmouth Heritage Trail section transitions between forest and residential neighborhoods.

Beginning inland at Oakshades Park at Gerard Avenue and Broadway, this section connects trail users to the nearby waterfront, providing uninterrupted views of Sandy Hook Bay, bridge crossings over numerous creeks, and a route to Atlantic Highlands. The eastern endpoint of this trail segment is Avenue D and NJ 36.

Bayshore Trail: 2.1 miles

After a gap of 0.7 mile, the next segment of trail begins at Bay Avenue, just south of Earle Pier. Considered part of the Henry Hudson Trail system, the Bayshore Trail continues east to Popamora Point. This section is paved for its first 0.6 mile; after that, as the trail traces the shoreline, the surface changes to gravel and sand. This area can also be subject to flooding, so check for trail conditions after heavy rains.

The trail is open sunrise–sunset. Dogs must be on a leash. There is one restroom in Atlantic Highlands at the Henry Hudson Trail Activity Center on NJ 36. Parking is also available at the activity center. No other restrooms or water fountains exist on the trail itself.

CONTACT: monmouthcountyparks.com/page.aspx?ID=2525

DIRECTIONS

To reach the southernmost trailhead in Freehold from I-95, take Exit 8 for NJ 133/Hightstown toward Freehold. Continue onto NJ 133, using the middle lane to stay on NJ 133. In 0.2 mile take the exit toward Hightstown/Freehold. Keep right at the fork and merge onto NJ 33 E. Go 11.1 miles, and take the exit for County Road 537 in Freehold. Turn right onto W. Main St., and go 2 miles. The trailhead will be on your left next to a gas station.

To reach the trailhead with parking near Oakshades Park, take Garden State Pkwy. to Aberdeen Township. If heading southbound, take Exit 118 toward Aberdeen, turn left onto Lloyd Road, go 0.3 mile, and turn left onto Gerard Ave. In 0.2 mile, Oakshades Park will be on your right. If heading northbound, take Exit 117 to merge onto NJ 35 S toward Hazlet/Aberdeen. In 0.2 mile take a sharp left onto NJ 35 N, and go 0.1 mile. Use the left lane to take the Pkwy./Clark St. exit, and go 0.3 mile. Turn right onto Clark St., and go 0.4 mile. The trailhead is next to the gas station on Broadway and Clark St. across from Oakshades Park.

To reach the Bayshore Trail eastern endpoint and parking lot at Popamora Point from Garden State Pkwy., take Exit 117 toward NJ 36. Follow signs to stay on NJ 36 E/S for 11.8 miles. Take a slight right onto Serpentine Dr., followed by an immediate right onto CR 8. In 0.1 mile, continue straight onto S. Linden Ave., and go 0.3 mile. Turn left onto Waterwitch Ave., and immediately turn left onto Shore Dr. in Highlands. Parking is available at Popamora Point at the end of Shore Dr. in 0.6 mile.

The village of Smithville, upon which the Historic Smithville Park (open 8 a.m.–30 minutes after sunset) sits, has a long and colorful past—and some important connections to the history of bicycles in America. Originally settled by the Lenni-Lenape tribe, the land was taken over by a Colonial settler in 1676. A dam, sawmill, and gristmill were built during the Colonial period, making it ideal for the Shreve brothers to establish a textile factory and workers' village when they bought the land in 1831. The factory eventually went bankrupt; in 1865, Hezekiah Bradley Smith bought the property and turned it into a modern industrial village to produce his woodworking machinery technology.

The manufacturing company produced the American Star Bicycle as the industry was taking off in the 1880s. The Star bicycle featured a small front wheel and large back wheel—which overcame the problem of

The green-blazed trail skirts Smithville Lake, which offers several fishing spots on the water.

County
Burlington

Endpoints
Historic Smithville Park visitor center at Meade Lane and Smithville Road to E. Railroad Ave., just west of Fir Lane (Eastampton Township)

Mileage
3.9

Roughness Index
2–3

Type
Rail-Trail/Greenway

Surfaces
Boardwalk, Dirt, Gravel, Sand, Wood Chips

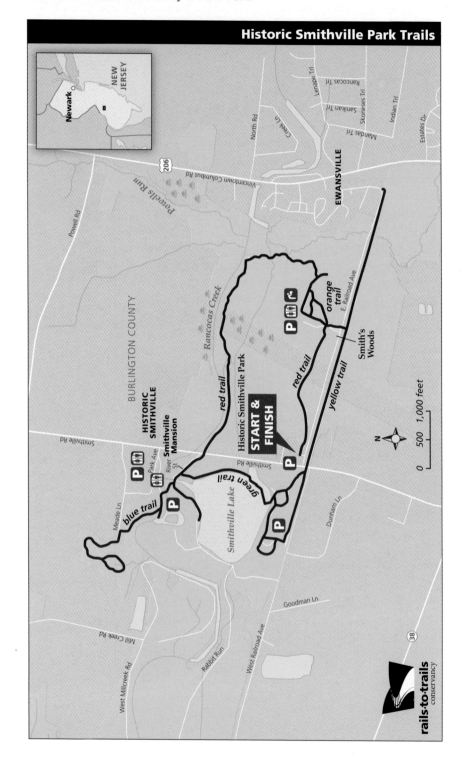

Historic Smithville Park Trails

NEW JERSEY

Newark

BURLINGTON COUNTY

Powell Rd

Powells Run

206

Vincentown Columbus Rd

North Rd

Creek Ln

Lenape Trl

Rancocas Trl

Sankian Trl

Skoneses Trl

Indian Trl

Estates Dr

Mandas Trl

EWANSVILLE

Rancocas Creek

orange trail

E. Railroad Ave

Smith's Woods

red trail

yellow trail

red trail

Historic Smithville Park

HISTORIC SMITHVILLE

Smithville Rd

Smithville Mansion

Park Ave

River St

Smithville Rd

START & FINISH

N

0   500   1,000 feet

blue trail

Meade Ln

green trail

Smithville Lake

Dunham Ln

Goodman Ln

Mill Creek Rd

West Millcreek Rd

Rabbit Run

West Railroad Ave

38

rails-to-trails
conservancy

tipping forward that was common among high-wheel bicycles at the time. An iron sculpture of the Star can be seen on River Street, close to the start of the Ravine Nature Trail in the park.

Starting at the municipal lot on the corner of Smithville Road and East Railroad Avenue, head east on the red trail (the trails are marked with color-coded signage) as it enters the woods and leaves the sound of cars behind. The wooded trail passes through a brief section of open fields where a transmission line intersects above; interpretive signage emphasizes the importance of the vegetation in this area as pollinator habitats. About 0.3 mile from the start, you come to a parking lot and a trail intersection. If you turn right, the orange trail will take you across East Railroad Avenue and connect to the yellow trail. If you turn left, the orange trail will take you down to the Smith's Woods Area, which includes picnic pavilions and a butterfly garden, planted with species known to attract pollinators. Continue straight along the red trail as the path winds around the opposite side of these amenities, intersecting with a playground before reentering its forested surroundings.

The forested path offers the perfect setting for a diversity of trail users—on this section, you may encounter everything from families with children on a hike to friends walking their dogs together. About 0.45 mile from the start, the red trail veers left.

Continuing along the red trail, you will encounter a staircase with a smooth ramp for wheeled items like bicycles. Almost 0.7 mile from the start, there is another split in the trail; bear left to continue along the red trail, emerging from the forest to travel parallel to the Rancocas Creek as it winds toward Smithville Lake. The trail crosses busy Smithville Road and continues to wind its way through the park, crossing two bridges before ending at the boat launch on River Street.

In this area by the boat launch, you'll begin to see interpretive signage that tells the story of historic Smithville and different aspects of life in the industrial village, such as the first bicycle railway. Modified bicycles served as individual pods for users and sat along a fencelike track as users pedaled their way to their destinations. At a time when most roads were unpaved and easily became muddy, the bicycle railway offered a way to get from nearby communities to the industrial center of Smithville in less than 10 minutes.

Next to the boat launch is the beginning of the blue-blazed Ravine Nature Trail. Users should note that this walking-only path is off-limits to bicycles. The change in surface to bumpy wood chips also discourages wheeled use. Shortly into the trail, a set of stairs helps users climb the steep hillside as the route winds through the trees, emerging along Meade Lane. Cross the road and turn left to continue down the trail in an open, grassy field. Entering the woods again, you will encounter densely packed trees and hilly terrain along the ravine, while bridges help you cross the water channels below. There is a small loop at the

On the blue-blazed trail (walking only), pedestrians will encounter forested and hilly terrain along the ravine, and bridges over the water.

end of the trail; regardless of which way you come, you will very soon return to where you started and need to double back to the beginning.

On the way back, if you wish to turn left at Meade Lane, you will reach several parking lots, a farm complex, and a mansion complex. Smithville Mansion—where Hezekiah Smith and his family resided—is open for tours during the summer season on particular days of the week. Consult its website, **smithvillemansion.org,** for details.

To reach the green trail, first take the red trail back over the bridge. As you saw earlier, a large gravel lot and several brick buildings appear to your right. Interpretive signage notes them as industrial buildings where the machinery was made and provides information about what it was like to work for the company. Turn down the lane and over the bridge, now on a spur section of the green trail, which leads to the lake and several fishing spots on the water.

After taking the time to admire the view on a nearby bench, double back to the red trail, go over the second bridge, and turn right at the next gravel lot to head down the main green trail. While the green trail can accommodate bicycles, the multiple, steep staircases at the end near West Railroad Avenue could make it difficult to traverse on wheels.

This stretch offers views of Smithville Lake on your right. Rabbits hop across the trail, and bullfrogs call to each other from the muddy banks. A floating section over the water provides a panoramic view of the lake. On warm, sunny days, you might even spot blue herons and other waterfowl dancing across the lake in search of a meal.

Mind the stairs as you exit the floating section, as the trail splits again. Turn left and you'll head up a set of stairs, then down a steep sloping hill and up again to meet the yellow trail. Turn right and you'll also encounter a set of stairs, as the trail splits once more. To the left, the green trail leads toward the yellow trail. To the right, it continues to wrap around the lake, and not long after, you will see a staircase that leads down to another pavilion overlooking the lake. With the staircase on your right, turning left is the quickest exit to the West Railroad Avenue trailhead. Continue straight and the trail creates a short loop through the woods, surrounding a small gazebo in the middle. Exiting the loop, you'll want to turn right to reach the end of the green trail and the beginning of the yellow trail on your left.

The yellow trail, the only pathway in the park that permits equestrian use, parallels Railroad Avenue. Take care when crossing over Smithville Road before continuing straight. In this section, trees separate the path from the nearby road and, dampening the noise, offer a quiet respite. There are plans to continue the path, but for now the yellow trail ends just 0.8 mile from its start, with a cut-through providing access back down to the road.

CONTACT: co.burlington.nj.us/948/Historic-Smithville-Park

DIRECTIONS

To reach the W. Railroad Ave. trailhead from I-295 N, take Exit 43 (from I-295 S, take Exit 43A). Head southeast on Creek Road, following signs for Rancocas Woods. Continue 1.3 miles, and turn left onto Marne Hwy. Continue another 1.6 miles, and turn right onto Lumberton Road. After 0.4 mile, turn left onto NJ 38 E. Head straight 3.9 miles before turning left onto Smithville Road. In 0.4 mile turn left onto W. Railroad Ave. In 0.2 mile, the parking lot will be visible on the right.

To reach the municipal lot on Smithville Road, follow the directions above to Smithville Road. Turn left onto Smithville, and go 0.45 mile; the parking lot will be on your right.

To reach the parking lots on Meade Lane near the mansion and farm complexes, follow the directions above to Smithville Road. Turn left onto Smithville, and go 0.8 mile. Turn left onto Meade Lane, and parking lots A and B will be visible.

To reach the Smith's Woods trailhead, follow the directions above to Smithville Road. Turn left onto Smithville, go 0.4 mile, and turn right onto E. Railroad Ave. Continue straight 0.4 mile. The entrance will be on your left.

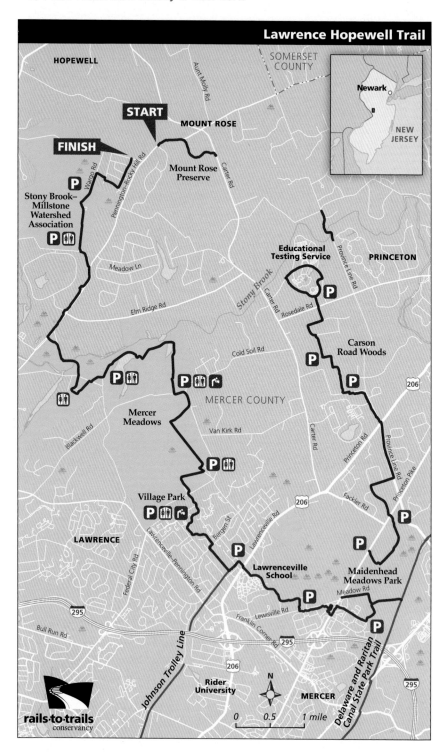

Lawrence Hopewell Trail

HOPEWELL

SOMERSET COUNTY

Newark

NEW JERSEY

MOUNT ROSE

START

FINISH

Mount Rose Preserve

Stony Brook–Millstone Watershed Association

Meadow Ln

Elm Ridge Rd

Stony Brook

Educational Testing Service

PRINCETON

Province Line Rd

Rosedale Rd

Carter Rd

Carson Road Woods

206

Cold Soil Rd

MERCER COUNTY

Mercer Meadows

Van Kirk Rd

Blackwell Rd

Princeton Rd

Carter Rd

Village Park

Bergen St

Lawrenceville Rd

206

Fackler Rd

Province Line Rd

Princeton Pke

LAWRENCE

Federal City Rd

Lawrenceville–Pennington Rd

Lawrenceville School

Maidenhead Meadows Park

Meadow Rd

295

Bull Run Rd

Lewisville Rd

Franklin Corner Rd

295

Delaware and Raritan Canal State Park Trail

206

Johnson Trolley Line

Rider University

MERCER

295

rails·to·trails
conservancy

0   0.5   1 mile

The Lawrence Hopewell Trail (LHT) offers more than 19 miles of pathway on a developing loop through public and private land in Lawrence and Hopewell Townships, about 5 miles north of Trenton. The route links business districts, parks, schools, historical villages, and playing fields, and it provides views of farmland and woodlands. Though the trail's surface is largely porous pavement (which offers better stormwater control than traditional pavement), there are some crushed-stone sections, such as through Carson Road Woods, Maidenhead Meadows Park, and Mercer Meadows.

The planned 22-mile route is nearly complete with four gaps remaining, some of which traverse busy roads. The trail is anticipated to be finished in 2021. Additional connections to adjacent communities are also being planned, and the trail is part of a developing network in the Greater Philadelphia and Camden region called the Circuit Trails, which will encompass 800 miles of trail when complete.

The LHT is broken into 16 named segments, each with its own unique historical and natural features and trail characteristics. The first one, called the Mount Rose Distillery Segment—a 1.1-mile excursion through the wooded Mount Rose Preserve—begins at the north end of the trail in Hopewell.

County
Mercer

Endpoints
Pennington–Rocky Hill Road and Bailey Ct. to Carter Road, 0.4 mile south of Pennington–Rocky Hill Road (Hopewell); Province Line Road at Pretty Brook Road to Province Line Road, 0.25 mile south of Stony Brook Lane (Princeton); ETS Dr. at Research Road to Princeton Pike, 0.4 mile southwest of Fackler Road (Lawrence); Princeton Pike at Meadow Road (Lawrence) to Weldon Way at Moores Mill Mount Rose Road (Hopewell)

Mileage
19.2

Type
Greenway/Non-Rail-Trail

Roughness Index
2

Surfaces
Asphalt, Crushed Stone

This peaceful journey lies halfway between two of the East Coast's biggest cities: New York City and Philadelphia.

Moving clockwise around the loop from there, you can pick up the trail again in Lawrence on the Educational Testing Service campus. After looping around the property, you'll continue another 4 miles south to the end of this section at Princeton Pike. Along the way, you'll traverse Carson Road Woods, which includes numerous walking paths throughout the pristine preserve, and pass the campus of another major employer, Bristol-Myers Squibb. As you approach the end of this section, use caution as you travel through Maidenhead Meadows Park; the trail here can be challenging to navigate with a road bike or hybrid.

A gap of less than a mile separates this section from the next. Pick up the trail farther down Princeton Pike at Meadow Road. You'll now begin the longest continuous section of trail. In 0.5 mile, you'll come to a T-junction; head right to continue on the LHT. Go left to reach the Delaware and Raritan Canal State Park Trail (see page 21) in 0.3 mile; the expansive trail stretches nearly 70 miles and takes travelers into Trenton.

If you stayed on the LHT, you'll pop out of the trees into a business park environment. Soon, you'll be on a northwest course winding through the Lawrenceville School campus, with its redbrick buildings, and Village Park, a popular spot with numerous athletic facilities and playgrounds. A highlight of the route is passage through Mercer Meadows, a sprawling 1,600-acre park with native grasses and wildflowers, lush woodlands, and two lakes, where you might spot deer, rabbits, and other wildlife. A unique attraction in the park is the Pole Farm, a historical relic of a telecommunications company once located here. Mercer Meadows also offers equestrian riding opportunities, including on portions of the LHT.

Approaching trail's end, you'll enter Hopewell again, passing through the nature reserve of the Stony Brook–Millstone Watershed Association, and end just 0.4 mile from where you started.

CONTACT: lhtrail.org

DIRECTIONS

To reach the parking lot in the Mount Rose Distillery Segment from the intersection of US 206 and Princeton Pike in Trenton, head north on US 206. In 4.8 miles you'll reach the unincorporated community of Lawrenceville, where you'll take a left onto Carter Road. Follow Carter Road north 4.2 miles to the trailhead, which will be on your left. From the intersection of US 202 and US 206 in Somerville, head south on US 206, and go 14.2 miles. Turn right onto Cherry Valley Road, and go 4.75 miles. Turn left onto Carter Road. Go 0.4 mile, and the trailhead will be on your right.

To reach parking at the Watershed Institute in the Stony Brook–Millstone Watershed Reserve, take I-295 to Exit 72. Follow NJ 31 northbound 1.4 miles. Make a slight left to continue on NJ 31 N, and go 3.1 miles. Turn right onto Titus Mill Road; follow it 1.2 miles east to the parking lot.

It's hard to believe that a noisy locomotive once ran through here, given that stillness is a defining characteristic of the Middlesex Greenway. Even when people pour onto the trail from the adjacent neighborhoods, it remains a tranquil escape shielded from the everyday hum of the suburbs and the hubbub of the industries nearby.

The rail-trail sits on a corridor that once held trains moving anthracite coal from Pennsylvania to New Jersey. The Easton and Amboy Railroad was a subsidiary of the Lehigh Valley Railroad; it was active in some form or other from 1875 through 1991. When it ceased operations, some motivated citizens immediately recognized the potential of having a corridor that cut close to their neighborhoods. Twenty years of effort later, the rail-trail finally opened in 2012.

The Middlesex Greenway is a great trail for a leisurely stroll with a dog (leashed, of course), an evening jog, or a bike ride. Because of its location, it's a natural draw for families, and you will see users of all ages enjoying a shady trip through history. Currently, the trail runs from Metuchen through Edison to Woodbridge.

County
Middlesex

Endpoints
Middlesex Ave., 0.1 mile northeast of Memorial Pkwy. (Metuchen), to 0.2 mile east of Crows Mill Road, just south of E. William St. (Woodbridge)

Mileage
3.6

Type
Rail-Trail

Roughness Index
1

Surface
Asphalt

Shielded by trees, the trail provides a relaxing outing amid the surrounding suburbs.

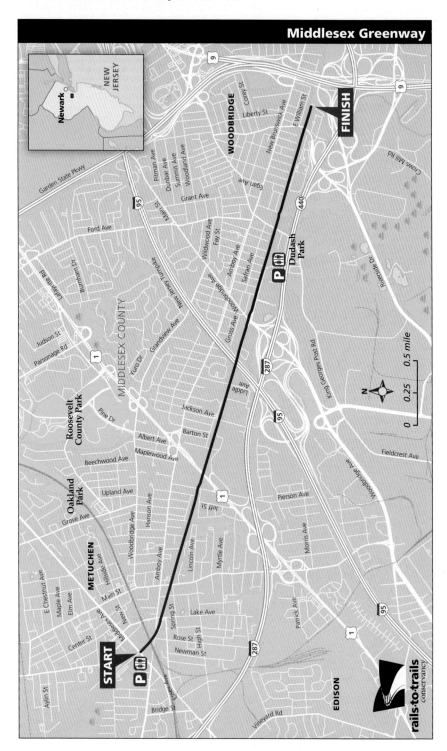

Middlesex Greenway

NEW JERSEY

Newark

WOODBRIDGE

FINISH

Corey St

Liberty St

E William St

New Brunswick Ave

9

9

Crows Mill Rd

Garden State Pkwy

Pitman Ave

Dunbar Ave

Summit Ave

Woodland Ave

Grant Ave

Egan Ave

95

Neily St

Ford Ave

440

Riverside Dr

Burnham Dr

Lafayette Rd

New Jersey Turnpike

Wildwood Ave

Fay St

Amboy Ave

Safran Ave

Woodbridge Ave

Dudash Park

P

Gross Ave

MIDDLESEX COUNTY

Judson St

Parsonage Rd

1

Yuro Dr

Grandview Ave

King Georges Post Rd

287

Pine Dr

Liddle Ave

95

Roosevelt County Park

Jackson Ave

Barton St

N

0   0.25   0.5 mile

Fieldcrest Ave

Beechwood Ave

Maplewood Ave

Albert Ave

Oakland Park

Upland Ave

Hanson Ave

Woodbridge Ave

Jeff St

1

Pierson Ave

Woodbridge Ave

Grove Ave

Morris Ave

E Chestnut Ave

Maple Ave

Elm Ave

METUCHEN

Hillside Ave

Main St

New St

Middlesex Ave

Amboy Ave

Lincoln Ave

Myrtle Ave

Spring St

Lake Ave

Patrick Ave

95

Center St

Rose St

High St

Newman St

287

1

Aylin St

Bridge St

Essex Ave

Vineyard Rd

EDISON

START

P

rails-to-trails conservancy

A good place to begin your journey is the Metuchen trailhead on Middlesex Avenue, with parking and a trail kiosk. A gateway with the trail's name signifies its start, and you will see this motif replicated at other trail entry points; seven of these entrances are wheelchair accessible. The path stretches out before you flat and wide, hemmed in by native plantings and giant trees. Mile-marker posts whiz by every 0.25 mile, along with a sign to let you know which of the three municipalities you are in at that time. Colorful and detailed interpretative signage can also be found strategically placed at access points, narrating the history of the railroad and the region.

In Edison, about 1 mile in, you may spot the logo of the East Coast Greenway; this portion of the trail is part of that developing effort to connect trails on a 3,000-mile route between Maine and Florida. Edison is also where you'll find the lone pedestrian bridge on the trail; the rest of the crossings are either underneath vehicular traffic or at street level. (The Woodbridge Avenue crossing is the widest of the on-road crossings, so approach with caution.) The bridge arches over US 1 before depositing you safely on the other side of the highway.

In Woodbridge, more than 2.5 miles into your journey, you will see on your right side a redbrick wall with faded lettering looming above the bushes. A historical marker reveals this to be the old Fords Porcelain Works building, constructed in 1906. This factory produced bathroom fixtures, including sinks, bathtubs, and toilets, but shut down in the 1960s. Although the trail dead-ends unceremoniously shortly thereafter, you can always turn right back around and disappear into the shady coolness of the greenway.

CONTACT: middlesexcountynj.gov/About/ParksRecreation/Pages/PR/Middlesex-Greenway.aspx

DIRECTIONS

To reach the western end of the trail in Metuchen from I-287 S, take Exit 3 for New Durham Road/County Road 501 toward New Durham/Metuchen. Turn left onto New Durham Road/CR 501, and stay on it 1.3 miles, then turn left onto Middlesex Ave. The Greenway Park parking lot will be on your right. From I-287 N, take Exit 2A, and merge onto NJ 27 N/Essex Ave. In 400 feet, turn left onto Bridge St. In 0.1 mile turn right onto Middlesex Ave., and go 0.4 mile to Greenway Park.

Although there is no trailhead for the eastern end of the trail in Woodbridge, you can park at Dudash Park in Edison. From I-287 S, take Exit 1B for US 1 S toward CR 531/Trenton. Merge onto Main St./CR 531, heading south, and stay on it 0.8 mile. Make a left onto Woodbridge Ave., and follow it 1.4 miles. Use the right lane to take the I-95/I-287/New Jersey Turnpike ramp. Keep right, and then turn right onto May St. Dudash Park will be on the left in 0.4 mile. Once you have parked, follow the park pathway to the Middlesex Greenway entrance. From I-95, take Exit 10 for NJ 440 E, and keep left at the fork, then right, following signs for I-287 N/CR 514 E. Turn right onto May St., and go 0.4 mile to Dudash Park.

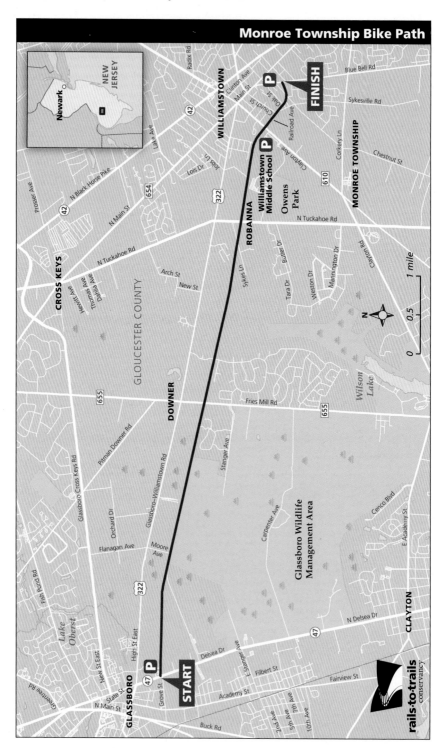

The Monroe Township Bike Path carries visitors through the tranquil woodlands of the Glassboro Wildlife Management Area as it connects the southern New Jersey suburban towns of Glassboro and Williamstown. The pathway is part of the Circuit Trails, an expansive regional trail network across nine counties, including Gloucester County, which will eventually encompass 800 miles of trails.

The borough of Glassboro's name reflects the glass-making industry that thrived here throughout the 19th century. In fact, the 6.3-mile paved trail owes its existence to that boom. The route follows the former corridor of the Pennsylvania-Reading Seashore Lines, which in 1933 acquired tracks originally laid by the Williamstown Railroad (later the Williamstown & Delaware River Railroad) in the 1870s and early 1880s. Originally conceived to serve the many glass and bottle makers in

The dense understory of the Glassboro Wildlife Management Area creates a haven for birds.

County
Gloucester

Endpoints
Delsea Dr. S/NJ 47 between Awalt Dr. and Grove St. (Glassboro) to Blue Bell Road/County Road 633 between Virginia Ave. and Chestnut St. (Williamstown)

Mileage
6.3

Type
Rail-Trail

Roughness Index
1

Surface
Asphalt

the area, the railroad later connected to other lines to carry tourists to the Jersey Shore destinations of Atlantic City, Ocean City, Wildwood, and Cape May.

Unlike some other eastern rail corridors that follow meandering streams, the railroad followed the shortest-distance rule that results in today's nearly arrow-straight trail.

Beginning on the south side of Glassboro, the trail heads east through a commercial-industrial complex before entering the northern edge of a hardwood forest in the Glassboro Wildlife Management Area. The 2,300 acres are popular for squirrel, grouse, and deer hunting in season. The tree cover makes for shady trail travel in the summer.

The vegetation screen thins out a bit after 1.3 miles at Moore Avenue, then gets heavy again until the path crosses County Road 655 in another 1.3 miles. After a 0.5-mile jaunt through a neighborhood, the forest becomes dense again for nearly a mile until the outskirts of Williamstown, a one-time glass-manufacturing center in its own right. The trail passes a sprawling educational campus before passing through a leafy residential neighborhood around the old station site on Railroad Avenue.

You may see a plaque near the trailhead designating this section as the George F. McDonald Sr. Memorial Bike Path, named for the 1975–1978 mayor. A nearby convenience store is a good place to stock up on snacks before heading back to Glassboro.

CONTACT: mtprnj.org/bike-path

DIRECTIONS

To reach the trailhead in Glassboro from I-76/North-South Fwy./NJ 42, take Exit 13 onto NJ 55 S. Go 6.7 miles to Exit 53A, and merge onto County Road 553/Woodbury-Glassboro Road, which becomes N. Woodbury Road and then S. Woodbury Road. Go 2.4 miles and merge onto Delsea Dr./NJ 47. Go 1.9 miles, turn left onto Awalt Dr., and look for on-street parking. The trail is just south of Awalt Dr.

To reach parking for the eastern trailhead at Williamstown Middle School from North-South Fwy./NJ 42 S (or from the Atlantic City Expy.), keep left to get on the Atlantic City Expy. Take Exit 38, and head southwest on Williamstown Road. Go 2 miles (the road will become CR 536 Spur/Sicklerville Road and then Clayton Road). Turn right into the Williamstown Middle School parking lot. Bear right to find parking closest to the trail at the north end of the lot. Once on the trail, turn right and go 0.7 mile to find the eastern trailhead on Blue Bell Road.

The Paulinskill Valley Trail follows a creek by the same name through a section of rural New Jersey with a strong German influence. In fact, the word *kill* is Dutch for "riverbed or stream channel." German refugees from European wars settled along the Paulins Kill during the Colonial period, and their influence survives in communities along the 27-mile trail. Visitors will see plentiful wildlife, such as bear, bobcat, mink, and deer, along the path, and sightings of more than 100 species of birds have been documented. Fishing is also available in the Paulins Kill.

The New York, Susquehanna and Western Railway laid tracks down the valley between Kittatinny Mountain and the New Jersey Highlands in 1886. Trains hauled coal from Pennsylvania and carried passengers, produce, and dairy products from the agricultural valley until hard times hit in 1962, and the railroad removed the tracks west

When the snow arrives, skiers, snowshoers, and even dog sled teams hit the route.

Counties
Sussex, Warren

Endpoints
Brugler Road, 0.2 mile north of Warrington Road (Knowlton Township), to Sparta Junction, 0.6 mile southeast of Sunset Inn Road and Limecrest Randazzo Road (Sparta Township)

Mileage
27.1

Type
Rail-Trail

Roughness Index
2–3

Surfaces
Ballast, Cinder, Dirt, Grass

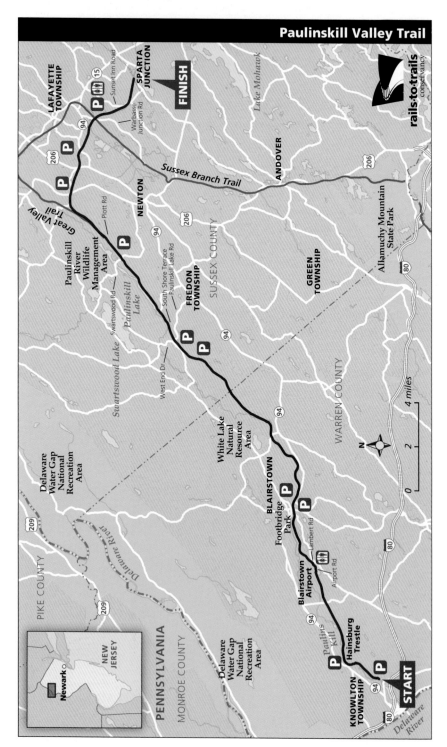

Paulinskill Valley Trail

rails-to-trails
conservancy

LAFAYETTE TOWNSHIP

15

Sunset Inn Road

SPARTA JUNCTION

FINISH

Lake Mohawk

Warbasse Junction Rd

206

ANDOVER

206

Sussex Branch Trail

Great Valley Trail

Plott Rd

NEWTON

206

94

SUSSEX COUNTY

Paulinskill River Wildlife Management Area

Swartswood Rd

Paulinskill Lake

South Shore Terrace

Paulinskill Lake Rd

FREDON TOWNSHIP

94

GREEN TOWNSHIP

Allamuchy Mountain State Park

80

Swartswool Lake

West End Dr

WARREN COUNTY

Delaware Water Gap National Recreation Area

209

White Lake Natural Resource Area

94

BLAIRSTOWN

Footbridge Park

Lambert Rd

80

Delaware River

PIKE COUNTY

209

Blairstown Airport

Airport Rd

94

PENNSYLVANIA

MONROE COUNTY

Paulins Kill

Hainsburg Trestle

94

START

KNOWLTON TOWNSHIP

80

Delaware River

Delaware Water Gap National Recreation Area

N

0   2   4 miles

NEW JERSEY

Newark

of Sparta Junction. Used unofficially as a trail for many years, the corridor was purchased by the state in 1986 and became a state park in 1992. The remains of icehouses, creameries, and depots can be spotted from the trail.

The path runs from near the Paulins Kill confluence with the Delaware River in the west to active railroad tracks at Sparta Junction in the east. The trail's primarily cinder surface is better suited to bikes with wide tires. Note that the tips of the trail are where you will encounter different surfaces; there is a short section (about 20 feet) of ballast at the trail's western end, and a 0.6-mile section of dirt and grass from Sunset Inn Road to the trail's eastern end.

Start on the west end at the Brugler Road trailhead in Knowlton Township. In 1.1 miles the trail arrives at the massive Paulinskill Viaduct, also known as the Hainesburg Trestle. Built by the Delaware, Lackawanna & Western Railroad in 1910, the viaduct soars 115 feet above Paulins Kill and Station Road as seven arches carry it 1,100 feet across. At one time, it was the world's largest reinforced concrete structure.

In 4 miles, you'll arrive at Blairstown Airport, which interrupts the trail. Take Airport and Lambert Roads to resume the trail in 0.6 mile. Footbridge Park in Blairstown is 2 miles ahead, where you can find something to eat or

The pathway is truly multiuse, offering opportunities for exploration by foot, wheel, hoof, or ski.

explore the town's historic district that features a gristmill dating to 1825. This is the last chance to stock up on trailside snacks.

Crossing the creek four times in the next 4.5 miles, the trail also passes the 400-acre White Lake Natural Resource Area. Nine miles past Blairstown, trail users descend a side path to cross West End Drive/Paulinskill Lake Road, and then go left a short distance to South Shore Terrace, where they regain the railroad grade. The trail provides an elevated view of 3-mile-long Paulinskill Lake. The path crosses Swartswood Road/County Road 622 in 2.2 miles in the Paulinskill River Wildlife Management Area. You can access the Great Valley Trail in 0.9 mile at Plott Road, just north of Newton; it makes a 13-mile loop with the Paulinskill Valley and Sussex Branch Trails. The Paulinskill Valley Trail is also part of the September 11th National Memorial Trail that connects 9/11, Flight 93, and Pentagon Memorials.

Continuing 4.9 miles from that road crossing, you'll intersect the Sussex Branch Trail (see page 62) just past Warbasse Junction Road in Lafayette Township. That trail runs 18 miles between Branchville and Allamuchy Mountain State Park (go 1 mile left on the Sussex Branch Trail to reach restaurants in Lafayette). The last 0.6 mile can be overgrown and includes stream crossings on narrow footbridges. The trail ends at an active rail corridor with no public road access.

CONTACT: njparksandforests.org/parks/kittval.html and pvtc-kvsp.org

DIRECTIONS

To reach the western trailhead on Brugler Road from I-80, take Exit 4C-A or 4C, and merge onto NJ 94 N. Go 1.3 miles, and turn right onto Brugler Road. Go 1.2 miles, and look for parking just past the bridge in 0.4 mile. A parking permit is required from Knowlton Township (**knowlton -nj.com**) at the Brugler Road and Station Road trailheads.

To reach the eastern trailhead at Warbasse Junction Road from I-80 in Lafayette Township, take Exit 25 toward Newton. Merge onto US 206 N, go 10.9 miles, and turn left to stay on US 206/Main St. Go 1 mile, and turn left onto US 206/Spring St. Then go another 0.1 mile, and bear right onto US 206/NJ 94/Water St. Go 2.2 miles, and turn right onto NJ 94/Morris Farm Lafayette Road. Go 2 miles, and turn right onto Warbasse Junction Road. Go 0.5 mile, and look for trail parking on the right.

The Pleasantville to Somers Point Bike Path connects four cities along 8.2 miles of trail: Pleasantville, Northfield, Linwood, and Somers Point. The path travels through city centers, neighborhoods, and tree-lined parks, ending in Somers Point a few blocks away from the Atlantic Ocean.

Trailside memorials and ice cream shops provide ideal spaces to take a break along the way. Much of the route travels through residential neighborhoods and past schools. Often, you can see students using the path as a safe walking route between home and school, as well as other residents out enjoying the trail for both exercise and leisure—for a quick ride or a stroll into town.

The north end of the trail begins in Pleasantville, the most urban of the communities. Beginning off Devins Lane, the path travels behind various retailers until it makes an abrupt right turn just before Chestnut Avenue. The path utilizes an inactive railroad bridge to cross over busy US 40/Black Horse Pike. After crossing the highway, the trail continues alongside Fuae Avenue in Northfield.

Once in Northfield, the path travels through residential neighborhoods. At Zion Road, it leaves Fuae Avenue and begins to parallel Wabash Avenue.

Extending into Linwood along Wabash Avenue, the bike path (occasionally called the Linwood Bike Path) evokes a pleasant community feel. The bike path takes the center of a wide median that divides Wabash Avenue; the eastern side is one-way northbound, and the western side is one-way southbound. Linwood offers a variety of attractions, including All Wars Memorial Park and the Linwood Arboretum.

As the path approaches Somers Point, the surroundings shift from residential to urban. The trail ends outside of the Somers Point city clerk's office but can be taken all the way into the historic district of Somers Point via on-road facilities.

County
Atlantic

Endpoints
Devins Lane between Noahs Road and Washington Ave. (Pleasantville) to NJ 52 and County Road 559 (Somers Point)

Mileage
8.2

Type
Rail-Trail/Rail-with-Trail

Roughness Index
1

Surface
Asphalt

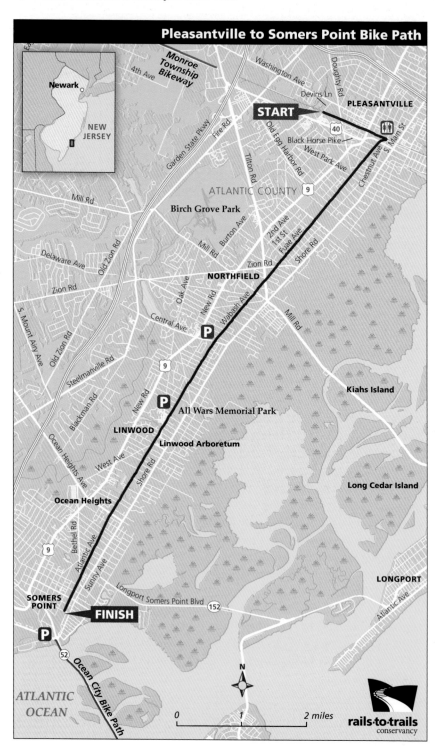

Pleasantville to Somers Point Bike Path

Newark

NEW JERSEY

Monroe Township Bikeway

4th Ave

Washington Ave

Doughty Rd

Devins Ln

PLEASANTVILLE

START

Garden State Pkwy

Fire Rd

40

Black Horse Pike

S. Main St

Chestnut Ave

West Park Ave

Old Egg Harbor Rd

Tilton Rd

Mill Rd

ATLANTIC COUNTY

9

Birch Grove Park

Burton Ave

2nd Ave

1st St

Fuae Ave

Shore Rd

Mill Rd

Delaware Ave

Old Zion Rd

Mill Rd

Zion Rd

NORTHFIELD

Zion Rd

Oak Ave

New Rd

Wabash Ave

Mill Rd

S. Mount Airy Ave

Old Zion Rd

Central Ave

P

Kiahs Island

Steelmanville Rd

9

Blackman Rd

P

All Wars Memorial Park

New Rd

LINWOOD

Linwood Arboretum

Long Cedar Island

Ocean Heights Ave

West Ave

Shore Rd

Ocean Heights

Bethel Rd

9

Atlantic Ave

Sunny Ave

Longport Somers Point Blvd

152

LONGPORT

Atlantic Ave

SOMERS POINT

FINISH

P

52

Ocean City Bike Path

ATLANTIC OCEAN

N

0   1   2 miles

rails·to·trails
conservancy

The trail connects neighborhoods and parks across four cities.

CONTACT: atlantic-county.org/tourism/cycling.asp

DIRECTIONS

To reach the north end of the trail in Pleasantville, take the Atlantic City Expy. to Exit 5. Head southwest on US 9/S. New Road, and go 0.8 mile. Turn left onto Decatur Ave. There is limited curbside parking.

To reach the southern end of the trail in Somers Point, take the Atlantic City Expy. to Exit 5. Head southwest on US 9/S. New Road, and go 3 miles. Turn left onto W. Mill Road. In 0.5 mile turn right onto Shore Road, and continue 4.3 miles. Turn right onto W. New Jersey Ave. Turn right onto First St. Parking is on the right.

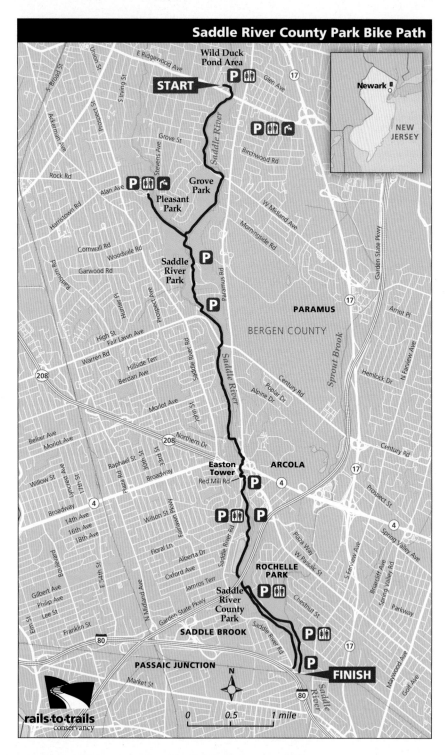

Saddle River County Park Bike Path

Wild Duck
Pond Area

START

Glen Ave

17

Saddle River

E Ridgewood Ave

S Broad St

Union St

S Irving St

Prospect St

Ackerman Ave

Grove St

Stevens Ave

Birchwood Rd

Newark

NEW
JERSEY

W Midland Ave

Rock Rd

Grove
Park

Morningside Rd

Alan Ave

Pleasant
Park

Harristown Rd

Cornwall Rd

Woodvale Rd

Garwood Rd

Saddle
River
Park

Paramus Rd

PARAMUS

BERGEN COUNTY

Garden State Pkwy

Radburn Rd

Hunter Pl

Prospect Ave

Saddle River Rd

Sprout Brook

Arnot Pl

17

High St

Fair Lawn Ave

Warren Rd

Hillside Terr

Berdan Ave

Saddle River

Century Rd

Poplar Dr

Alpine Dr

Hemlock Dr

N Fairview Ave

208

Morlot Ave

John St

Northern Dr

Century Rd

Bellair Ave

Morlot Ave

Willow St

Lyncrest Ave

17th Ave

Raphael St

30th St

33rd St

Broadway

208

**Easton
Tower**

Red Mill Rd

ARCOLA

4

17

Prospect St

Broadway

4

14th Ave

16th Ave

18th Ave

Plaza Rd

Fairlawn Pkwy

Wilson St Ln

Floral Ln

Alberta Dr

Saddle River Rd

4

Spring Valley Ave

E 54th St

Oxford Ave

Jamros Terr

**ROCHELLE
PARK**

Plaza Way

W Passaic St

S Fairview Ave

Briarcliff Ave

Spring Valley Rd

Parkway

Gilbert Ave

Philip Ave

Lee St

Franklin St

N Midland Ave

Garden State Pkwy

**Saddle
River
County
Park**

Chestnut St

17

Maywood Ave

Elm St

80

SADDLE BROOK

Saddle River Rd

PASSAIC JUNCTION

Market St

N

0   0.5   1 mile

80

Saddle River

FINISH

Goll Ave

rails·to·trails
conservancy

The Saddle River County Park Bike Path is a beautiful suburban trail that winds alongside the Saddle River. Most of the trail runs through moderately dense suburban development, with residential and commercial buildings along the length of the trail. Portions of the route are slightly more wooded and secluded. While traveling through the green landscape and along the waterway, you may see geese, ducks, squirrels, and deer.

Due to its proximity to local neighborhoods, cyclists, runners, walkers, in-line skaters, families, dogs, and children commuting to and from school all enjoy the Saddle River County Park trail. Enhancing the journey is the fact that nowhere along the path will you have to cross traffic; instead, the trail has several over- and underpasses for roads, which facilitate a safe and enjoyable trail experience.

The bike path offers an easy, seamless journey with multiple crossings above and below streets and over the Saddle River.

County
Bergen

Endpoints
Saddle River County Park/Wild Duck Pond Area, just east of Pershing Ave. and E. Ridgewood Ave. (Ridgewood), to Railroad Ave., between Saddle River Road and Rochelle Ave. (Rochelle Park)

Mileage
7.6

Type
Greenway/Non-Rail-Trail

Roughness Index
1

Surface
Asphalt

Leaving from the northern trailhead in the Wild Duck Pond Area, the pathway begins just past the parking area; follow signs to Glen Rock/Fair Lawn/Dunkerhook—the path is well signed along its entire length. At 0.8 mile, bear left as the path follows Grove Street and then passes under it. At 1.6 miles, the trail crosses over a stream and arrives at a T-intersection—go left, pass a small dam, and cross over the river, following signs to Dunkerhook/Fair Lawn. At the next T-intersection, go left and follow signs for Saddle Brook/Rochelle Park. Continue to follow the river, and at mile 2.3, you will cross over the Saddle River again. Continue following signs to Saddle Brook/Rochelle Park.

Just past mile 4, you will come upon the historical Easton Tower, built in 1899 on the site of a former gristmill. Go right, cross over a bridge, and, at the intersection of Red Mill Road, turn left to travel under the road. Continue to follow the river and signs to Rochelle Park. You will pass several ball fields along the way and a path that leads to parking. The trail circles a pond at mile 5. At that point, bear left and pass under the Garden State Parkway. From here, there will be paths that follow the river on both sides. Remain on the west side of the river, passing more ball fields and grassy open areas until you reach Rochelle Park.

The length of the trail is dotted with several restrooms, drinking fountains, and parking facilities. Additionally, users can access the playgrounds, a water park, and picnic spaces all along the trail route. These amenities make the Saddle River County Park Trail an excellent experience for residents and visitors seeking a shady space for exercise and recreation.

CONTACT: co.bergen.nj.us/parks-recreation-areas/saddle-river-county-park

DIRECTIONS

To reach the northern trailhead at the Wild Duck Pond Area (1133 E. Ridgewood Ave., Ridgewood), head southeast on Garden State Pkwy., and take Exit 165 for Ridgewood Ave. Turn right onto E. Ridgewood Ave., and follow it 0.7 mile. Turn left to stay on E. Ridgewood Ave. another 0.1 mile. Make a slight left to stay on E. Ridgewood Ave. 0.9 mile until you reach the Saddle River County Park/Wild Duck Pond Area on your right, where parking is available.

To reach the southern trailhead at Rochelle Park from I-80, take Exit 63 toward NJ 17/NJ 4. Head northeast on Riverview Ave., and almost immediately turn left onto Essex St. After 0.3 mile, turn right onto Saddle River Road. In 0.4 mile turn right onto Railroad Ave. After 0.1 mile, turn left and Rochelle Park will be on the left; parking will be 0.1 mile farther inside the park.

The Sandy Hook Multi-Use Pathway travels 8.7 miles alongside the picturesque beaches and historical monuments of the Sandy Hook peninsula. The pathway begins in the Gateway National Recreation Area and loops around the historic Fort Hancock. Traveling south alongside Hartshorne Drive/Ocean Avenue, the route also offers beach access and unique glimpses of the Sandy Hook Lighthouse, the oldest working lighthouse in the United States.

Fort Hancock is a former U.S. Army installation that housed 12,000 soldiers at its peak during World War II. The fort was built to protect New York Harbor, but its uses have changed over time. Once deactivated, the fort was turned over to the National Park Service (NPS), eventually becoming part of the three-part Gateway National Recreation Area, where former landfills have been converted into wildlife habitat and recreation areas.

The northern trailhead is east of the intersection of Atlantic Drive and Ford Road, with parking in nearby Lot G. This trailhead features beach access, restrooms, drinking fountains, and a bike-maintenance station, as well as food trucks throughout the summer.

Starting at the northern trailhead, you'll find sand dunes and trees that provide small pockets of shade throughout the ride. Immediately before Ford Road, the trail diverges into two pathways. The multiuse path continues to the right. To the left a bike path follows Knox Road and features a sandy outdoor gym area with exercise equipment. The two pathways converge at the intersection of South Bragg Drive and Knox Road. This northern portion of the peninsula also houses an array of unnamed multiuse trails that split off from the Sandy Hook Multi-Use Pathway.

The pathway continues toward the western edge of the peninsula to loop around Fort Hancock. Here, the trail winds past Sandy Hook Chapel to the right and History House to the left, a lieutenant's quarters built in 1898 that the NPS maintains to depict an officer's life at Fort Hancock during World War II. Heading south, the

County
Monmouth

Endpoints
Gateway National Recreation Area near Atlantic Dr. and Ford Road (Highlands) to NJ 36/Ocean Ave., 0.4 mile north of Shrewsbury River Bridge (Sea Bright)

Mileage
8.7

Type
Greenway/Non-Rail-Trail

Roughness Index
1

Surface
Asphalt

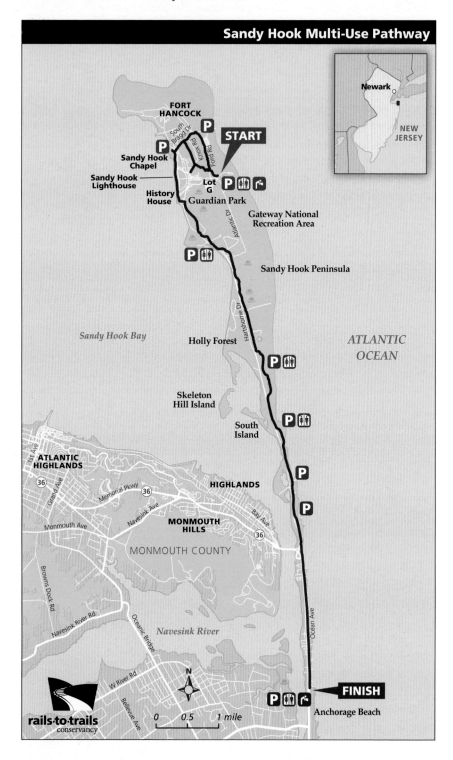

Sandy Hook Multi-Use Pathway

A beautiful view of the Sandy Hook Bay is a highlight of the route.

pathway follows the shoreline, providing a beautiful view of the Sandy Hook Bay. About 0.7 mile south of Sandy Hook Chapel, you will pass Guardian Park and two Nike missiles, honoring the Cold War missile men of the U.S. Army.

Continuing to follow Hartshorne Drive 4.5 miles from the missiles, the sun-dappled pathway travels south past various beaches with public access until Hartshorne Drive merges with Ocean Avenue. Here, the trail travels adjacent to the road past private beaches and residential homes. The trail ends just before Anchorage Beach, which lies 0.3 mile south of the terminus. The beach features public parking, outdoor showers, restrooms, and public beach access for a fee.

CONTACT: sandyhookfoundationnj.org/visit/mup.htm

DIRECTIONS

To reach parking near the northern endpoint in the Gateway National Recreation Area, take I-195 E to its end, and near mile marker 36, exit onto Garden State Pkwy. Keep left to head north on the parkway, and go 11.5 miles. Take Exit 109, and continue straight (slight left) onto Half Mile Road. In 0.6 mile turn right onto W. Front St., and go 0.8 mile. Turn left onto Hubbard Ave., and go 0.6 mile. Turn right onto Navesink River Road, which curves left and becomes Locust Point Road in 4.4 miles. In 0.5 mile continue straight onto Locust Ave., and go 0.4 mile. Turn right onto Monmouth Ave., which almost immediately curves left and becomes Navesink Ave. In 0.9 mile turn right onto NJ 36 S. Go 1.7 miles to the Sandy Hook peninsula, and make a slight right to loop around and head north on Ocean Ave./Hartshorne Dr., which continues 3.5 miles straight into the Gateway National Recreation Area (note that there is a $15 entry fee to enter the park). Take a right onto Atlantic Dr., and follow it 1.2 miles to Lot G on the left. The trailhead is located across Atlantic Dr., behind a restroom building to the left.

To reach the closest parking to the southern endpoint, follow the directions above to the Sandy Hook peninsula, and make a slight right to loop around and head north on Ocean Ave./Hartshorne Dr. In 0.2 mile, take a right off Hartshorne Dr. into Lot A.

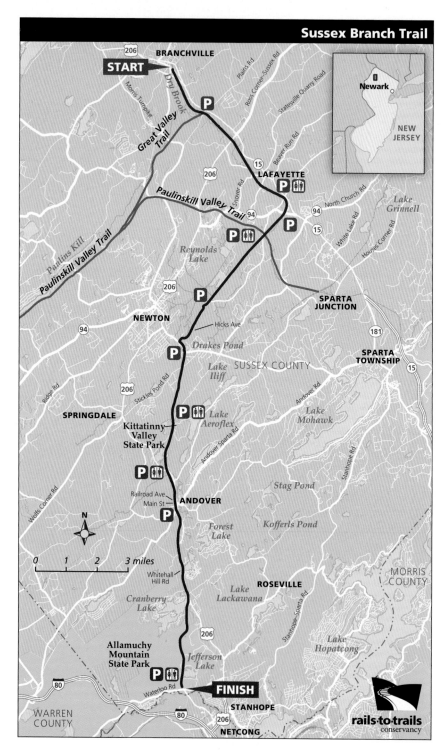

The corridor now home to the Sussex Branch Trail was originally the narrow-gage, mule-drawn Sussex Mine Railroad, which opened in 1851 to haul iron ore from mines in Andover to the Morris Canal. After several upgrades and expansions, the line eventually merged with the Delaware, Lackawanna & Western Railroad. That railroad's merger with the Erie Railroad to form the Erie Lackawanna Railroad in 1960 marked the beginning of the end of the Sussex Branch, and the final train ran on the line in 1966. Fortunately, the State of New Jersey subsequently purchased the right-of-way for trail use and now administers the Sussex Branch Trail as part of Kittatinny Valley State Park.

Begin your trip in Branchville, where the trail starts just south of downtown due to a couple of missing railroad bridges. The rustic trail moves southeast, paralleling Dry Brook before emerging into classic Garden State farmland. This stretch is sometimes overgrown with weeds—and bears have been spotted in the adjacent woods—so trail users should exercise caution. Just before Augusta Hill Road, the trail crosses the Great Valley Trail, an unpaved 3.5-mile route that heads southwest.

Bridges provide dry passage as you approach Lafayette, which offers several food, drink, and antiques shopping options not far from the trail. South of Lafayette, the path

County
Sussex

Endpoints
Mill St., east of Newton Ave. (Branchville), to Waterloo Road and Continental Dr. (Byram Township)

Mileage
18.0

Type
Rail-Trail

Roughness Index
2

Surface
Cinder, Dirt, Grass

Dense woodlands envelop much of this rustic, unpaved pathway.

travels through dense and quiet woodlands, so you may be surprised when you reach an intersection with the Paulinskill Valley Trail (see page 49) and a subsequent road crossing. The peaceful wooded route soon resumes, though, traveling to the outskirts of Newton. While the trail continues unmaintained on the rail corridor another 0.5 mile, a large sign directs you to an on-road detour via Hicks Avenue/County Road 663 to continue on the main route. The road portion is short (1.1 miles) but treacherous, particularly for hikers, as cars move quickly, and only a narrow shoulder provides a perhaps false sense of security.

Back on the former rail corridor, you'll again be enveloped by trees, and a cut through bedrock is spectacular. Soon you'll reach access to campgrounds and Lake Aeroflex in Kittatinny Valley State Park.

As you enter Andover, another short on-road detour on low-stress Railroad Avenue is required. Where the trail resumes adjacent to Main Street, low-hanging branches, tree roots, and a narrowed width may prove to be a challenge. At Whitehall Hill Road, trail users may find that vegetation has completely consumed the trail, so another short on-road detour may be desired. (Note that while Whitehall Hill Road is not a busy road, it *is* hilly.)

You will be rewarded for your determination once you reach scenic Cranberry Lake, whose eastern shore the trail closely follows. Pause to watch boaters enjoying the crystal-clear water. The path widens considerably after the lake and the surface improves, so you'll likely encounter many more trail users along this final stretch. After passing Jefferson Lake, you'll soon reach the trail's end at a large trailhead and parking lot on Waterloo Road. Those hoping to visit Stanhope or Netcong—the closest towns to the trail's southern end—can continue south via a side path along Continental Drive.

CONTACT: state.nj.us/dep/parksandforests/parks/kittval.html

DIRECTIONS

There is no official parking at the trail's northern end in Branchville. To reach the Augusta Hill Road trailhead from I-80, take Exit 25, and head north on US 206 toward Stanhope/Newton. Travel 10.9 miles, then make a slight left onto Main St. in Newton. After 0.9 mile, turn left onto Spring St., then immediately turn slightly right to stay on Spring St. In 0.1 mile take the first left onto Mill St., and drive 4.4 miles as it becomes County Road 519/Newton Halsey Road. Veer right onto August Hill Road; parking can be found on your left after 1 mile.

To reach the southern trailhead in Byram Township from I-80, take Exit 25 for US 206 N toward Stanhope/Newton. Immediately take the first exit toward International Trade Center/Waterloo Village, and merge onto International Dr. After 0.2 mile, turn right onto Waterloo Valley Road. Travel on Waterloo Valley Road 1.1 miles as it becomes Continental Dr. When you reach the road's end, cross Waterloo Road to enter the parking lot.

Running alongside a New Jersey Transit passenger line, the Traction Line Recreation Trail has been around since 1986, when Jersey Central Power & Light donated portions of the land to the Morris County Park Commission. Even though this trail runs parallel to an active transit line, the land was first owned by the Morris County Traction Company, which ran trolleys between Newark and Dover 1914–1928. The trolleys also used to take vacationers to the old Bertrand Island Amusement Park at the northern end of the line.

The Morris & Essex Line, which now parallels the trail (a configuration known as rail-with-trail), has a train station along the route that allows residents and tourists alike to access this trail for commuting to work or school, as well as for taking recreational trips to nearby places of interest.

The Traction Line Recreation Trail spans nearly 3 miles between Morristown and Madison. The northern end of the

This rail-with-trail parallels a New Jersey Transit passenger line for its entire length.

County
Morris

Endpoints
Morris Ave. and Washington Ave. (Morristown) to Danforth Road and Beech Ave. (Madison)

Mileage
2.7

Type
Rail-Trail/Rail-with-Trail

Roughness Index
1

Surface
Asphalt

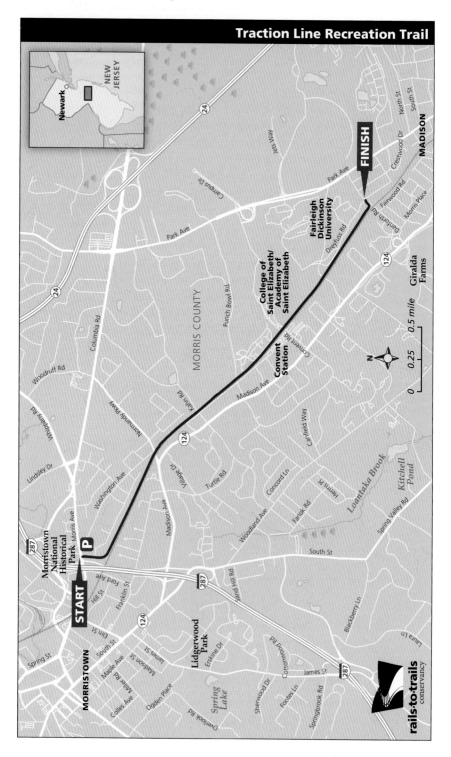

trail begins at Morris Avenue, across from Morristown National Historical Park, a worthwhile side excursion to explore sites significant to the American Revolution. Look for the trail entrance right before you cross Washington Avenue; a green BIKE ROUTE sign marks the start.

From the Morris Avenue entrance, you'll enjoy a pleasant walk or ride on smooth asphalt, with much of the path lined with greenery, where you may see wildlife such as deer, rabbits, and chipmunks. The trail is flat without any hills or steep grades, so it is accessible to users with different abilities and needs. It also offers 10 workout stations, called Fit-Trail stations, along the route, which provide opportunities to complete cardio, stretching, and strength-training exercises.

After 1.8 miles, you'll pass Convent Station, accessible via an at-grade, marked railroad crossing. Trail users, as well as vehicles on Convent Road, can cross the tracks to reach the train station. On the other side of the trail, across from the train station, is the entrance to the Academy of Saint Elizabeth, as well as the College of Saint Elizabeth. The trail continues farther southeast to end at Danforth Road, adjacent to Fairleigh Dickinson University. Eventually, the path will continue south of Danforth Road to Drew University in Madison.

CONTACT: m66.siteground.biz/~morrispa/index.php/parks/traction -line-recreation-trail

DIRECTIONS

To reach parking near the northern end of the trail from I-287 N, take Exit 36A for County Road 510 E/Morris Ave. Take a right onto Morris Ave., then immediately bear right onto Washington Ave. In 200 feet, take a right onto W. Valley View Dr. In 380 feet, take a right onto Howell Pl., which dead-ends into the trailhead parking lot. From I-287 S, take Exit 36. Keep left to merge onto Lafayette Ave., and in 300 feet, turn left onto Ridgedale Ave. In 0.1 mile turn left onto Morris St., which becomes Morris Ave. Go 0.3 mile to Washington Ave., and then follow the directions above from there.

Although there isn't a parking lot at the southern end of the trail, on-street parking is available along Beech Ave. To reach it from I-287 S, take Exit 37 to NJ 24 E. Go 1.3 miles on NJ 24 E, and take Exit 2A for County Hwy. 510 W toward Morristown. Merge onto the Columbia Turnpike. In 0.1 mile turn left onto Park Ave. In 1.5 miles turn right onto Danforth Road. Go 0.2 mile, turn left onto Beech Ave., and look for parking; the trail entrance is at the intersection of Beech Ave. and Danforth Road. From I-287 N, take Exit 35, and turn right onto South St. In 400 feet, turn left onto Woodland Ave. Go 1.3 miles, and turn left onto Kitchell Road. Go 0.7 mile, and turn right onto Madison Ave./NJ 124. In 0.6 mile, turn left onto Danforth Road. Take a left onto Beech Ave. and look for parking; the trail entrance is at the intersection of Beech Ave. and Danforth Road.

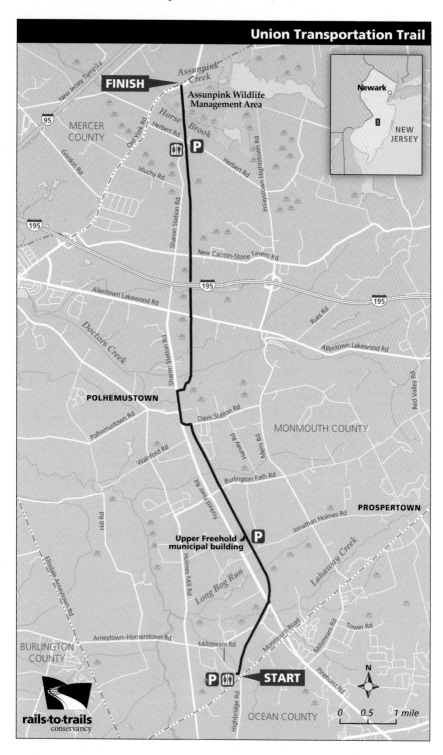

Union Transportation Trail

FINISH

Assunpink Creek

Assunpink Wildlife Management Area

Newark

NEW JERSEY

MERCER COUNTY

New Jersey Turnpike

95

195

Gordon Rd

Old York Rd

Horse Brook

Herbert Rd

Hluchy Rd

Sharon Station Rd

Herbert Rd

Imlaystown Hightstown Rd

New Canton-Stone Tavern Rd

195

Allentown Lakewood Rd

195

Rues Rd

Allentown Lakewood Rd

Red Valley Rd

Doctors Creek

Sharon Station Rd

POLHEMUSTOWN

Polhemustown Rd

Davis Station Rd

Harvey Rd

Meirs Rd

MONMOUTH COUNTY

Walnford Rd

Burlington Path Rd

PROSPERTOWN

Hill Rd

Forked River Rd

Jonathan Holmes Rd

Lahaway Creek

Upper Freehold municipal building

Ellisdale Arneytown Rd

Holmes Mill Rd

Long Bog Run

Millstream Rd

BURLINGTON COUNTY

Arneytown–Hornerstown Rd

Millstream Rd

Monmouth Road

Millstream Rd

Tower Rd

START

Highbridge Rd

Pinehurst Rd

OCEAN COUNTY

N

rails·to·trails
conservancy

0   0.5   1 mile

The Union Transportation Trail follows the path of the former Pemberton & Hightstown Railroad, which began operating in 1868. The original purpose of the railroad was to allow local farms and dairies to more easily ship goods by providing access to larger railroad hubs. The times haven't changed much in this part of the Garden State—today, the Union Transportation Trail still traverses farmland and countryside along its route.

In 1888 the Union Transportation Company—after which the trail is named—leased the line and used it for several decades. Passenger service ceased in 1931, but freight rail service continued until 1977, after which Jersey Central Power & Light acquired the line. The current trail operates as an easement granted by the utility company, and the power line runs along the length of the trail. Users heading out on a hot summer day should take precautions;

The trail offers several picturesque stream crossings through the rural countryside.

County
Monmouth

Endpoints
8 Millstream Road at Monmouth Road (Cream Ridge) to Old York Road between Sharon Road and Windsor Perrineville Road (Hightstown)

Mileage
9.3

Roughness Index
2

Type
Rail-Trail

Surface
Crushed Stone

a hat and extra water are in order because the trees are trimmed back due to the power line, and there is no shade along the trail. The trail is part of a developing network in the Greater Philadelphia region called the Circuit Trails, which will encompass 800 miles of trail when complete.

Starting from the southern terminus at the Millstream Road trailhead, you will cross Millstream Road itself before continuing through wooded areas, and it isn't long before the first farmland scene appears. About 0.8 mile into the trail, you will see a small horse farm on your right—and perhaps even a horse or two grazing beyond the fence that abuts the path. Nearly another 0.4 mile farther, the trail crosses Forked River Road. Trail users can activate flashing beacons to warn oncoming drivers, but take care when crossing this higher-speed road. The path continues, flanked by trees on either side that obscure the farm fields that lie beyond them. Another 0.9 mile farther, after you cross Jonathan Holmes Road, a trailhead lies to your right. Not long after, a spur trail on the left leads to the parking lot of the Upper Freehold municipal building.

Heading north, the trail passes more fields and a tree farm and crosses Burlington Path Road before passing by a small suburban development on the right, beginning about 3.5 miles from the start of the trail. The trail crosses Davis Station Road before turning sharply to the left to parallel it. The path turns right again and, in this section, parallels busy Forked River Road. Vast farmland flanks your right, while a small shopping center and green fields appear on your left. In this section, the trail goes up and down several gentle hills, which may result in some huffing and puffing for inexperienced or infrequent trail users.

At 4.7 miles from the start, the route turns back to the right and enters a short, wooded area—the only portion of the trail offering significant shade. Even in this small space, wildlife thrives. Frogs sing to each other from a muddy pond beside the trees. Immediately after this quiet respite, you pass over a bridge, and the sky opens up again as you go up a short but steep hill and head back to the familiar, flat railroad grade of the trail.

From here on, you'll encounter eight more bridges as the trail crosses many small streams. About 5 miles into the trail, the trees on either side make the space feel wooded, but farmland is never far away—farm vehicles and equipment can be seen peeking through the trees. Another 0.9 mile ahead, the path crosses a creek via a small bridge before going through an underpass, with I-195 overhead. The underpass itself contains clues to the wildlife and people that frequent the trail. Horse hooves from equestrian users mingle with deer tracks and smaller paw prints—perhaps left by a bobcat or a fox—imprinted in the trail's crushed-stone surface.

At about 6.75 miles from the start, you'll pass more fields that, in summertime, are planted with tall corn stalks on either side, spreading far and wide. Farther down the trail, you may even see farmers hard at work; take care as large tractors cross from one side of the trail to the other. After another 0.75 mile, the trail passes over another bridge to cross a stream, but the countryside views continue for 2 miles—this time with short, verdant green crops on either side.

You will see the Sharon Station Road trailhead on your left, 8 miles from the start. The path crosses Herbert Road and soon enters the Assunpink Wildlife Management Area. You'll know when you reach it, as the swampy Horse Brook flanks either side of the trail bridge. As you overlook the wetlands here, the sounds of cars and farm equipment fall away, with frogs taking their place, talking to each other as waterfowl fly overhead. Not long after, you will cross over Assunpink Creek, thick with vegetation on either side, and soon reach the end of the trail at Old York Road.

CONTACT: monmouthcountyparks.com/page.aspx?ID=3777

DIRECTIONS

There is no parking available at the northern terminus. The closest parking is located 0.9 mile south at the intersection of Sharon Station and Herbert Roads. To reach the Sharon Station Road trailhead from the New Jersey Turnpike/I-95, take Exit 8 and merge onto NJ 133. In 0.1 mile take the Milford Road exit, and merge onto Milford Road, heading south. Continue 1 mile, and turn right onto Etra Road. In 0.2 mile make the next left onto Cedarville Road, and continue 1.4 miles. Turn right onto Windsor Perrineville Road, and continue 1 mile. Turn left onto Old York Road, and go 2 miles. Turn left onto Herbert Road, and go 0.7 mile. The trailhead is located on the right at the intersection of Herbert and Sharon Station Roads.

To reach the Jonathan Holmes Road trailhead from I-195, take Exit 11 and head south on Imlaystown Hightstown Road. In 0.8 mile, turn right onto County Road 526, and continue 1.4 miles. Turn left onto Sharon Station Road, which becomes Forked River Road. Continue 3.8 miles. Turn left onto Jonathan Holmes Road, and the trailhead will be located on the left, just after the trail crossing in 0.2 mile. Alternatively, while on Forked River Road, just before reaching Jonathan Holmes Road, users may also turn into the Upper Freehold municipal building lot and park there; a spur trail leads from the parking lot to the main trail.

At the southern terminus, to reach the Millstream Road trailhead from I-195 W, take Exit 16 and turn left (from I-195 E, take Exit 16A) onto CR 537 W/Monmouth Road. Continue 6.9 miles. Turn right onto Millstream Road, and go about 400 feet. The trailhead is located on the left.

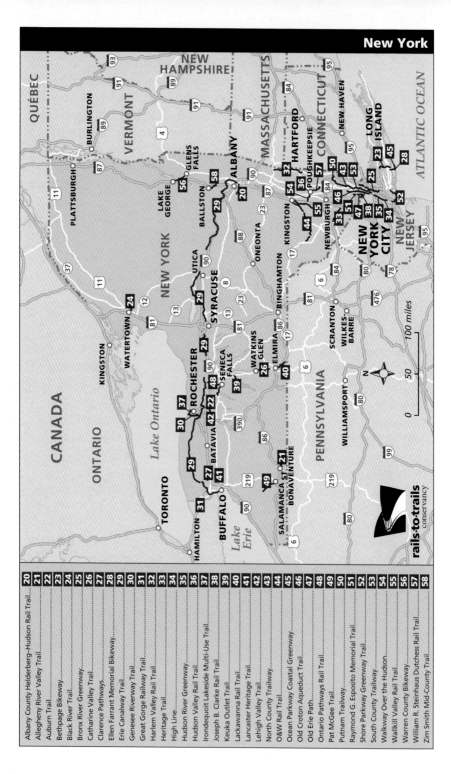

New York

Part of the Heritage Trail parallels overgrown railroad tracks (see page 121) .

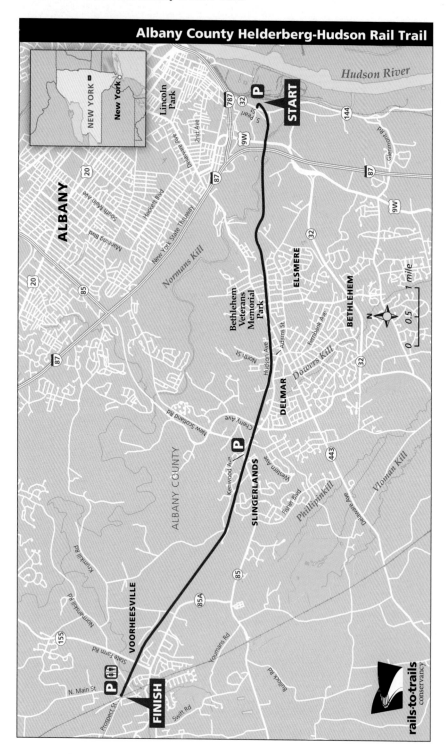

Albany County Helderberg-Hudson Rail Trail

Hudson River

NEW YORK

New York

Lincoln Park

START

ALBANY

ELSMERE

BETHLEHEM

Bethlehem Veterans Memorial Park

DELMAR

Normans Kill

Dowers Kill

SLINGERLANDS

Phillipinkill

Vloman Kill

ALBANY COUNTY

VOORHEESVILLE

FINISH

N. Main St

rails-to-trails
conservancy

0   0.5   1 mile

N

Following the route of the former Delaware & Hudson (D&H) Railway, the Albany County Helderberg-Hudson Rail Trail serves as a scenic oasis and community connector for residents living southwest of Albany. In 2018 the final section of the trail was paved; now, 9 miles of flat, asphalt-surfaced pathway is available through several of the state capital's suburbs. Although largely traversing residential areas, the pathway offers views of picturesque bridges, creeks, and woodlands throughout. Watch for deer, turkeys, bald eagles, and other wildlife along the way.

Starting just south of Albany—where there's a trail-specific parking lot—the trail heads west, quickly crossing under the I-87/New York State Thruway. This eastern end of the trail is not far from the Hudson River, and the trail's grade gently climbs as it moves away from

A bridge above the Albany County Helderberg-Hudson Rail Trail provides travelers a safe, uninterrupted route.

County
Albany

Endpoints
NY 32/S. Pearl St. and Old S. Pearl St. (Albany) to Grove St., 190 feet east of S. Main St. (Voorheesville)

Mileage
9.0

Type
Rail-Trail

Roughness Index
1

Surface
Asphalt

the river. A mile from the start, you'll cross an old railroad bridge over Normans Kill (*kill* being a Dutch term for "creek").

From the bridge, it's 2.2 miles to Bethlehem Veterans Memorial Park, which includes several benches to rest and enjoy the peaceful setting. From Bethlehem west, you'll also find three trailside workout stations. As you continue, the trail passes within blocks of the center of the pleasant hamlet of Delmar, which provides a variety of services, such as restaurants and shopping.

Artwork is being added to the trail, and as you pedal through Delmar, you'll see a whimsical mural of bright flowers and trees painted by a local artist near the intersection of Adams Street and Hudson Avenue. A mile farther down the trail, as you travel under Cherry Avenue, you'll also see the pillars of the overpass painted with floral motifs.

After continuing through Slingerlands, where there is a parking lot on Kenwood Avenue behind the Slingerlands Fire District, you have 3.7 miles more to go before reaching Voorheesville. At the end of the trail in Voorheesville, travelers will find a pavilion that harks back to the railway station that once occupied the space.

CONTACT: mohawkhudson.org/helderberg-hudson-rail-trail and
albanycounty.com/Government/Departments/CountyExecutive/RailTrail.aspx

DIRECTIONS

To reach the Albany trailhead from I-787 S, take Exit 2 for S. Pearl St. Merge onto Green St., and go 0.1 mile. Turn left onto S. Pearl St., and go 0.7 mile. A parking lot for the trail is just south of the intersection with Old S. Pearl St. and Kenwood Road. From I-787 N, take Exit 2, and turn left onto Vine St. Immediately turn left onto Green St., go 0.4 mile, and follow the directions above.

To reach the trailhead in Voorheesville from I-90, take Exit 1S and merge onto Adirondack Northway, heading south. In 0.8 mile turn right onto US 20 W/Western Ave. Go 0.2 mile, crossing over I-87/New York State Thwy., and make the next left onto Church Road. Stay on Church Road 1.5 miles, then turn left onto Johnston Road/County Road 203. Johnston Road becomes Normanskill Road and then Voorheesville Road/CR 306. Stay on these for a total of 3.5 miles. Turn right onto Grove St., and drive 0.2 mile, almost to the end of Grove, near the train tracks. The parking lot and rail-trail pavilion will appear on the right.

The towns of Allegany and Olean (OH-lee-an) sat at the hub of river, railroad, wagon road, and canal traffic during New York's early history. It's no wonder that today the area is home to a popular trail that connects the two towns.

The Allegheny River Valley Trail comprises a 5-mile main loop and a 1-mile cutoff around St. Bonaventure University in Allegany, and a 2-mile connector on paths and sidewalks into Olean. The entire 8 miles is paved, traveling along the wooded Allegheny River shoreline for about 3 miles, encircling the college campus, and passing through the industrial and retail center of Olean to a trailhead brewery.

The main loop trail dates back to the 1990s, when local businessman Joseph Higgins conceived a loop trail using the southern edge of a sprawling rail yard. He helped negotiate an agreement among the Town of Allegany, the City of Olean, and St. Bonaventure University. The extension through Olean was added later.

The popular Allegheny River Valley Trail connects the towns of Allegany and Olean.

County
Cattaraugus

Endpoints
Bonaventure Road and
E. Union St. (Allegany)
to E. Greene St. and
Edwards Ct. (Olean)

Mileage
8.1

Type
Greenway/Rail-with-Trail

Roughness Index
1

Surface
Asphalt

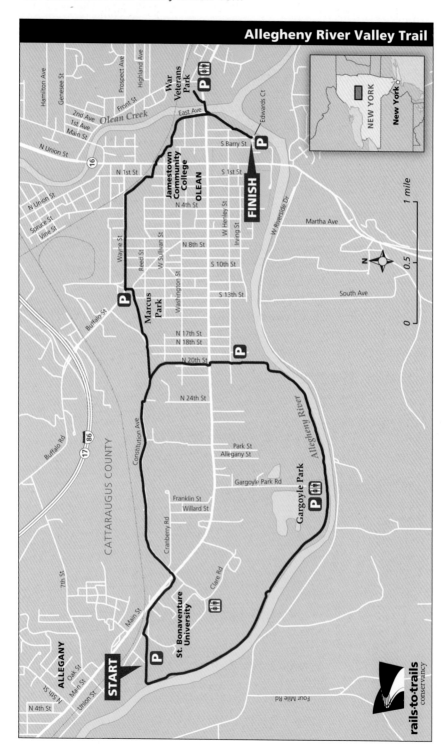

Allegheny River Valley Trail

Starting at the trailhead near the tennis courts at St. Bonaventure University, take the trail to the left to reach the Allegheny River in about 0.25 mile. The river carried early settlers west and brought commerce to the region.

Oak, maple, ash, and cherry trees provide welcome shade in the summertime. At 1.2 miles, you'll pass a mile-long trail on your left that offers a loop around the university and can serve as a shortcut back to the trailhead. On the main loop, you'll cross a few bridges over small tributaries and experience short dips and climbs.

At 2 miles, you arrive at Gargoyle Park, which has parking, athletic fields, and restrooms. East and west of the park you'll see earthen berms—all that's left of a 368-acre oil tank facility that held some 300 tanks until the early 1940s. The 4.5-foot embankments surrounded each tank in case of fire or a rupture. Company owners created the park for tank farm workers and their families.

The trail turns away from the river at 3 miles and heads north along an unshaded utility right-of-way for about a mile to a trail fork. A right turn goes 2 miles through residential and retail areas of Olean on paths and sidewalks along Constitution Avenue, Wayne Street, and an active railroad line to the local campus of Jamestown Community College, where you'll see a 1940s vintage Pennsylvania Railroad passenger station. The trail continues south along Olean Creek to a sidewalk on Adams Street that ends at Edwards Court.

A left turn at the previously mentioned fork follows the main loop. After crossing Constitution Avenue, you'll pass a popular ice cream shop and travel within sight of the rail yard. You'll return to the St. Bonaventure campus about a mile after the fork and arrive at your starting spot in about another 0.5 mile.

CONTACT: allegany.org/index.php?alleganytowntrail

DIRECTIONS

To reach the trailhead at St. Bonaventure University in Allegany from I-86/Southern Tier Expy., take Exit 24, and head south on W. 5 Mile Road. Go 0.4 mile, and turn left onto NY 417/W. State Road. Go 0.8 mile, and stay straight as the road becomes NY 417/Main St. Go 0.5 mile, and turn right onto S. Seventh St. Then go 0.1 mile, and turn left onto E. Union St. Go 0.4 mile, and turn right onto Bonaventure Road; look for parking on the right. The trail is adjacent to the parking lot.

To reach the trailhead in Olean from I-86/Southern Tier Expy., take Exit 26 and turn right onto NY 16/N. Union St. Ext. Go 0.6 mile, turn left onto Front St., and then go 1.2 miles. Turn right onto E. State St. Go 0.3 mile, turn left onto Fulton St., and then go 0.2 mile. Bear right onto Adams St. Go 0.1 mile to E. Greene St., and look for parking at Four Mile Brewing, which allows trail parking.

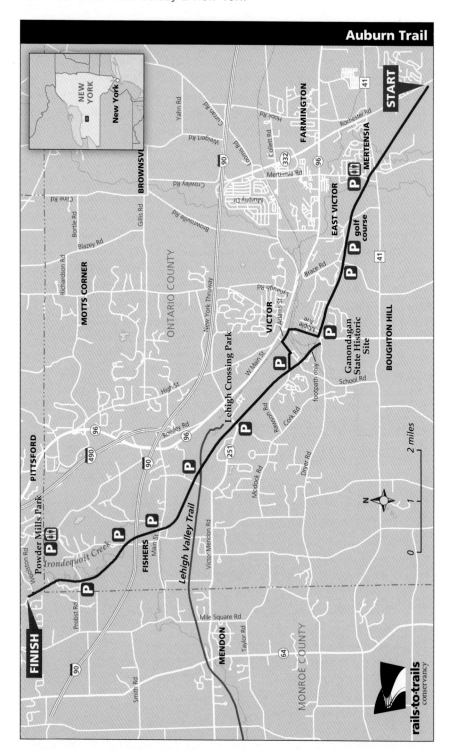

Auburn Trail

There are so many reminders from the heyday of the railroad age on the nearly 10-mile Auburn Trail that visitors might imagine they're chugging through villages and countryside at the throttle of a locomotive. An old depot, a pump house, waiting shelters, and concrete mileage markers (two are original) are just some of the relics from the old days.

The crushed-stone trail follows the corridor of a New York Central line from Farmington to Pittsford. There are two gaps in Victor, but work is under way to close them. One on-shoulder detour takes an interesting jaunt past shopping and old buildings in the village of Victor.

Near the southern end of the trail, Mertensia Park offers a convenient starting point, with parking at the entrance next to the trail. Turn right to follow the trail northwest, or take a new 3-mile section that heads southeast toward NY 332 and the Auburn Meadows subdivision.

Heading northwest, you'll reach a 0.8-mile detour onto East Victor Road. The town of Victor plans to close this gap with a foot trail across golf course property. If it's

Along the rail-trail, concrete mileage markers indicate the distance in railroad miles from Syracuse.

Counties
Monroe, Ontario

Endpoints
NY 332/Rochester Road and Canandaigua Farmington Town Line Road (Farmington) to Woolston Road and Railroad Mills Road (Pittsford)

Mileage
9.6

Type
Rail-Trail

Roughness Index
2

Surface
Crushed Stone

not completed, turn right onto East Victor Road, left onto Break of Day Road, and left onto Brace Road. Look for the trail on the right.

The Auburn Trail goes just over a mile to the site of a circa 1840 railroad depot of the Auburn and Rochester Railroad, which lends its name to the trail. A number of mergers resulted in its acquisition by New York Central Railroad in 1853. This corridor's sections closed in 1960 and 1978. The depot is privately owned, as is an adjacent boxcar.

Another detour starts at the depot, although plans call for closing this gap with a trail alongside railroad property. If that's not complete, turn right onto the bike lane on Maple Avenue; go 0.5 mile and turn left onto Adams Street (or go another block to Main Street through the historical Victor Village); and then turn left onto School Street and pass two breweries en route to the trail in 0.5 mile on the right.

Back on the Auburn Trail, you'll cross the dirt Seneca Trail for hikers on the right past Rawson Road, and in about 2 miles you'll come to Lehigh Crossing Park and cross under the Lehigh Valley Trail (see page 150), which heads west 15 miles to the Genesee Valley Greenway.

You'll arrive on Main Street in Fishers about a mile past the Lehigh Valley Trail junction. The small cobblestone building on the north side of the trail is a pump house built for the Auburn and Rochester Railroad in 1845 to supply water to steam locomotives.

The final leg to Woolston Road passes through rural countryside, crossing Irondequoit Creek on two stone-arch bridges and a 90-foot steel bridge. A painted mural graces the trail's I-90/New York Thruway underpass. Facilities are available at the 380-acre Powder Mills Park, after you turn right onto Woolston Road and travel 0.3 mile to the park entrance.

CONTACT: victorhikingtrails.org/map/trails/auburn.php

DIRECTIONS

To reach the Mertensia Park trailhead in Farmington from I-90, take Exit 44 toward Canandaigua, and merge onto NY 332. Go 1.4 miles, turn right onto NY 96, and then go 0.5 mile. Turn left onto Mertensia Road. Go 0.8 mile, and turn right into the park entrance at Fawn Meadow St. Trail parking is at the entrance.

To reach the trailhead in Pittsford from I-490 S, take Exit 28 and veer right onto NY 96 N. Go 0.2 mile, and turn left onto Fisher Road. From I-490 N, take Exit 29, and turn right onto NY 96 N. Go 2.6 miles, and turn left onto Fisher Road. From Fisher Road, go 0.5 mile, and turn right onto Woolston Road/County Road 29. Go 0.7 mile, and look for parking on the left or right in Powder Mills Park. After parking, continue another 0.3 mile on the shoulder of Woolston Road, and look for the trail on your left.

The nicely paved Bethpage Bikeway runs alongside suburban roads for long segments of the route, but it's much more than a suburban trail. Each on-road suburban stretch is broken up by one of three beautiful parks in the Long Island region: Trail View State Park, Bethpage State Park, and Massapequa Preserve.

Beginning at the northern terminus on Woodbury Road, the asphalt path follows the highly trafficked Sunnyside Boulevard Extension for the first mile, passing a corporate office park on the left before curving sharply right to remain on Sunnyside Boulevard. The shared-use path then crosses over Northern State Parkway and down a short, steep hill. After crossing Sunnyside Boulevard at a traffic signal on Fairchild Avenue, the path turns left onto the Long Island Expressway North Service Road. The path parallels this service road 0.7 mile over a series of undulating hills.

The Bethpage Bikeway offers a mixture of suburban neighborhoods and parkland.

County
Nassau

Endpoints
Manetto Hill Road and Woodbury Road (Woodbury) to Merrick Road and Ocean Ave. (Massapequa)

Mileage
13.4

Type
Greenway/Non-Rail-Trail

Roughness Index
1

Surface
Asphalt

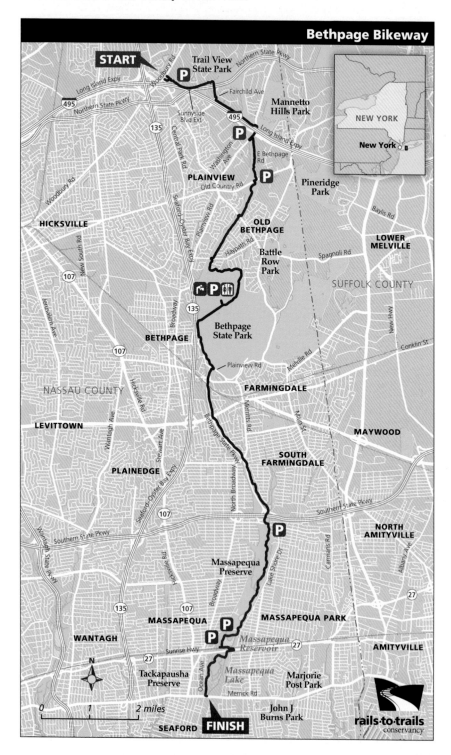

The path turns right at Washington Avenue and crosses under the Long Island Expressway. To the right in 0.2 mile is a parking area for the trail. From here, the trail crosses Washington Avenue and parallels East Bethpage Road, opposite an industrial park. In 0.8 mile, the path crosses Old Country Road and enters the southern section of Trail View State Park. Hiking and mountain biking trails run along the bike path, and the trail experience is much greener as it follows the edge of the park, crossing over a few well-marked neighborhood roads, such as Old Bethpage and Haypath Roads.

In 1.4 miles, the path enters Bethpage State Park at Haypath Road. The path skirts the park for 0.5 mile before entering a lovely wooded section of the route. In this section, which runs roughly 2 miles, you'll share the trail with riders, walkers, and runners. Both Trail View State Park and Bethpage State Park feature cross-country skiing trails. A side path from the picnic area in the center of the park leads to restrooms and water fountains. The path travels next to a golf course before popping out on the other side of the park. Here, you will cross the moderately trafficked Plainview Road, where flashing lights alert drivers to the bike crossing.

After crossing Plainview Road, the path follows the right-of-way of Bethpage State Parkway for 2.5 miles. This on-road segment feels similar to the beginning of the route, traveling alongside traffic until it crosses over Southern State Parkway and enters Massapequa Preserve. Arguably the nicest segment of the bikeway, the shaded, well-paved preserve is dotted with lakes, ponds, reservoirs, and marshland. This well-maintained section of the trail offers the best opportunity to escape into nature.

After rounding Massapequa Reservoir, the path crosses Sunrise Highway and turns right to complete the final mile through the preserve. Shoreline fishing is popular at the reservoir, though Nassau County has seasonal restrictions in place for black bass and other fish. The trail's southern terminus is at Massapequa Lake, where Ocean Avenue meets Merrick Road. If you're interested in continuing your journey down to Jones Beach, the northern endpoint of the Ellen Farrant Memorial Bikeway (see page 101) is only 2.1 miles west of Massapequa Lake.

CONTACT: www.dot.ny.gov/bicycle

DIRECTIONS

To reach parking near the northern entrance to Trail View State Park from I-495 E/Long Island Expy., take Exit 46 for Sunnyside Blvd. toward Plainview. In 0.3 mile, keep right, following signs for Sunnyside Blvd. In 0.2 mile, continue onto Executive Dr./S. Service Road; then follow the directions below. From I-495 W, take Exit 46, and merge onto N. Service Road. Go 0.2 mile, turn left onto Sunnyside Blvd., and immediately turn left onto Executive Dr./S. Service Road. Go 0.8 mile, following signs for Washington Ave. Turn right onto S. Service Road, go 500 feet, then turn left onto Washington Ave. In about 0.1 mile, take a right at the first traffic light onto Executive Dr. Trailhead parking can be found at the first entrance on your right.

To reach parking near the southern entrance to Trail View State Park from I-495/Long Island Expy., take Exit 48 toward Round Swamp Road/Old Bethpage. In 0.2 mile, merge onto Service Road and go 0.1 mile. At the first traffic light, head south onto Old Country Road. In 0.5 mile, turn right onto E. Bethpage Road, and take the first left for trailhead parking. The path continues north and south from this parking lot.

To reach parking at Bethpage State Park from I-495/Long Island Expy., take Exit 44, and merge onto NY 135 S toward Seaford. Travel south 4.3 miles to Exit 8 for Powell Ave. toward Bethpage. In 0.2 mile, turn left onto Powell Ave./Plainview Road. The second entrance on your left leads to Bethpage State Park (note that there is a parking fee). Travel up the park entrance road to a parking fee booth to access the path and park facilities.

To access the bikeway using light rail, take the Long Island Rail Road (LIRR) Babylon Branch to the Massapequa train station, which is 0.3 mile west of the trail's southern terminus. Visit **mta.info** for more information.

This paved scenic trail, converted from the New York Central Railroad, follows a small portion of the Black River's 114-plus miles. Originating in the Adirondack foothills, the Black River flows west to empty into Lake Ontario, near the Thousand Islands region between northern New York State and southeastern Ontario.

If you are starting your trip at Watertown and heading east to the village of Black River, consider exploring the downtown area before you set out. Watertown reached its peak during the Gilded Age, when it was rumored to have a higher percentage of millionaires than any other city in the United States thanks to its status as a manufacturing center. Nature lovers can explore the urban Thompson Park, designed by Frederick L. Olmsted and donated to the city by industrialist John C. Thompson in 1889. The park includes walking trails and houses the New York State Zoo.

Shortly after leaving Watertown, and for most of the Black River Trail's journey east, travelers will be surrounded by a wooded landscape.

County
Jefferson

Mileage
4.5

Endpoints
Dead end of Walker Ave., just east of NY 3/Eastern Blvd. (Watertown), to Black River trailhead and parking lot off NY 3/E. Rutland St. between NY 342 and Stone Dr., just before NY 3/E. Rutland St. crosses the Black River (Black River)

Type
Rail-Trail

Roughness Index
1

Surface
Asphalt

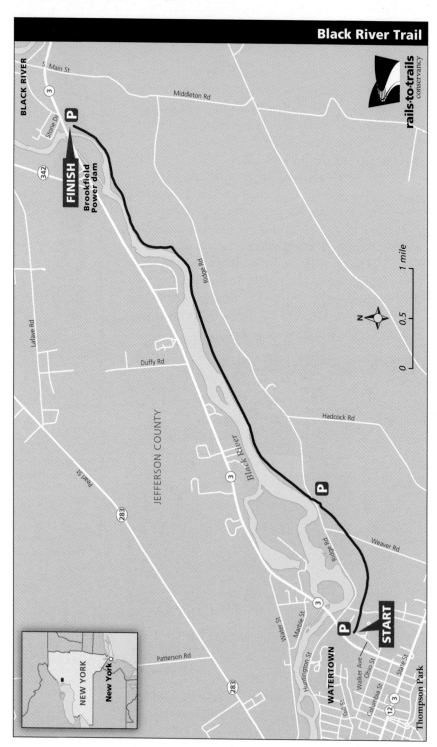

Black River Trail

rails·to·trails
conservancy

BLACK RIVER

S. Main St

Middleton Rd

Stone Dr

FINISH

Brookfield
Power dam

342

Ridge Rd

LaFave Rd

Duffy Rd

JEFFERSON COUNTY

Hadcock Rd

Pearl St

Black River

283

1 mile

0.5

0

N

Weaver Rd

Ridge Rd

Water St

Marble St

START

Huntington St

WATERTOWN

Walker Ave

Ohio St

State St

Patterson Rd

283

Gill St

Columbia St

12   3

Thompson Park

NEW YORK

New York

Near the heart of downtown Watertown, the western endpoint of the Black River Trail can be found behind an apartment complex at the dead end of Walker Avenue. The western trailhead includes a small parking lot with an information panel and a map.

The Black River Trail is smooth, flat, and well maintained, making it ideal for a relaxing stroll or bike ride following the river east. It has numerous scenic views and overlooks, as well as several drop-in points for canoe and kayak portage or fishing. In winter, the path is also suitable for snowshoeing.

After 4.5 miles, your journey ends at the eastern endpoint in the village of Black River. The small community began in the early 1800s with the erection of a mill on the south side of the river. Today, it includes two small river islands and a park that overlooks the town and river. Just before NY 3/East Rutland Street meets the river, the trail ends at the Black River Trailhead, where parking can be found.

As you approach Black River, you'll be greeted by a picturesque view of the Brookfield Power dam, nearby rapids, and the Poors Island Recreation Area. Poors Island is located 1 mile northeast of the eastern trailhead, heading toward the village of Black River, and boasts the best views of the river and dam. To top it off, an area complete with grill, picnic tables, and additional parking makes Poors Island the perfect spot for a picnic lunch.

CONTACT: parks.ny.gov/parks/199

DIRECTIONS

Parking is available at either end of the trail. An additional trailhead with parking is located 0.5 mile east of the western endpoint, where the trail intersects Ridge Road.

To access the western endpoint in Watertown from I-81, take Exit 45 toward Arsenal St./Watertown/NY 3. If heading northbound, turn right onto Arsenal St.; if southbound, turn left onto NY 3 E/Arsenal St. In 1.8 miles, continue onto Public Square, which turns into NY 12/State St. in 0.2 mile. In 1.4 miles, turn left onto NY 3 E/Eastern Blvd., heading toward the river. In 0.2 mile, turn right onto Ohio St., then take an immediate left onto Walker Ave. Follow Walker Ave. through the apartment complex until it dead-ends at the parking lot for the trail.

To access the eastern endpoint from I-81, follow the above directions to the intersection of NY 12/State St. and NY 3 E/Eastern Blvd. Turn left and follow NY 3 E/Eastern Blvd. 4.8 miles (during which Eastern Blvd. becomes Rutland St. and Rutland St. crosses the Black River into the village of Black River). Parking at the eastern trailhead is on the right immediately after crossing the bridge.

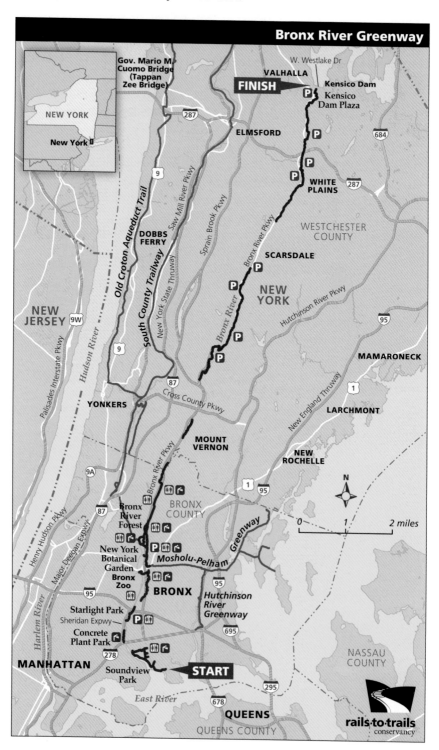

Bronx River Greenway

The Bronx River travels from the mouth of the East River north to the Kensico Dam, providing views of the natural history of the area. Because the trail is under development, there are several gaps between its completed sections. Therefore, carrying a trail map with you (or on your smartphone) is recommended; a detailed map of the Bronx River Greenway can be found on **TrailLink.com** or **bronxriver.org.**

Beginning at the trail's southern end, you'll explore a restored salt marsh at the mouth of the Bronx River. You can access the trail at the eastern entrance to Soundview Park at Leland and O'Brien Avenues. The path travels

This view of the Bronx River in Scarsdale is one of many scenic sights along the trail.

Counties
Bronx, Westchester

Endpoints
Soundview Park at Leland Ave. and O'Brien Ave. (Bronx) to Kensico Dam Plaza at 1 Bronx River Pkwy. (Valhalla)

Mileage
23.3

Type
Greenway/Non-Rail-Trail

Roughness Index
1

Surface
Asphalt

uninterrupted 1.5 miles through the park, which is well used by families from around the area. This trail segment ends at Lafayette Avenue.

There's a 0.5-mile gap to reach the next section of trail, which traverses Concrete Plant Park. Walkers can use the sidewalks along city streets to bridge this gap, but thru-cyclists will need to be comfortable with on-street biking until the trail is completed here. Concrete Plant Park, finished in 2009, shows a unique and thought-provoking mix of industrial uses and public space that shouldn't be missed.

After traveling 0.4 mile through Concrete Plant Park, the trail continues as an on-street connection along the access road of Sheridan Expressway 0.4 mile to the southern end of Starlight Park, where you'll find one of the many attractive river access points for boats. The Bronx River Alliance is completing Phase 2 of Starlight Park, which will fill this gap with an off-street trail, anticipated to be finished by the end of 2019. In the park, plan a stop at the Bronx River House, the new headquarters of the Bronx River Alliance, for maps, restrooms, and a water fountain.

The stone wall and log fence flanking the Bronx River Greenway give a rustic feel to the paved path.

Continue north from Starlight Park, where the trail jogs east as the Bronx River enters the Bronx Zoo and the New York Botanical Garden. If time permits, spend an afternoon off the trail wandering through the zoo or the famous botanical garden and its living museum. You can also enjoy the multitude of free public parks that dot the trail throughout this 2-mile section. Not to be missed is the Bronx River Forest, just north of the botanical garden, which is being restored by the New York City Department of Parks and Recreation and the Bronx River Alliance and provides an oasis of green in one of the nation's most urban areas.

The trail continues north to the Kensico Dam, listed on the National Register of Historic Places. There are four on-street connections along the remaining journey to the Kensico Dam, ranging in length from 0.5 to 2 miles. Side streets can complete these connections until the trail is constructed, but there are no signs to guide you through them to the next section of trail, so bringing a map will be important for doing a thru-journey on the Bronx River Greenway.

Once you make it to the Kensico Dam, end your journey on the Bronx River Greenway by heading up to West Westlake Drive, the road on top of the Kensico Dam, which is open only to walkers and bikers. You'll get a unique view of Kensico Dam Plaza and a great sense of accomplishment.

CONTACT: bronxriver.org

DIRECTIONS

To reach the southern terminus in the Bronx from I-95, take Exit 4B for Rosedale Ave. to Bronx River Pkwy. From I-95 W, merge onto E. 177th St. and turn right onto Rosedale Ave. in 0.2 mile. From I-95 E, turn left onto Rosedale Ave. From Rosedale Ave., go 0.1 mile, and turn right onto E. 174th St. Go another 0.1 mile, and turn left onto Bronx River Pkwy. Go 0.7 mile, and take Exit 2E for Bruckner Expy. toward I-278 E. Go 0.2 mile, and turn right onto Sound View Ave. After 0.8 mile, take a slight right onto Leland Ave. The trail begins at the intersection of Leland Ave. and O'Brien Ave. in 0.3 mile.

To reach the northern terminus in Valhalla from I-287, take Exit 4, and head north on NY 100A/Knollwood Road. In 1.8 miles turn right onto NY 100 S/Grasslands Road. After 1.3 miles, turn left onto Virginia Road. Travel 0.4 mile, and take a sharp left onto the Bronx River Pkwy. At Kensico Cir. in 0.2 mile, take the second exit onto Park Dr. In about 0.1 mile turn left onto Park Dr. W, and follow it 0.2 mile to the Kensico Dam Plaza parking area.

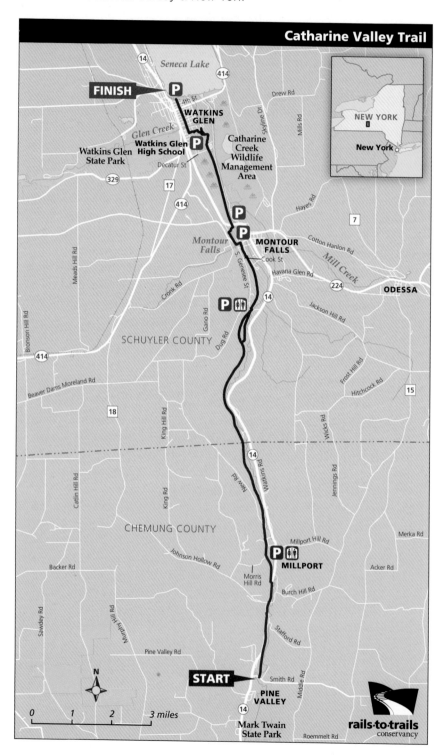

Enjoy a smooth ride along the Catharine Valley Trail, a well-maintained multiuse pathway that provides a comfortable and shaded biking experience through Upstate New York. High points include entering the historical town of Montour Falls, with its incredible downtown vista featuring several striking civic buildings complemented by a waterfall backdrop, and the view as you enter the Watkins Glen marina, which is a treat.

The Catharine Valley Trail follows segments of the former Northern Central Railway and Chemung Canal towpath from Smith Road on the north end of Pine Valley to Seneca Lake, but an extension of the trail to continue the route south to Horseheads is under development. The majority of the trail is wooded, with a solidly packed crushed-limestone surface; there are a few short paved sections as you enter Montour Falls and Watkins Glen.

From Pine Valley, you'll follow NY 14 north, screened from the roadway by trees and brush. At mile 1.8, you'll cross the roadway on a pedestrian bridge and continue through the forest canopy and peaceful environs. A half mile after the bridge, you'll reach Morris Hill Road and traverse Millport.

In 6 miles, you'll reach Montour Falls, where there are trailheads at South Genesee and Cook Streets. After leaving Montour Falls, the trail skirts the Catharine Creek Wildlife Management Area. There are two restrooms spaced out along the trail and quite a few historical landmarks to be discovered.

At Decatur Street, just past Watkins Glen High School, turn right and follow the roadway to the marina, which offers an excellent view of beautiful Seneca Lake. Watkins Glen is the perfect ending to your trail journey, as it's a lovely town and very walkable, with a harborside restaurant and many shops to browse. Watkins Glen State Park is also close at hand; its spectacular waterfalls and hiking trails make it well worth a visit.

Counties
Chemung, Schuyler

Endpoints
Smith Road, 0.2 mile east of Watkins Road/ NY 14 (Pine Valley), to N. Decatur St. and First St. (Watkins Glen)

Mileage
12.9

Type
Rail-Trail

Roughness Index
1

Surfaces
Asphalt, Crushed Stone

Travelers cross this pedestrian bridge on their way north along the Catharine Valley Trail from Pine Valley to Millport.

CONTACT: parks.ny.gov/parks/80

DIRECTIONS

The closest parking to the southern terminus is in Millport. From I-86, take Exit 52B for NY 14 N. Merge onto County Road 64, and in just a few hundred feet, turn left onto NY 14 N/ Westinghouse Road. Go 1.5 miles, and turn left to remain on NY 14. Continue 6.0 miles, and turn left onto Crescent St. Travel 0.1 mile to Maple St. Turn right; in 240 feet you'll reach a trail kiosk and limited parking at the end of Maple St.

To reach the northern terminus from I-86, take Exit 40 for NY 226 N toward Savona. Head east on NY 226/E. Lamoka Ave., and continue 13.1 miles; take a right onto CR 23. Travel 8.0 miles, then make a right turn onto CR 28. In 1.0 mile, take a left onto Bath St. Go 0.3 mile, and turn right onto NY 14/N. Madison Ave. In 0.4 mile, turn left onto First St. and then make your next left onto Decatur St., which will bring you to the large parking lot of the Watkins Glen marina.

Two former rival railroad corridors that crossed in Buffalo's eastern suburbs now form a nearly 18-mile paved trail system called Clarence Pathways in Clarence, Newstead, and Akron.

Five trails make up Clarence Pathways: West Shore Trail/Newstead-Akron Bike Path, Peanut Line Trail, Waterford Trail, and Spaulding Green Trail. They connect suburban neighborhoods with parks, town centers, and local workplaces. In the winter, snowmobiling is allowed on two of these routes: the Peanut Line Trail between Goodrich Road and Salt Road, and the West Shore Trail/Newstead-Akron Bike Path between Salt Road in Clarence and Cedar Street in Akron.

The longest stretch is known as the West Shore Trail/Newstead-Akron Bike Path. It follows the route of the West Shore Railroad Company (originally the New York,

County
Erie

Endpoints
West Shore Trail/ Newstead-Akron Bike Path: Wehrle Dr. between Barton Road and Faber Lane (Clarence) to Cedar St. between Railroad St. and Eckerson Ave. (Akron). **Peanut Line Trail:** NY 78/Transit Road between Old Post Road W and Woodbridge Lane (Clarence) to West Shore Trail, 0.9 mile southeast of Barnum Road and Clarence Center Road (Akron). **Waterford Trail:** Peanut Line Trail at Heise Road and Clarence Center Road to Roll Road and Dana Marie Pkwy. (Clarence). **Spaulding Green Trail:** Goodrich Road between Roll Road and Greiner Road to Meadowglen Dr. between Golden Aster Ct. and Glenview Dr. (Clarence)

Mileage
17.9

Type
Rail-Trail

Roughness Index
1

Surface
Asphalt

The Peanut Line Trail offers a ride through a bucolic backdrop.

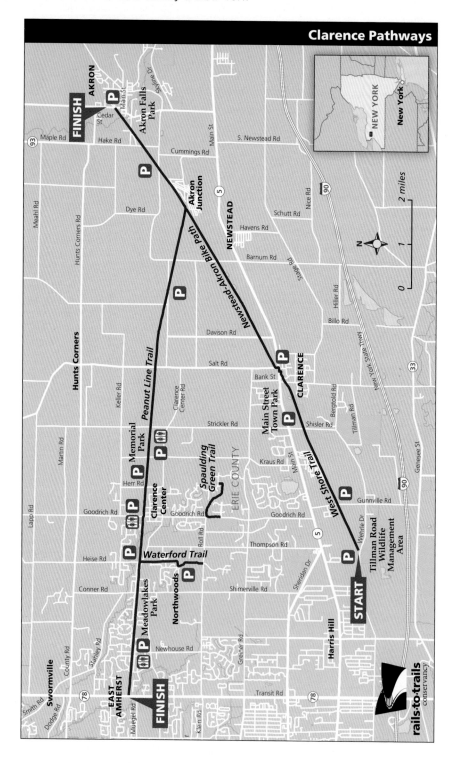

Clarence Pathways

NEW YORK

New York

2 miles

N

AKRON

FINISH

Maple Rd

93

Meahl Rd

Hunts Corners Rd

Hunts Corners

Martin Rd

Lapp Rd

County Rd

Smith Rd

Dodge Rd

Swormville

78

Muegel Rd

Klein Rd

EAST AMHERST

FINISH

Stahley Rd

Conner Rd

Heise Rd

Goodrich Rd

Herr Rd

Keller Rd

Dye Rd

Hake Rd

Cedar St

Main St

Akron Falls Park

Skyline Dr

Akron Falls Dr

Cummings Rd

Akron Junction

Newstead-Akron Bike Path

NEWSTEAD

Main St

S. Newstead Rd

5

Havens Rd

Barnum Rd

Davison Rd

Salt Rd

Clarence Center Rd

Strickler Rd

Kraus Rd

Main St

Goodrich Rd

Thompson Rd

Shimerville Rd

Newhouse Rd

Rolf Rd

Goodrich Rd

Peanut Line Trail

Memorial Park

Clarence Center

Spaulding Green Trail

ERIE COUNTY

Waterford Trail

Meadowlakes Park

Northwoods

Greiner Rd

Sheridan Dr

5

Bank St

Main Street Town Park

CLARENCE

Shisler Rd

Bergtold Rd

Tillman Rd

West Shore Trail

Gunnville Rd

Wehrle Dr

START

Tillman Road Wildlife Management Area

Harris Hill

Transit Rd

78

Schutt Rd

Nice Rd

90

Hiller Rd

Billo Rd

Speas Rd

New York State Thwy

33

Genesee St

90

rails-to-trails conservancy

West Shore & Buffalo Railway Company), which ran freight and passengers from the western shore of the Hudson River to Buffalo beginning in the 1880s. Passenger service arrived in Clarence in 1884.

The Peanut Line Trail follows the corridor of New York Central's (NYC's) Batavia Line, also known as the Peanut Line because of its relative insignificance in NYC's railroad empire. The line was acquired by NYC in the 1850s. The parent railroad didn't want competition in the region from the West Shore and bought that railroad too in 1885.

Starting on the **West Shore Trail** on Wehrle Drive in Clarence, you'll pass through a forest to a crossing at Gunnville Road in 0.9 mile; this is the former site of a railroad station. For the next couple of miles, trees screen the trail from Clarence High School and a residential neighborhood before you arrive at Main Street Town Park. Here you'll find the Clarence Historical Museum and the Goodrich-Landow Log Cabin, moved from Goodrich Road, where it was built in 1825. In another 1.3 miles, the trail name changes to **Newstead-Akron Bike Path** as it crosses Davison Road.

At a fork at Akron Junction in 2.5 miles, you can go left onto the **Peanut Line Trail,** which heads to the East Amherst boundary in 8.3 miles, or right to remain on the Newstead-Akron Bike Path, which ends in Akron in 2.1 miles.

Heading right, the trail ends on Cedar Street, just a couple of blocks south of regional ice cream maker Perry's. Perry's doesn't offer tours, but products are served locally at a pastry shop on Akron's Main Street, located 0.2 mile south.

If you chose the left fork, you'll head west on a rail corridor that once carried vacationers to Niagara Falls. The Peanut Line Trail passes through farmland for the first 2.2 miles and then reenters Clarence and continues through forest and farmland as it arrives at Memorial Park, 4 miles past the fork.

About 2 miles past the park, the paved trail on your left is the **Waterford Trail,** which passes through the Northwoods community. In 2.3 miles you'll pass residential neighborhoods before arriving at the trail's end in East Amherst, where you can visit a drive-in diner just to the north.

Disconnected from the other trails in the system, the **Spaulding Green Trail** links the Clarence Town Hall and public library on Goodrich Road to the Spaulding Green housing project, built around an old quarry.

CONTACT: www2.erie.gov/clarence/index.php?q=parks-department

DIRECTIONS

To reach the West Shore trailhead in Clarence from I-90, take Exit 49, and turn left onto NY 78/Transit Road. Go 0.6 mile, and turn right onto Wehrle Dr.; then go 2.5 miles and look for trailhead parking on the left.

To reach the Newstead-Akron Bike Path trailhead in Akron from I-90, take Exit 48A, and turn right onto NY 77. Go 0.7 mile, and turn right onto NY 5/Main St. Go 5.0 miles, and turn right onto NY 93/Buell St. Go 1.6 miles, turn right onto NY 93/Main St., and then immediately turn left onto NY 93/Buffalo St. Go about 400 feet, turn right onto NY 93/John St., and then immediately turn left onto NY 93/Cedar St. Go 0.1 mile and use on-street parking on the left across from Eckerson Ave.

To reach the junction of Newstead-Akron Bike Path and the Peanut Line Trail, follow the directions above to the Akron trailhead. Take the trail 2.1 miles and turn right onto the Peanut Line Trail.

To reach the Peanut Line Trail western trailhead from I-90, take Exit 4, and head east on N. French Road. Go 3.1 miles, and turn right onto NY 78/Transit Road. Go 1.6 miles, and turn left onto Clarence Center Road. Then go 1.1 miles, and turn left onto Clarence Town Park. Go 0.1 mile to the circle in Meadowlakes Park, bear right, and look for parking. A 400-foot path goes to the Peanut Line Trail; turn left, and go 1.2 miles to the western trailhead.

When Jones Beach State Park opened on Long Island's South Shore in the late 1920s, a series of scenic parkways was built on infill dredged from nearby towns to connect New Yorkers to the new public recreation spot. These scenic byways allow motorists to experience the park even while zipping along the blacktop. The north–south Wantagh State Parkway, terminating at Jones Beach, was the first parkway to be completed. A parallel path was also designed for nonmotorists to access what would quickly become one of the most beloved recreational areas in New York. The beach features historical bathhouses, a wooden boardwalk, an iconic water tower, and a waterfront amphitheater. The Ellen Farrant Memorial Bikeway, sometimes referred to as the Jones Beach Bikeway or Wantagh Parkway Shared-Use Path, is a relatively straight and flat path, curving around trees here and there. The challenge in riding it comes from the mild slopes as one approaches the bridges, as well as from the lack of shade on the path.

In Cedar Creek Park, an unassuming opening in the fence serves as the entrance to the north end of the trail. There, an interpretive display tells the history of the parkway's development. In no time, you will find yourself on the historical byway and, depending on the time of day,

County
Nassau

Endpoints
Cedar Creek Park at Merrick Road and Larch St. (Seaford) to Jones Beach State Park, southeast corner of Field 5, at Ocean Pkwy. and Wantagh State Pkwy. (Wantagh)

Mileage
5.5

Type
Greenway/Non-Rail-Trail

Roughness Index
1

Surface
Asphalt

The trail's three bridges—over Flat Creek, Goose Creek, and Sloop Channel—supply bay and marsh views.

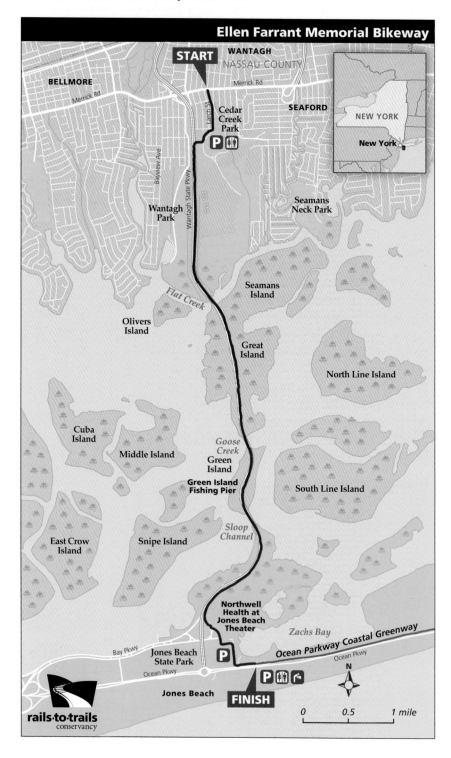

Ellen Farrant Memorial Bikeway

START

WANTAGH
NASSAU COUNTY

BELLMORE

Merrick Rd

Merrick Rd

Larch St

Cedar
Creek
Park

SEAFORD

NEW YORK

New York

P

Bayview Ave

Wantagh
Park

Wantagh State Pkwy

Seamans
Neck Park

Flat Creek

Seamans
Island

Olivers
Island

Great
Island

North Line Island

Cuba
Island

Middle Island

Goose
Creek
Green
Island

Green Island
Fishing Pier

South Line Island

East Crow
Island

Snipe Island

Sloop
Channel

Northwell
Health at
Jones Beach
Theater

Zachs Bay

Ocean Parkway Coastal Greenway

Bay Pkwy

Jones Beach
State Park

P

Ocean Pkwy

Ocean Pkwy

P

N

Jones Beach

FINISH

0   0.5   1 mile

rails·to·trails
conservancy

in the path of incessant winds. Depending on which direction it's blowing, the wind may be a challenge or an ally; check the weather forecast before you set off.

The trail's three bridges offer the best scenery of the journey. In 1.3 miles, the first crossing traverses Flat Creek. The trail narrows, and signs urge users to walk their bikes up the slope and across the bridge, where you'll catch sight of Seamans Island to the east. The second crossing, over Goose Creek, comes at the 2.5-mile mark. Here, you'll get glimpses of marsh and tidal flats. Before you reach the final bridge, a detour takes you down to the Green Island Fishing Pier, popular with anglers of all stripes. A state fishing permit can be purchased at the Jones Beach administrative offices. The final bridge on your way south is the drawbridge over Sloop Channel. It has the longest span and widest sea views of the three. White fishing boats dot the water below.

Near the end of the trail, the Northwell Health at Jones Beach Theater can be seen towering over the trees. As your journey comes to a close, 5.5 miles from where you began, you emerge into the parking lot for the open-air theater. There is a connection along the edge of the lot to Zachs Bay and, a little farther than that, the entrance to the Ocean Parkway Coastal Greenway (see page 162), which runs perpendicular to the Ellen Farrant Memorial Bikeway. You can extend your ride along that trail or head through the underpass for Ocean Parkway to reach Jones Beach, a popular and lively destination.

CONTACT: parks.ny.gov/parks/jonesbeach

DIRECTIONS

To reach Cedar Creek Park in Seaford from Southern State Pkwy., take Exit 27S for Wantagh State Pkwy. toward Jones Beach State Park. Go 2.4 miles, keeping right. Take Exit W6 for Merrick Road. Follow it east 0.2 mile. Turn right onto the Cedar Creek Park access road, and travel 0.3 mile south to the Field 1 parking lot. Note that non–Nassau County residents pay a fee to park there on weekends and holidays in summer. The trail can be accessed across the street.

If you choose to start your trail ride from the southern end, you can park at Jones Beach State Park, but be aware that there is an entrance fee; rates can be found at **parks.ny.gov /parks/jonesbeach**. From I-495, take Exit 40W, and head southwest on Jericho Turnpike. Almost immediately, turn left onto Brush Hollow Road. In 0.8 mile, turn left onto Wantagh State Pkwy. toward Jones Beach. In 13.0 miles, at the traffic circle, take the second exit onto Ocean Pkwy. E. Continue 0.8 mile, then make a slight right to enter parking for Field 6. To reach the starting point of the trail, go 0.2 mile along the Jones Beach Boardwalk to the East Bathhouse building. Take the underpass beside the bathhouse across Ocean Pkwy. and onto the Ocean Parkway Coastal Greenway. Turn left when you emerge from the underpass. The Ellen Farrant Memorial Bikeway is perpendicular to the greenway and begins where the latter ends, heading north from the Field 5 parking lot.

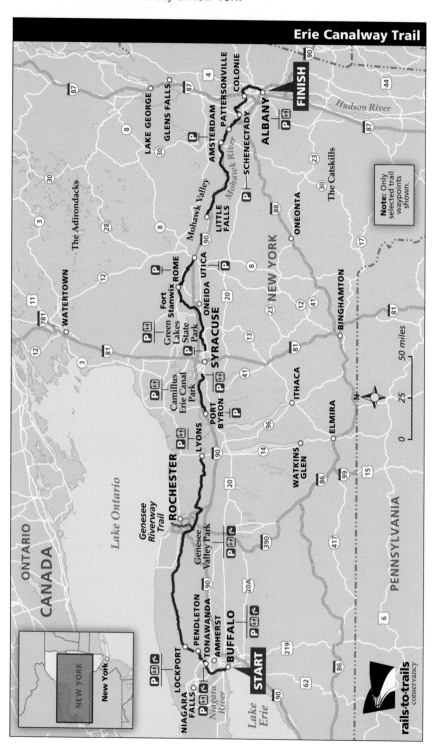

Erie Canalway Trail

When complete, the Erie Canalway Trail will run 365 miles in Upstate New York—from Buffalo in the west to Albany in the east—linking many other communities along the way, including Rochester, Syracuse, Rome, Utica, and Schenectady. The route currently comprises nearly 292 miles of open trail and has a few remaining gaps. In 2018 a 5-mile gap on the eastern side of the trail was closed when a new section of the trail opened between Amsterdam and Pattersonville.

The expansive pathway is also part of an even larger trail system, the developing 750-mile Empire State Trail, which will connect trails from New York City to Canada and Buffalo to Albany to create the longest multiuse state trail in the country.

The Erie Canalway Trail follows its namesake, which opened in 1825. At the time of the canal's construction,

Counties
Albany, Cayuga, Erie, Herkimer, Madison, Monroe, Montgomery, Niagara, Oneida, Onondaga, Orleans, Schenectady, Wayne

Endpoints
Erie St. and Lakefront Blvd. (Buffalo) to Corning Riverfront Park and Quay St. near US 9 (Albany) *Note:* This developing route is not yet fully contiguous; please refer to the interactive maps on the websites below to bridge the gaps.

Mileage
291.9

Type
Canal/Rail-Trail/Rail-with-Trail

Roughness Index
1–2

Surfaces
Asphalt, Concrete, Crushed Stone, Gravel

The Erie Canal, opened in 1825, is a National Heritage Corridor and is on the National Register of Historic Places.

railroads were just coming into vogue. The Mohawk and Hudson, New York's first railroad, opened in 1831 and ran from Albany to Schenectady. At first, the railroads were seen as competition for the precious canal, so the state's lawmakers permitted trains to carry freight only during the winter when the canal was closed. But this restriction was soon lifted, and by the late 1800s trains had clearly won the battle of transportation supremacy. Today, about one-third of the Erie Canalway Trail (more than 100 miles) is built on these former railways, largely consisting of the West Shore Line on the trail's eastern end.

As most of the trail follows these canal and rail corridors, it is nearly level, with an average grade of 1%. A few steeper grades and hill climbs can be found in the Mohawk Valley section on the trail's eastern half. Large sections of the path are surfaced in stone dust from crushed limestone; however, some stone-dust sections are being converted to asphalt paving. A range of bike types—including mountain and hybrid bikes, as well as road bikes equipped with wider tires (28 millimeters or more recommended)—can be used effectively on the trail. The two longest paved sections are at either end of the trail: from Albany to Schoharie Crossing and from Buffalo to Pendleton. There are a few on-road gaps throughout the trail, but most are easily navigable with trail signage and road markings. The trickiest on-road gap, which may be more difficult for novice

The trail offers an unforgettable way to view the autumn colors of Upstate New York.

riders, is the section through Syracuse. The Syracuse gap is being improved with on- and off-road biking facilities as part of the Empire State Trail project, scheduled to be completed in 2020.

For those who want to cross-country ski, the western and central portions of the trail receive the most snowfall on average. The trail is open year-round, but it's up to each municipality whether they wish to plow, so check with the local government if you plan to use the trail in the winter months, especially if you want to snowmobile, which is permitted in some of the more rural areas.

The western segment of the Erie Canalway Trail is also referred to as the Shoreline Trail. It begins in downtown Buffalo and travels about 13 miles north to Tonawanda. Part of the route includes the Riverwalk along the Niagara River, which is quite scenic and provides access to two popular recreational amenities in Buffalo: LaSalle Park and Riverside Park, both offering athletic fields and places to picnic. In this section, you'll find overlooks and viewing platforms to stop and enjoy the breathtaking sights of both the Niagara River and Lake Erie, one of the country's Great Lakes. In Buffalo, you can also cross the river into Canada on the Peace Bridge.

Between North Tonawanda and Lyons, the Erie Canalway Trail continues nearly seamlessly for more than 100 miles. For history buffs, a worthwhile side trip in this section is the Buffalo Niagara Heritage Trail Museum, located just off the trail in Amherst, a suburb of Buffalo. Costumed interpreters and tours of the buildings throughout this 35-acre historical village—including homes, a one-room schoolhouse, and a working blacksmith shop—provide a tangible sense of 19th-century life here.

Plan to spend some time in Lockport as well. To accommodate the 600-foot elevation change from one end of the canal to the other, dozens of locks were built along the waterway. In the city's famous "flight of five," you'll have the unique opportunity to see one of the few remaining original locks alongside a modern working lock.

Another unforgettable sight is watching one of the lift bridges ascend and lower to accommodate the passage of a boat. Many of these low bridges can be found in the central part of the trail in the Rochester area. The bridges, which are just a few feet above the water, required passengers to duck, as memorialized in the popular folk song "Low Bridge, Everybody Down," written in 1905.

On the south side of Rochester, you'll find another of the trail's gems: Genesee Valley Park. The 800-acre park was designed by Frederick Law Olmsted, the famous landscape architect who helped create New York City's Central Park. In Genesee Valley Park, you can connect to the Genesee Riverway Trail (see page 110), which heads north to downtown Rochester and to Lake Ontario, another Great Lake.

In addition to connecting dozens of communities between Buffalo and Albany, this cross-state trail links numerous parks and other beautiful green spaces.

A 30-mile gap in the trail exists between Lyons and Port Byron, where the trail picks up again. From Port Byron to the outskirts of Syracuse, the trail stretches about 20 miles. As the canalway approaches Syracuse from the west, the Camillus Erie Canal Park is a notable attraction. The park includes the stunning Nine Mile Creek Aqueduct, listed on the National Register of Historic Places, and Sims Store, a replica of a mid–19th-century store that serves as a museum and gift shop. Those interested in learning more of the corridor's history should also explore the Erie Canal Museum in Syracuse.

There is a 12-mile gap in the trail across Syracuse, but the path continues east of the city, where you'll soon come to Green Lakes State Park. The park, sprawling nearly 2,000 acres, makes for a pleasant excursion. It's centered on two beautiful blue-green lakes that are open for swimming and boating, and there are hiking and camping opportunities in the park's lush forests.

This eastern section of the trail—spanning more than 50 miles through Chittenango (hometown of L. Frank Baum, author of *The Wonderful Wizard of Oz*), Oneida, Rome, and Utica—is one of its most picturesque, with the Adirondacks to the north and the Catskills to the south. In the early 1800s, a critical component of the Erie Canal was its passage through Mohawk Valley, a natural break in the mountains that separated the busy Eastern Seaboard from the country's developing interior. A popular stop here is Fort Stanwix, where you'll find American Revolution–era costumed guides who provide a glimpse of life in the 18th century.

A gap of about 20 miles lies between Utica and the final leg of the trail, which picks up in Little Falls. Between Little Falls and Albany, this section of the trail, also known as the Mohawk-Hudson Bikeway, stretches 39 miles and is paved with some on-road connections.

In Schenectady, you'll enjoy the tree-lined Stockade Historic District, with restored 17th- and 18th-century homes and churches along Union Street. Continuing east, the trail goes through the town of Colonie, which offers a pleasantly wooded interlude, with undulating lowlands and small hillsides as it runs along the Mohawk River. The Canalway Trail leaves the Mohawk Valley in Cohoes and turns south into the Hudson Valley. As the trail approaches its end in Albany, it runs through woodlands along the Hudson River and connects with the city's popular Corning Riverfront Park. Continue south through Corning Riverfront Park and use the bike and pedestrian overpass to visit downtown Albany, including the State Capitol building.

CONTACT: cycletheeriecanal.com, canals.ny.gov/trails, and **eriecanalway.org**

DIRECTIONS

As the Erie Canalway Trail passes through more than 200 communities, there are a considerable number of access points and places to park. The Parks & Trails New York's **cycletheerie canal.com** website offers comprehensive details about parking and other amenities. **TrailLink .com** also provides an interactive map of the trail, with dozens of parking waypoints marked.

On the west end of the trail, parking is available in Buffalo's LaSalle Park. To reach the park from I-190 S, take Exit 9, and turn right onto Porter Ave. Almost immediately, turn left onto DAR Dr. Travel 0.3 mile to the LaSalle Park parking lot, which will be on your left. The trail borders the park along the Lake Erie waterfront. From I-190 N, take Exit 9, and continue straight onto Sheridan Terr. In 0.3 mile take a slight right onto Busti Ave, and go 0.5 mile. Turn right onto Porter Ave., and go 0.3 mile. Turn left onto DAR Dr., and follow the directions above.

On the east end of the trail, parking is available in Albany's Corning Riverfront Park. From I-787 N, take Exit 4, and merge onto Quay St. Go 0.5 mile to the Corning Riverfront Park parking lot, which will come up on your right. The trail borders the parking lot on the side closest to the river. From I-787 S, take Exit 3B, and turn left onto Broadway. Continuing on Broadway, you will see an underpass for I-787 that is signed HUDSON RIVERFRONT in 0.2 mile. Head under the interstate to reach Quay St. in less than 500 feet. Turn left onto Quay, and follow it 0.6 mile to the parking lot for Corning Riverfront Park.

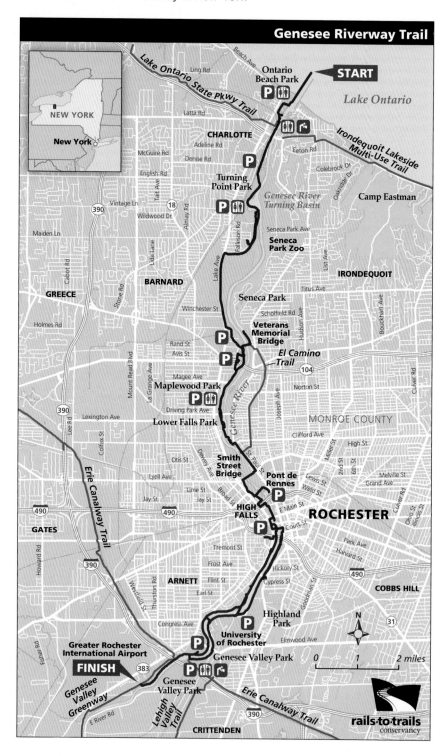

By the early 1800s, Rochester had earned the nickname of Flour City because of its numerous mills that allowed the young town to rapidly become the largest flour producer in the United States. The flour mills were located along the Genesee River, whose waterfalls provided power to keep them running. Now, the Genesee Riverway Trail closely follows the river on its north–south course through Rochester, providing stunning vistas of the falls on the way.

While the waterfalls near the midpoint of the trail are a main attraction, there's plenty more to see along the well-used trail. Begin your trip in the north at Ontario Beach Park, where the trail juts out into Lake Ontario along a pier offering panoramic views. Back on land, you'll pass the park's historical—and still operating—carousel from 1905. Follow signs to continue through the oft-crowded park and parking lots to meet the Genesee River for the first time. For a short distance, you'll course between riverside docks and a rail line, in a configuration known as rail-with-trail.

Soon you'll arrive in Turning Point Park, where a long and winding boardwalk transports trail users across the marshy Genesee River Turning Basin, which once served as a turnaround point for boats before they reached the river's waterfalls, as well as a loading dock for ferries transporting rail cars full of coal. Back on land, the trail continues south as a rail-trail on the former line, eventually curving to meet Lake Avenue, where the trail then parallels the roadway. (Cyclists will need to pay attention, as the pathway eventually becomes unidirectional on both sides of the road, requiring a crossing for those traveling southbound.)

After transitioning briefly to sidewalks and bike lanes, the multiuse trail continues, unsigned, at Maplewood Drive. Signs resume where a turn to the left will take you across a trail bridge; take the turn for river views or direct access to the Seneca Park Zoo, designed by Frederick Law Olmsted. Back on the main route, the trail narrows as it passes under the granite-arched Veterans Memorial Bridge before emerging into a wooded corridor that displays

County
Monroe

Endpoints
Ontario Beach Park on Lake Ontario at Beach Ave. and Lake Ave. to the Genesee Valley Greenway, 0.5 mile southeast of NY 383/Scottsville Road and Air Park Dr. (Rochester)

Mileage
22.8

Type
Rail-Trail/Rail-with-Trail

Roughness Index
1

Surfaces
Asphalt, Concrete

Bring a camera to capture the views at Lower Falls Park, a highlight of the Genesee Riverway Trail.

spectacular colors in the fall months. You'll be able to glimpse the river again too—while you began alongside boats docked in the river, the water now courses at a significant distance below you. The trailside Maplewood Park along this stretch provides an excellent stopping point, with a rose garden (and restrooms) likely to beckon.

Immediately after crossing Driving Park Avenue, you'll reach your first waterfall. Lower Falls Park delivers spectacular views of the eponymous waterfall and attractive Driving Park Bridge, as well as interpretive signage. Just to the south, the Middle Falls lack views but provide an excellent reminder of the importance of the falls to Rochester, as you cross via the top of an active hydroelectric dam. Now on the eastern side of the river, the trail soon transitions once more to bike lanes and sidewalks on St. Paul Street that direct trail users to another crossing of the Genesee River on the Smith Street Bridge. Pause on the bridge to take in impressive views of downtown Rochester.

Back on the western side of the river, the trail again uses a former rail corridor to pass through industrial parts of the city before merging into the road network of the charming High Falls District—one of the oldest neighborhoods in Rochester. Pont de Rennes is a necessary visit; the converted road bridge offers cyclists and pedestrians unobstructed views of the High Falls from their namesake neighborhood. Look for physical reminders of Rochester's industrial past in the gorge that surrounds the 96-foot waterfall—the main driver of the city's industrial past.

Just before the trail passes through the High Falls District, it loses signage; trail users are advised to consult a map to proceed through Rochester's downtown. Several sections are on sidewalk or road, while at other times the trail is a riverside promenade that will challenge cyclists and wheelchair users with stairs. At Court Street, the trail splits, offering trail users an option on either side of the Genesee River. No matter which route you choose, the river will be just a stone's throw away, and you'll marvel at the stillness of the water so close to the High Falls.

The eastern route passes through the campus of the University of Rochester, but two trail bridges spanning the river offer direct access to trail users on the western side. Those on the eastern side will need to cross the river at Genesee Valley Park (another Olmsted design), as the alternative will send you eastbound on the Erie Canalway Trail (see page 104). Back on the Genesee River's western bank, the trail continues a short distance to its end at a signed junction with the Genesee Valley Greenway near Greater Rochester International Airport.

Other trails to explore in this scenic area include the Lehigh Valley Trail (see page 150), the Irondequoit Lakeside Multi-Use Trail (see page 134), and the Lake Ontario State Parkway Trail.

CONTACT: cityofrochester.gov/article.aspx?id=8589936619

DIRECTIONS

Parking at the trail's northern end is available in Ontario Beach Park. To reach the park from I-490, take Exit 21 for I-590 S/NY 590 N. Follow signs for, and merge onto, NY 590 N. Travel 5.4 miles on NY 590 until you reach a traffic circle. At the circle, take the second exit onto Sea Breeze Dr., and travel 1.1 miles, continuing on Sea Breeze Dr. through two traffic circles along the way. At the third traffic circle, take the third exit onto Durand Blvd., and continue straight as it becomes Sweet Fern Road, Pine Valley Road, and Lake Shore Blvd. After 3.3 miles, turn right onto St. Paul Blvd. then immediately turn left onto Pattonwood Dr. Go 0.9 mile, crossing the Genesee River, and turn right onto Lake Ave. After 0.6 mile, turn right onto Corrigan St. to drive directly into Ontario Beach Park's parking lots. The trail begins along the pier at the park's northeast corner.

Parking near the trail's southern end can be found in Genesee Valley Park. To reach the park from I-390 S, take Exit 16A for E. River Road toward NY 15/W. Henrietta Road, and turn right onto E. River Road. In 0.1 mile proceed through the traffic circle, then in 0.3 mile take your first right onto Hawthorne Dr. Follow Hawthorne Dr. 0.3 mile, then turn right onto Moore Road. Cross the Erie Canal, then take your first left into the park.

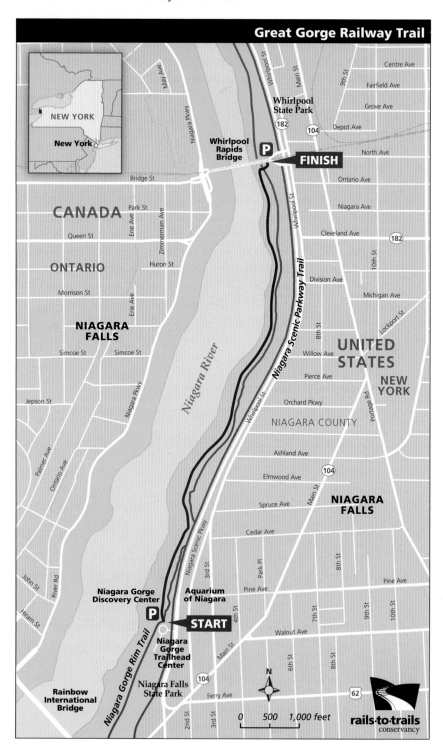

The Great Gorge Railway Trail is truly a gem. Nestled between the Niagara River and the Niagara Scenic Parkway, this short but stunning rail-trail offers unparalleled access and views of one of North America's greatest and most famous natural wonders. Located in a well-populated area and heavily frequented tourist destination, the trail offers a fun outing for families and vacationers hoping to find spectacular views while venturing away from the larger crowds buzzing around Niagara Falls.

The best starting point is located adjacent to the Niagara Gorge Discovery Center, on the northeast end of Niagara Falls State Park. A number of intersecting footpaths and park trails are in the vicinity, so be sure to stop by the Niagara Gorge Trailhead Center across from the Discovery Center and grab a map, which includes useful information about all the available trails surrounding the park and waterfalls. Hiking tours are offered through the Discovery Center mid-May–October.

The Niagara River yields scenic vistas of the United States–Canada border.

County
Niagara

Endpoints
Niagara Gorge Discovery Center, 0.25 mile north of Niagara Scenic Pkwy. and NY 104/Main St., to Whirlpool Rapids Bridge at Bridge Ave. and Whirlpool St. (Niagara Falls)

Mileage
1.2

Type
Rail-Trail

Roughness Index
1

Surface
Crushed Stone

Note that this will be an out-and-back experience of 1.2 miles each way. The crushed-stone trail begins by crossing under a footbridge that leads guests to the Aquarium of Niagara. Hikers are quickly removed from the hustle and bustle of the attractions nearby as they travel the smooth and easy-to-follow pathway that parallels the Niagara River and slopes gently down from the canyon edge to the riverbank.

Along the hike, trail users will find multiple lookout points that deliver stunning vistas of the river, the falls, and impressive bridges connecting the United States to Canada and the city of Niagara Falls, Ontario. Other highlights of the journey include remnants of the mills, factories, and infrastructure that relied on the power of the falls during the height of the Industrial Revolution in America.

As the trail continues down toward the river, a few spurs offer hikers a slightly more adventurous and challenging route to the river's edge; to stay on the Great Gorge Railway Trail, follow signs with that name and marked #4. The trail hugs the cliff face for its duration.

The trail hits a dead end directly beneath the aptly named Whirlpool Rapids Bridge. Travelers will want to take a few moments to absorb the view of the immense rapids at this point in the river before returning to the trailhead.

Just before the end of the trail, a large staircase leads back up to the top of the cliff. If hikers want a slightly easier route back to the trail center, the Niagara Scenic Parkway Trail (marked as trail #1) and the Niagara Gorge Rim Trail (trail #2) provide a less strenuous alternative to the Great Gorge Railway Trail, which is uphill in its entirety for the return trip. A parking lot is also accessible at the top of this staircase.

CONTACT: niagarafallsstatepark.com/attractions-and-tours/discovery-center-and-hiking-trails

DIRECTIONS

To reach the parking lot adjacent to the Niagara Gorge Trailhead Center from Buffalo, take I-190 N to Exit 21, and merge onto Niagara Scenic Pkwy. Go 3.2 miles. At the traffic circle, exit right onto John Daly Blvd. and continue 0.4 mile. Turn left onto Niagara St., and continue 0.5 mile. Turn right onto First St., which becomes Niagara Scenic Pkwy. The parking lot for the Niagara Gorge Trailhead Center will be on your left in 0.3 mile. From I-190 S, take Exit 22. Follow the service road 0.2 mile, and turn right onto US 62/Niagara Falls Blvd. Go 3.4 miles, and turn left onto NY 104/Main St. Go 0.2 mile, and turn right onto Niagara Scenic Pkwy. The Niagara Gorge Trailhead Center will be on your left in 0.2 mile.

To reach the parking lot near the north end of the trail from I-190, take Exit 24 for NY 31 W. Head west on NY 31, which becomes College Ave. after 1.2 miles. Follow College Ave. 1.0 mile. Take a left onto NY 104/Lewiston Road, and follow it 0.4 mile to a right turn onto Findlay Drive. Take your next left onto Whirlpool St., and continue 0.5 mile to the parking lot, which will be on your left.

Paralleling the Connecticut and Massachusetts borders, which lie only a few miles away, the Harlem Valley Rail Trail is a beautiful paved wooded pathway along the former New York & Harlem Railroad corridor that is accessible to users of many types and abilities.

Trail advocates ultimately envision a 46-mile trail from Wassaic in Dutchess County to Chatham in Columbia County. Currently, three segments totaling just over 17 miles have been built. Funding to close the 8-mile gap between Millerton and Under Mountain Road will help the trail surpass the halfway mark to completion. According to the Harlem Valley Rail Trail Association, the trail segment to close that gap has been designed and funded and should be opened by 2020.

Overall, the trail is bucolic and easygoing throughout. The asphalt pavement is well maintained and mostly flat. Scenery is generally wooded, though the path passes

Counties
Columbia, Dutchess

Endpoints
Wassaic Station at NY 22/NY 343, 0.5 mile north of Deep Hollow Road (Wassaic), to US 44/Main St. between NY 22 and S. Center St. (Millerton); Under Mountain Road, 0.25 mile east of NY 22 (Millerton), to Orphan Farm Road, 0.5 mile south of NY 22 (Copake Falls); Black Grocery Road, 0.3 mile east of Underhill Road, to Ford Lane and Anthony St. Ext. (Hillsdale)

Mileage
17.2

Type
Rail-Trail/Rail-with-Trail

Roughness Index
1

Surface
Asphalt

In summer, the tree canopy provides welcome shade along the former New York & Harlem Railroad corridor.

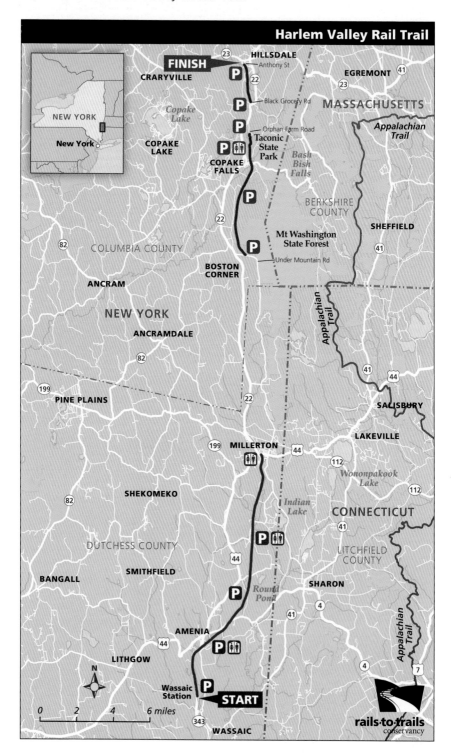

Harlem Valley Rail Trail

The trail's southern segment between Wassaic Station and Millerton highlights this beautiful vista.

through a variety of landscapes, including wetlands, creeks, some open grasslands, tree farms, and farmland. The trail features numerous parking lots and access points, mileposts, signage, and benches.

The 10.7-mile southern section begins at Wassaic Station, the northern terminus of the Metro-North Railroad Harlem Line, a commuter route. Because the Metro-North line ends here, the trail parallels the active rail line only a short distance. The northern endpoint of this trail section is Millerton, which offers a quaint downtown with restaurants, shops, and a historical one-room schoolhouse near the trail parking lot.

The next section picks up 8 miles north at Under Mountain Road and spans 5 miles to Orphan Farm Road in the hamlet of Copake Falls. There is a short (0.4-mile) portion where the trail—after passing another small parking lot—goes along an unpaved road before resuming. As it approaches Taconic State Park, it passes over the scenic Bash Bish Brook (Bash Bish Falls are about a mile east, over the Massachusetts border) before arriving at the entrance to the state park, which includes some public amenities. As the trail continues, the tree canopy opens up to reveal the Orphan Farm Meadow, flanked by mountains—including the Catskills—on two sides.

After a gap of 0.7 mile, the northern section of trail picks up at Black Grocery Road and continues north to Anthony Street in a residential area of Hillsdale. Currently this segment is only 1.5 miles long and is difficult to access. However, pleasant views along the way include vast fields of Christmas trees and other active farmland.

CONTACT: hvrt.org

DIRECTIONS

To reach the southern terminus at Wassaic Station from the intersection of NY 22 and NY 55 in Pawling, head north on NY 22, and go 6.8 miles. Keep left to remain on NY 22, and go 13.1 miles, past the hamlet of Wassaic. Following signs for the Metro-North commuter railroad, turn right into the Wassaic Station parking lot. Note that this is a paid parking lot. (Train travelers can also take the Metro-North Harlem Line from as far south as Manhattan to the last stop, Wassaic Station.)

To reach the north end of the southern segment, follow the directions above, and continue on NY 22 N another 11.2 miles to Millerton. Turn right onto US 44 E/Main St. The trail and parking lot are on the first block, within 500 feet, on your right.

To access the middle trail segment, follow the directions above to Millerton, and continue another 8.4 miles north on NY 22. Turn right onto Under Mountain Road. The trail and parking lot are 0.4 mile away, on your left.

To access the trail in Copake Falls, continue 5.9 miles north of Under Mountain Road on NY 22, and make a hard right onto Orphan Farm Road in Copake Falls. After 0.6 mile, the trail and parking lot are on your right.

To reach the trail at Black Grocery Road from NY 23/Main St. and NY 22 in Hillsdale, head south on NY 22. After 0.4 mile, make a sharp right onto Anthony St. and then an immediate left onto Underhill Road. Take Underhill 1.4 miles, then make a left onto Black Grocery Road. Go to the end of Black Grocery Road, where there is a parking area next to the trail.

To reach the northern terminus in Hillsdale from NY 23/Main St. and NY 22 in Hillsdale, head west 0.2 mile on NY 23/Main St., then turn left onto Anthony St. After 0.1 mile, at the intersection with White Hill Lane, go straight to continue on Anthony St. Ext. (do not go left to stay on Anthony St.). The trail is 100 feet up the hill on the left, in a residential area. Parking is available at a lumber store (312 White Hill Lane) by the rail-trail kiosk.

Built on the former Erie Railroad main line, the 15-mile Heritage Trail runs through the small Orange County towns of Goshen, Chester, Monroe, and Harriman. The shaded trail runs through different landscapes as it weaves through the area's villages and towns, ideal for a quick bite or gift shopping. Orange County is working to extend the trail to the city of Middletown, roughly 4.8 miles northwest of the current Hartley Road endpoint and 7 miles northwest of Goshen.

Starting at Hartley Road in Goshen, trail users can find limited parking for two or three cars. The trail starts off narrow and has a rural feel to it, with a compacted earth and crushed-limestone surface. In 0.9 mile, the trail crosses 6½ Station Road, where alternative parking is available. At this junction, trail users can also find the first of several scenic attractions along the trail. Here, nature

The sun-dappled Heritage Trail travels through a handful of Orange County communities and varied landscapes.

County
Orange

Endpoints
Hartley Road, 0.2 mile south of Echo Lake Road/Cheechunk Road and 0.2 mile east of the Wallkill River (Goshen), to Mary Harriman Park at Meadow Ave. and River Road (Harriman)

Mileage
15.1

Type
Rail-Trail/Rail-with-Trail

Roughness Index
1–2

Surfaces
Asphalt, Crushed Stone, Dirt

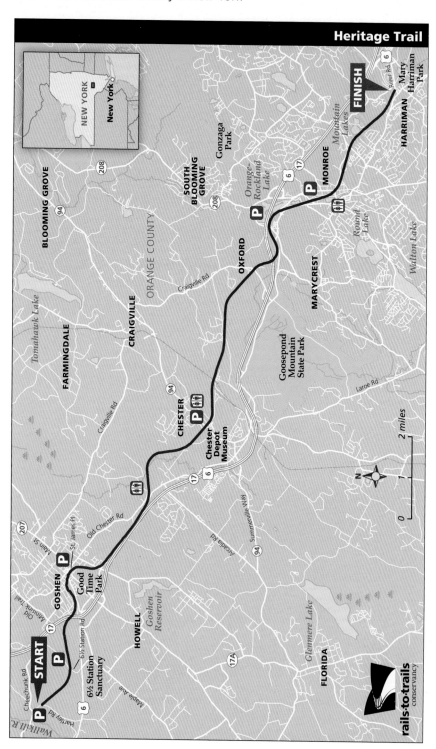

Heritage Trail

NEW YORK

New York

BLOOMING GROVE

208

94

SOUTH
BLOOMING
GROVE

Gonzaga
Park

208

Orange-
Rockland
Lake

FINISH

River Rd

6

Mary
Harriman
Park

HARRIMAN

6

17

MONROE

Mountain
Lakes

P

Round
Lake

Wilton Lake

OXFORD

ORANGE COUNTY

Craigville Rd

MARYCREST

CRAIGVILLE

Tomahawk Lake

FARMINGDALE

Goosepond
Mountain
State Park

Laroe Rd

Craigville Rd

CHESTER

94

P

Chester
Depot
Museum

2 miles

17   6

Summerville Way

N

0   1

St. James Pl

Old Chester Rd

207

Main St

94

Arcadia Rd

Glenmere Lake

Old Minisink Trail

17

GOSHEN

P

Good
Time
Park

HOWELL

Goshen
Reservoir

Maple Ave

174

FLORIDA

Cheechunk Rd

START

P

6½ Station Rd

6½ Station
Sanctuary

P

6

Hartley Rd

Wallkill R.

rails·to·trails
conservancy

lovers will enjoy passing through the 62-acre 6½ Station Sanctuary, a marshland that's home to more than 200 species of birds.

A mile after crossing 6½ Station Road, the trail passes beneath busy NY 17 as it approaches the town of Goshen. This mostly on-road section of trail is not very clearly marked, but in Goshen it changes to a paved, 10-foot-wide trail. As you travel through Goshen, you'll pass Good Time Park, a mile-long racetrack that hosted the Hambletonian Stakes horse race 1930–1956. For parking here, follow signs for St. James Place.

About 7 miles from the northern endpoint as you approach the town of Chester is the historical Chester Depot Museum. Owned and operated by the Chester Historical Society, the museum has become a convening place for charity walks, community cookouts, yard sales, and general community gatherings. The museum has parking, restrooms, and food.

Next the trail passes over several streams and brooks, including Seely Brook and Youngs Brook. The green fields and residential areas by this section of trail make the ride more enjoyable. As the trail approaches the town of Monroe, it passes Orange-Rockland Lake to the left at 10.8 miles. Just before the southern endpoint at Mary Harriman Park, you'll pass the playgrounds at Airplane Park and traverse a wooded stretch on your way to the village of Harriman.

CONTACT: orangecountygov.com/1475/heritage-trail

DIRECTIONS

To reach limited parking at the northern endpoint, take I-84 to Exit 3E for US 6/NY 17M E toward Goshen, and merge onto US 6 E. In 1.6 miles, turn left onto County Road 50, followed by a slight right in 0.6 mile onto Echo Lake Road. In 1.2 miles, turn right onto Hartley Road. In 0.2 mile, a small parking lot and the northern endpoint both come up on the left.

To reach parking near Good Time Park in Goshen, take I-84 to Exit 4E for NY 17 E toward New York City. Merge onto NY 17 E (which later joins US 6 E). In 5.0 miles, take Exit 124 for NY 207/NY 17A toward Florida/Goshen. Turn right onto NY 17A W/NY 207 E/Greenwich Ave., following signs for Goshen. In 0.8 mile, turn right onto Green St., and in 0.1 mile turn left onto St. James Pl., where there is a parking lot.

To reach parking at Airplane Park (also known as Crane Park) in Monroe from I-87, take Exit 16. Merge onto NY 17, and immediately take the first exit toward Nininger Road. Continue straight onto Nininger Road, and go 1.9 miles. Turn left onto Bakertown Road, and go 0.5 mile. Make a slight right to continue on Bakertown Road, and go 0.8 mile. Turn left onto Mapes Pl. In 0.1 mile turn right onto Carpenter Pl., and go 0.2 mile. Continue onto Lake St. Take the first right onto Millpond Pkwy., and go 0.4 mile to find parking on the right.

High Line

FINISH

High Line
at the Rail Yards

NEW YORK

New York

Hudson River

11th Ave

W 37th St

W 36th St

W 34th St

12th Ave

10th Ave

9A

W 29th St

W 31st St

W 28th St

W 30th St

W 27th St

W 29th St

11th Ave

Chelsea
Waterside Park

W 25th St

W 24th St

Chelsea
Park

W 26th St

9th Ave

W 29th St

W 23rd St

MANHATTAN

10th Ave

London
Terrace

9th Ave

NEW YORK COUNTY

8th Ave

Clement
Clarke
Moore Park

W 23rd St

W 22nd St

Chelsea
Grasslands

W 21st St

W 20th St

Hudson River Greenway

Chelsea
Market

9th Ave

W 17th St

8th Ave

W 19th St

7th Ave

11th Ave

10th Ave

Diller–
von Furstenberg
Sundeck

W 16th St

W 18th St

9A

W 15th St

Pier 54

N

W 14th St

START

Little West
12th St

W 13th St

Hudson St

0   0.125   0.25 mile

Whitney
Museum
of Art

Gansevoort St

Horatio St

7th Ave

Jane St

Washington St

Abingdon
Square

rails·to·trails
conservancy

The High Line trail runs 30 feet above the bustling Manhattan streets and sidewalks below, which for trail lovers makes it an attraction in the same league as the Statue of Liberty or the Empire State Building. In fact, this celebrated urban park and aerial greenway joined the Rail-Trail Hall of Fame in 2011.

The trail, developed on a former elevated freight line, offers more than just a place to walk on the Lower West Side. It's an aerial public park set amid brick buildings and glass-and-concrete skyscrapers where you can enter art museums, restaurants, and hotels or participate in an activity calendar chock-full of cultural events.

Visitors gain access to the High Line from nearly a dozen stairways and elevators along its 1.5-mile length. Once on the walkway, they're treated to displays of sculpture; well-tended gardens; and views of the Hudson River, docks, and a rail yard below.

The elevated railway came into existence in 1934 to get freight trains off the streets below. Dwindling use led to closure of the tracks by the 1980s, and a citizens group, Friends of the High Line, fought to block its demolition

Portions of the High Line artfully incorporate characteristics of the former railroad corridor.

County
New York

Endpoints
Gansevoort St. and Washington St. to W. 34th St. between 11th Ave. and 12th Ave. (New York City)

Mileage
1.5

Type
Rail-Trail

Roughness Index
1

Surface
Concrete

and raised money for its preservation. After years of struggle, CSX Transportation turned over the property to the city in 2005, and construction on the walkway began the following year.

The first section opened in 2009, running 10 blocks north from Gansevoort Street to 20th Street, with some sections passing through buildings. Two years later, another section opened from 20th Street to 30th Street. The final section—High Line at the Rail Yards—opened in 2014 and continued the trail from 30th Street to 34th Street.

As you start in the south at Gansevoort Street, imagine the railway passing through buildings in the Meatpacking District, where workers could unload livestock and load butchered meat. Today, the Whitney Museum of American Art stands next to the trail, displaying its collections from contemporary artists. The gardens of grasses and wildflowers here and throughout the trail represent the wild plants that sprouted as the elevated tracks sat dormant.

Crossing 13th Street, you can see the old Pier 54 archway on the Hudson, where passengers landed from transatlantic voyages. In another block, you'll walk through the Diller–von Furstenberg Sundeck, a popular gathering spot that combines outdoor furniture with steel planters full of wildflowers and grasses. Chelsea Market emerges on the streets below in the next block, at one time the location of the National Biscuit Co., later known as Nabisco.

A few blocks north, between 18th and 19th Streets, you'll stroll through the Chelsea Grasslands, and at 23rd Street you can see the sprawling brick London Terrace complex—at 1,700 units, it was once the largest apartment building in the world.

At 30th Street, the High Line swings left toward the Hudson River. A section of concrete deck has been removed here to reveal the steel beams and girders underneath. As the High Line parallels the Hudson, you have unobstructed views of river traffic to the west or 30 sets of track in the Long Island Rail Road yard to the east.

CONTACT: thehighline.org

DIRECTIONS

The High Line is open April, May, October, and November, 7 a.m.–10 p.m.; June–September, 7 a.m.–11 p.m.; and December–March, 7 a.m.–7 p.m.

You can reach the southern trailhead at Gansevoort St. and Washington St. via subway on the A, C, E, and L lines to 14th St. and Eighth Ave.; or the 1, 2, and 3 lines to 14th St. and Seventh Ave. To arrive by bus, you can take the M11 to Washington St. or Ninth Ave., or take the M14 to Ninth Ave.

You can reach the northern trailhead via subway by taking the 7 line to 34th St./Hudson Yards.

Choices for other trailheads can be found at **thehighline.org/visit/#/transportation.**

The Hudson River Greenway (HRG) is one of the most popular places to ride, walk, and jog in New York City. It makes up part of the Manhattan Waterfront Greenway loop, the cross-state Empire State Trail, and the multistate East Coast Greenway. The greenway is separated from traffic and runs through a series of parks along the Hudson River and the west side of Manhattan, offering beautiful views of the water and skyline along its two-lane, 12.9-mile paved path.

Beginning at the northern terminus in Inwood Hill Park, the HRG heads south 2 miles toward the George Washington (GW) Bridge. Before you get to the bridge, the trail takes a steep climb, 160 feet up, to Inspiration Point for views of The Palisades in New Jersey across the river and of the GW Bridge to the south. Follow the trail back down to the river, and pass underneath the GW Bridge. As you pop out from under the bridge, you will see the Little Red Lighthouse. Built in 1880, the lighthouse is listed on the National Register of Historic Places and was used for navigation along the Hudson River until it was decommissioned in 1948.

Along most of the route, you will notice that the trail has separated facilities for pedestrians and bicyclists. This division ensures that the thousands of HRG bicycle commuters can maintain safe speeds without negatively affecting those walking along the trail. The HRG passes through several parks along its route; each of these parks has a multitude of picnic areas with grills and benches, which are in frequent use during the summer months.

Follow the path another 2 miles south of the GW Bridge, where you will pass through Riverbank State Park and then enter Riverside Park. For the next mile, if it's springtime, you will travel through an expanse of cherry trees lining the Hudson River. Follow the greenway another mile, past the 79th Street Rotunda and under Henry Hudson Parkway. Restaurants and restroom facilities begin to dot the trail at this point, and around mile

County
New York

Endpoints
Dyckman St. and NY 9A/ Henry Hudson Pkwy. in Inwood Hill Park to Battery Pl. and West St. at Battery Park (New York City)

Mileage
12.9

Type
Greenway/Rail-with-Trail

Roughness Index
1

Surface
Asphalt

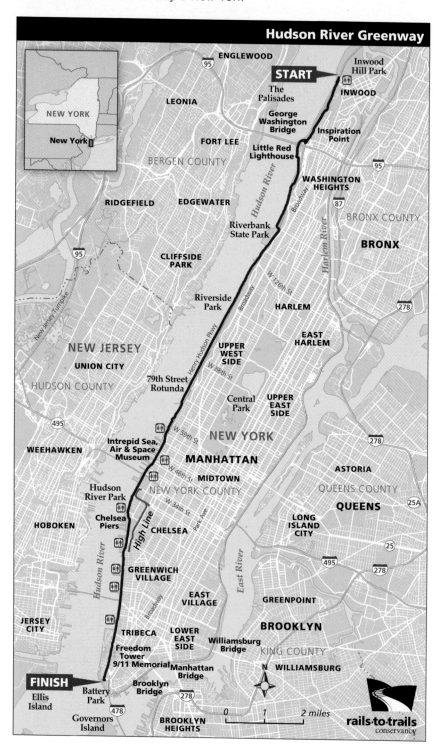

Hudson River Greenway

NEW YORK

New York

ENGLEWOOD

95

Inwood
Hill Park

START

The
Palisades

INWOOD

LEONIA

George
Washington
Bridge

Inspiration
Point

FORT LEE

Little Red
Lighthouse

95

BERGEN COUNTY

WASHINGTON
HEIGHTS

Hudson River

Broadway

87

RIDGEFIELD

EDGEWATER

BRONX COUNTY

Harlem River

BRONX

Riverbank
State Park

CLIFFSIDE
PARK

95

W 126th St

278

Riverside
Park

Broadway

HARLEM

New Jersey Turnpike

EAST
HARLEM

NEW JERSEY

Henry Hudson Pkwy

UPPER
WEST
SIDE

W 88th St

UNION CITY

HUDSON COUNTY

79th Street
Rotunda

Central
Park

UPPER
EAST
SIDE

495

W 59th St

NEW YORK

ASTORIA

WEEHAWKEN

Intrepid Sea,
Air & Space
Museum

W 46th St

MANHATTAN

QUEENS COUNTY

278

MIDTOWN

QUEENS

25A

Hudson
River Park

NEW YORK COUNTY

W 34th St

Park Ave

LONG
ISLAND
CITY

25

HOBOKEN

Chelsea
Piers

High Line

CHELSEA

Hudson River

GREENWICH
VILLAGE

495

278

EAST
VILLAGE

East River

GREENPOINT

JERSEY
CITY

Broadway

TRIBECA

LOWER
EAST
SIDE

Williamsburg
Bridge

BROOKLYN

N WILLIAMSBURG

KING COUNTY

Freedom
Tower

9/11 Memorial

Manhattan
Bridge

FINISH

Ellis
Island

Battery
Park

Brooklyn
Bridge

278

N

Governors
Island

478

BROOKLYN
HEIGHTS

0   1   2 miles

rails-to-trails
conservancy

Near the north end of the Hudson River Greenway, the George Washington Bridge—which allows vehicle, pedestrian, and bike traffic—connects New York to New Jersey.

7, the HRG leaves the highway and becomes an open-air trail for the rest of its route south to Battery Park.

Starting at West 59th Street, the second half of the trail is more densely populated with commuters, after-work recreators, and people getting in their evening runs and dog walks. Traveling through and along Hudson River Park, you will pass playgrounds, landscaped lawns, kayaking facilities, and basketball courts. Signals and directional signage become more prevalent here to ensure safe interactions between cars, bikes, and pedestrians. Highlights of this section include the Intrepid Sea, Air & Space Museum (at West 46th Street) and Chelsea Piers (near West 22nd Street), an area with a driving range and other attractions. Additionally, near Chelsea Piers, you will find yourself in the vicinity of the High Line, one of the nation's best-known converted rail corridors. The High Line is not connected to the HRG, but it's worth the detour to explore it. Note: The High Line is a pedestrian-only facility.

As you travel the final stretch toward Battery Park, you will pass Freedom Tower and the 9/11 Memorial. At the end of the trail in Battery Park, take a minute to look out over the Hudson River at the Statue of Liberty and take in New York City and all that it has to offer.

CONTACT: nycgovparks.org/facilities/bikeways

DIRECTIONS

As parking is limited in Manhattan, you will most likely want to take public transportation to the trail. Visit the Metropolitan Transportation Authority (**mta.info**) for information on the local bus and subway systems.

To reach the Inwood Hill Park access point from I-95, cross over the GW Bridge from New Jersey into Manhattan, and take Exit 1 for NY 9A/Hudson Pkwy. After 0.4 mile, follow signs for NY 9A N/Henry Hudson Pkwy./Riverside Dr. Merge onto NY 9A N/Henry Hudson Pkwy., and go 1.5 miles. Take Exit 17 toward Dyckman St. Continue onto Riverside Dr., and immediately turn left onto Henshaw St. In one block, you will reach Dyckman St.; the trail will be on your left in 0.1 mile. There is no public parking at Inwood Hill Park, but several public parking garages can be found near the trail access off Dyckman St.

To reach the Battery Park access point from I-478 N, take the underpass into Battery Park/Manhattan. Take the FDR Dr. exit to the left, and then turn left onto West St. Keep right to take the NY 9A/Battery Park exit, and go 0.1 mile to Battery Pl. Parking is not available, but garages can be found nearby. From I-78 E, take Exit 1 for NY 9A/West St., and merge onto Laight St. In 0.2 mile turn left onto West St. Go 1.1 miles, keep right to take the NY 9A/Battery Park exit, and go 0.1 mile to Battery Pl.

Offering a picturesque and family-friendly adventure, the Hudson Valley Rail Trail stretches 7.1 miles through hardwood forests, over Black Creek, and under two spectacular stone-arch bridges. Connecting the towns of New Paltz, Lloyd, and Highland, the rail-trail follows the former right-of-way of the New York, New Haven and Hartford Railroad. Two trailside cabooses, one dating to 1915 and the other to 1926, offer nods to the corridor's railroading past.

From North Putt Corners Road in New Paltz, you'll head east, paralleling NY 299 through a mixture of commercial areas and wooded canopy. A highlight of this section is passage through Tony Williams Park, where you'll find athletic facilities, picnic tables, and restrooms. Less than 0.5 mile from the park, the trail crosses over Black Creek, which is a popular waterway for kayakers and

Stone-arch bridges allow vehicular traffic to cross over the Hudson Valley Rail Trail.

County
Ulster

Mileage
7.1

Endpoints
N. Putt Corners Road at NY 299/Main St. (New Paltz) to Walkway Over the Hudson trailhead at 87 Haviland Road (Highland)

Type
Rail-Trail

Roughness Index
1

Surface
Asphalt

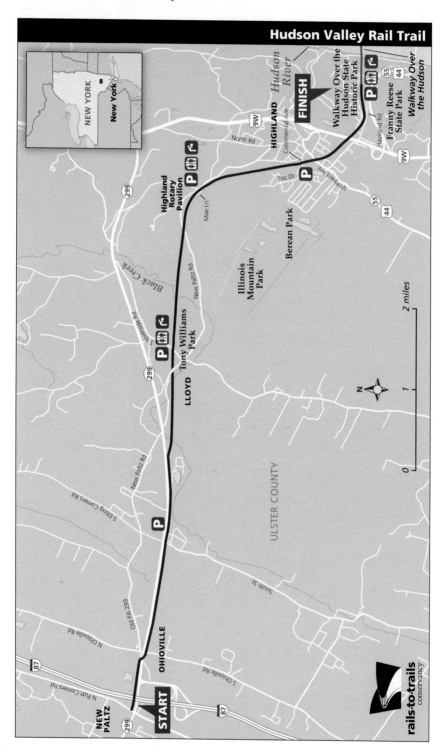

Hudson Valley Rail Trail

rails-to-trails
conservancy

canoeists. Farther on, the trail runs along a rock cut, where you'll find wildflowers blooming in the crevices in the spring. The cut also provides a cool spot to relax on hot summer days.

Near the trail's midpoint, two magnificent arched bridges carry New Paltz Road over the corridor. Shortly thereafter, you'll reach the Highland Rotary Pavilion, named for the Highland Rotary Club, which has made the Hudson Valley Rail Trail a primary project for more than a decade. The park setting offers restrooms, a large parking lot, picnic tables, and drinking water.

Along the route, signage invites you to explore the history of the trail and the communities it connects, while trailside exercise stations encourage you to pause for a health and wellness moment. You are now entering the hamlet of Highland and a more residential trail experience. A pedestrian bridge provides safe passage over US 44/NY 55/Vineyard Avenue as you continue through these more populated surroundings.

At its eastern end, the Hudson Valley Rail Trail meets the Walkway Over the Hudson State Historic Park (see page 193), which offers spectacular views from 212 feet above the Hudson River. Once on the east side of the river, travelers can make a seamless connection to the William R. Steinhaus Dutchess Rail Trail (see page 202) to continue riding another 13 miles from Poughkeepsie to Hopewell Junction. Together, the three trails were welcomed into Rails-to-Trails Conservancy's Rail-Trail Hall of Fame in 2016 and offer a seamless, combined route of just over 20 miles. They are also part of the Empire State Trail, a developing 750-mile trail network spanning the state from New York City to Canada and Buffalo to Albany.

CONTACT: hudsonvalleyrailtrail.net

DIRECTIONS

On its east end, the Hudson Valley Rail Trail shares a trailhead with the Walkway Over the Hudson at 87 Haviland Road in Highland. To reach the parking lot in Highland from I-87, take Exit 18 for NY 299 E. Continue on NY 299 for 5 miles, then turn right onto US 9W S. Continue on US 9W for 2.1 miles, then turn left onto Haviland Road. Parking will appear on your left in 0.5 mile.

Toward the west end of the trail, ample parking is provided in Tony Williams Park in Lloyd. To reach the park from I-87, take Exit 18 for Poughkeepsie and New Paltz. At the traffic light at the end of the exit, turn right onto NY 299 E, and go 2.3 miles. Turn right onto New Paltz Road, and go 0.7 mile. Turn left onto South Riverside Road; after 0.1 mile turn right into the parking lot entrance for Tony Williams Park.

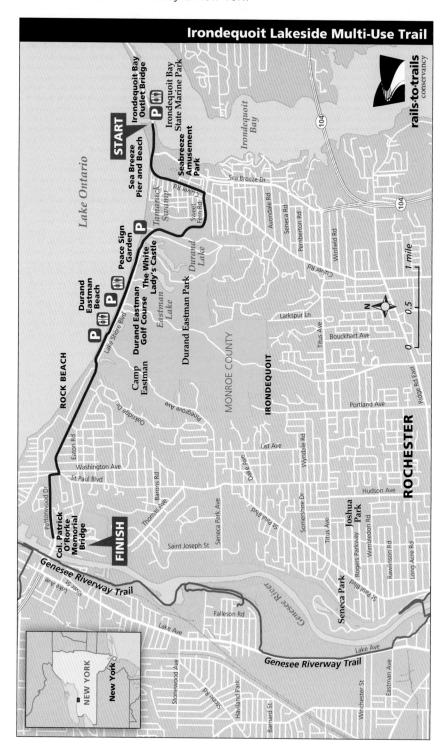

Irondequoit Lakeside Multi-Use Trail

rails-to-trails conservancy

START

Irondequoit Bay Outlet Bridge

Irondequoit Bay State Marine Park

Sea Breeze Pier and Beach

Seabreeze Amusement Park

Sea Breeze Dr

Irondequoit Bay

104

Tamarack Swamp

Culver Rd

Sweet Fern Rd

Avondale Rd

Seneca Rd

Pemberton Rd

Winfield Rd

104

Lake Ontario

Peace Sign Garden

The White Lady's Castle

Durand Lake

Durand Eastman Beach

Durand Eastman Golf Course

Durand Eastman Park

Eastman Lake

Larkspur Ln

Culver Rd

Titus Ave

Bouckhart Ave

1 mile

N

0   0.5

ROCK BEACH

Camp Eastman

MONROE COUNTY

IRONDEQUOIT

Portland Ave

Oakbridge Dr

Pinegrove Ave

Eaton Rd

Washington Ave

St Paul Blvd

Barons Rd

Thomas Ave

List Ave

Dale Ave

Seneca Park Ave

St Paul Blvd

Vyndale Rd

Somershire Dr

Titus Ave

Hudson Ave

Wyndale Rd

Ridge Rd East

ROCHESTER

Pattonwood Dr

Col. Patrick O'Rorke Memorial Bridge

FINISH

Genesee Riverway Trail

River St

Lake Ave

Saint Joseph St

Seneca Park

Joshua Park

Rogers Parkway

Wimbledon Rd

St Paul Blvd

Rawlinson Rd

Long Acre Rd

Falleson Rd

Genesee River

Lake Ave

Genesee Riverway Trail

Stonewood Ave

Stone Rd

Havilland Park

Barnard St

Saint Joseph St

Eastman Ave

Winchester St

NEW YORK

New York

Snaking along the shoreline of Lake Ontario, the Irondequoit Lakeside Multi-Use Trail provides a smooth journey infused with the region's rich natural and cultural heritage. The nearly 7-mile trail primarily runs through Rochester and one of its main suburbs, the town of Irondequoit. Framed by the Genesee River to the west, Lake Ontario to the north, and Irondequoit Bay to the east, the area is surrounded by water on three sides, which made its unique position valuable from early on. The trail's proximity to these and several other waterways also offers many opportunities for fishing.

For many years, the land was home to the Senecas, a tribe of the Iroquois Confederacy. Later it was pursued by the French, who were drawn to the area for its food supplies and trade benefits. Rochester and Irondequoit were founded in the early and mid-1800s, respectively.

The trail offers lush surroundings near Durand Lake.

County
Monroe

Endpoints
Culver Road, 0.25 mile east of Sea Breeze Dr. (Irondequoit), to Patton-wood Dr. and Joy Lane, before the Col. Patrick O'Rorke Memorial Bridge across the Genesee River (Rochester)

Mileage
6.9

Type
Rail-Trail

Roughness Index
1

Surfaces
Asphalt, Boardwalk, Concrete

Two wooden deer greet travelers near the entrance of the trail.

Decades later, the railroad brought trainloads of tourists to vacation along the beautiful shores and visit other attractions, such as the Seabreeze Amusement Park, which is the country's fourth-oldest amusement park and sits right near the easternmost endpoint of the trail.

Today, representations of the region's history can be found along the rail-trail from start to finish. From the east, you'll begin your adventure at the Irondequoit Bay State Marine Park by the Irondequoit Bay Outlet Bridge, a swing truss bridge. You'll be greeted by a kiosk and restrooms adjacent to the trail, as well as a pathway that leads to the dazzling Seabreeze Pier and Beach. From the trailhead, you'll head uphill on Culver Road 1 mile—traveling on the road or the sidewalk—passing restaurants and the amusement park.

At the 1-mile point, when Culver and Sweet Fern Roads meet, you will take a sharp right onto the trail, which is now an asphalt pathway and marked with a sign. You'll be heading downhill through comfortable, tree-lined shade; the lush surroundings are courtesy of the 977-acre Durand Eastman Park. Continue roughly 0.75 mile through the park on the paved path before reaching a timber boardwalk that navigates you through Tamarack Swamp. Immediately after exiting the swamp, the path will open up to reveal Lake Ontario on your right and Durand Lake on your left. Eastman Lake quickly follows on your left. Between the lakes, you'll spy a stark stone structure known as The White Lady's Castle, which is rumored to be haunted. Across from the spirited structure, you'll pass the Peace Sign Garden.

In 0.4 mile, you'll see the sandy shores of Durand Eastman Beach appear on your right, where you can enjoy the sight of glittering waters and happy beachgoers. As you glide past, the Durand Eastman Golf Course will be on your left. This section is also punctuated by slight hills, multiple parking areas, portable bathrooms, and informative signage, both for wayfinding and learning about the area.

Following the lakeshore views, the trail becomes a concrete pathway paralleling Lake Shore Boulevard for a mile before reaching Washington Avenue. Here you will need to exit the path and cross Lake Shore and St. Paul Boulevards; a traffic light and trail signage help guide you. Turn right onto St. Paul Boulevard, and follow the concrete pathway north. Continue another 0.1 mile; at the next light, cross the street, and take a sharp left onto Pattonwood Drive. Travel 0.5 mile more on Pattonwood Drive—be mindful of the traffic into Rochester—to reach the trail's western endpoint, marked by a kiosk and a bench shortly before the Colonel Patrick O'Rorke Memorial Bridge over the Genesee River.

For those wanting a longer adventure, or to reach parking at Ontario Beach Park, which lies along the Lake Ontario shoreline, head across the bridge's pedestrian path to connect with the Genesee Riverway Trail (see page 110) via a brief marked on-street route.

CONTACT: www2.monroecounty.gov/parks-trailmaps

DIRECTIONS

To reach the eastern trailhead in Irondequoit Bay State Marine Park from Rochester, get on I-490 and take Exit 21, following signs for NY 590 N; merge onto NY 590 N. Continue 5.4 miles north on the highway; at the traffic circle, take the second exit onto Sea Breeze Dr. Continue on Sea Breeze Dr. another 1.7 miles, going through three more traffic circles. You will pass Seabreeze Amusement Park before running into Culver Road. Take a right onto Culver Road, and continue 0.3 mile. You'll find the parking area and trailhead right before the Irondequoit Bay Outlet Bridge. The start of the trail is marked by a kiosk, which is next to a restroom and a path leading to the Seabreeze Pier and Beach.

For the western end of the trail, public parking is available in Ontario Beach Park, which is 1.1 miles away from the trail's terminus. Follow the directions above to Sea Breeze Dr., and travel 1.1 miles, continuing on Sea Breeze Dr. through two traffic circles along the way. At the third traffic circle, take the third exit onto Durand Blvd., and continue straight as it becomes Sweet Fern Road, Pine Valley Road, and Lake Shore Blvd. After 3.3 miles, turn right onto St. Paul Blvd. then immediately turn left onto Pattonwood Dr. Go 0.9 mile, crossing the Genesee River, and turn right onto Lake Ave. After 0.6 mile, turn right onto Corrigan St. to drive directly into Ontario Beach Park's parking lots. From the south end of the parking lot, take the Genesee Riverway Trail, which parallels River Road heading south. Follow this trail 1 mile to reach the Col. Patrick O'Rorke Memorial Bridge; cross the Genesee River. The entrance to the Irondequoit Lakeside Multi-Use Trail will be on your left at the end of the bridge.

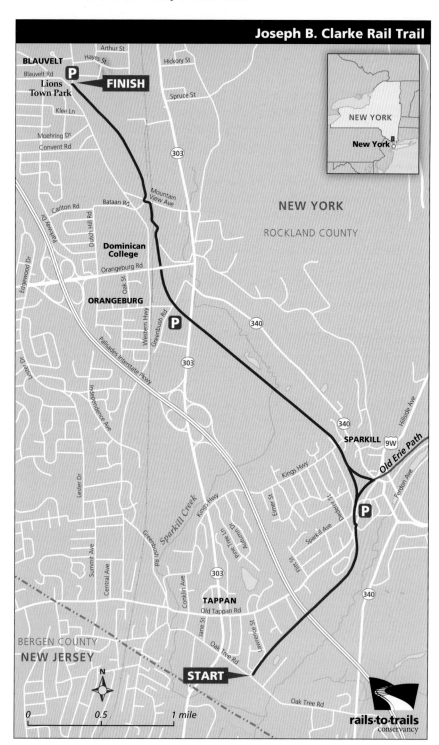

You might expect a 4-mile rail-trail that passes through three downtowns to be excessively urban, but the quaint town centers on the Joseph B. Clarke Rail Trail are compact and surrounded by woodlands, sanctuaries, and parks.

Beginning in Tappan, the trail runs through the hamlets of Sparkill, Orangeburg, and Blauvelt in Rockland County. Although it rolls inland, it joins two other rail-trails that overlook the Hudson River from The Palisades. Already popular with local residents, the trail is expecting more visitors with the 2019 opening of a multiuse path on the Gov. Mario M. Cuomo Bridge, formerly known as the Tappan Zee Bridge.

The trail is named for Joseph B. Clarke, the 1969–1996 superintendent for Orangetown's parks and recreation department. He saw the possibilities of using two former railroad corridors in the area for recreation and commuting. His interest also sparked the creation of the connecting Old Erie Path (see page 169) and the Raymond G. Esposito Memorial Trail (see page 182) in nearby riverfront communities.

Trees flank the trail between the town centers.

County
Rockland

Endpoints
Oak Tree Road between Lawrence St. and Rockland Park Ave. (Tappan) to Western Hwy. S between Blauvelt Road and N. Troop Road (Blauvelt)

Mileage
4.1

Type
Rail-Trail

Roughness Index
1

Surface
Asphalt

The three trails follow the corridors of the old New York & Erie Railroad and its affiliate, the Northern Railroad of New Jersey, which was primarily a passenger carrier. The Clarke trail traces the Northern Railroad from Tappan to Sparkill and the Erie main line from Sparkill through Orangeburg and Blauvelt. Northern's ridership dwindled in the 1930s. It was acquired by the Erie Railroad in 1942, and passenger service ended in 1966. The Erie survived under a variety of names until it became part of Conrail in 1976.

The trail starts in Tappan, a town steeped in Revolutionary War history. The DeWint House, which was built in 1700 and served as a temporary headquarters for George Washington during the war, is located 0.4 mile east on Oak Tree Road.

Heading north through hardwood forest alongside Sparkill Creek, the trail comes to a fork at Depot Square in Sparkill. The right fork joins the Old Erie Path, which follows the old Northern Railroad corridor to the riverfront villages of Piermont and Grand View-on-Hudson and connects to the Raymond G. Esposito Memorial Trail in South Nyack. Take the left fork to stay on the Clarke trail and follow the Erie Railroad's main line.

In 1.3 miles, the path arrives in Orangeburg at a pedestrian bridge over NY 303 and crosses Greenbush Road. The hamlet is the former home of Camp Shanks, where 1.3 million GIs stopped before being shipped out to Europe and North Africa from Piermont during World War II. A museum in a simulated barracks about 400 feet north at 20 Greenbush Road tells their story.

The newest 1.6-mile section passes beneath the Orangeburg Road bridge and crosses the CSX Railroad tracks on another pedestrian bridge before arriving in Blauvelt. On the way, the route passes Dominican College and ends across the street from the Lions Town Park and next door to the Blauvelt Free Library, located in the 18th-century home of Judge Cornelius Blauvelt.

CONTACT: orangetown.com/document/j-b-clark-rail-trail-extension

DIRECTIONS

To reach the endpoint in Tappan from I-87/I-287, take Exit 13S to merge onto Palisades Interstate Pkwy. heading south. Go 5.4 miles, and take Exit 5S onto NY 303 S. Go 1.2 miles, and turn left onto Oak Tree Road. Go 0.2 mile, and look for trail parking on the left.

To reach the endpoint in Blauvelt from I-87/I-287, take Exit 13S to merge onto Palisades Interstate Pkwy. heading south. Go 4.2 miles, and take Exit 6E onto Orangeburg Road/County Road 20. Go 0.5 mile east, and turn left onto Western Hwy. S/CR 15. Go 1.0 mile and look for the Blauvelt Free Library on your right. Trail parking is available here.

The Keuka Outlet Trail offers a sinuous route of nearly 7 miles between Penn Yan and Dresden in New York's Finger Lakes region. The rail-trail follows a railroad corridor that traced a former canal dug along the natural drainage of Keuka (KYOO-ka) Lake Outlet from Seneca Lake to Keuka Lake. Today, the millsite ruins along the watercourse add another dimension to the natural beauty of cascading waterfalls and rocky ravines.

Settlers moved into the area in the late 1780s, and by 1790 the first mill began operation on Crooked Lake Outlet, as it was then called, based on the "crooked" shape of Keuka Lake. By 1820 more than 20 mills operated along the stream. New York's canal-building boom led to construction in 1833 of the Crooked Lake Canal, which required 27 locks along its course. The canal never made money and was abandoned in 1873.

The Penn Yan and New York Railway Company opened a branch in 1884 that used the towpath as its corridor. Later

County
Yates

Endpoints
NY 54A/Elm St. between Burns Terr. and Lakeview Cemetery (Penn Yan) to Seneca St. between Main St. and Margaret St. (Dresden)

Mileage
6.7

Type
Rail-Trail

Roughness Index
1–2

Surfaces
Asphalt, Ballast, Dirt, Gravel

The Keuka Outlet Trail abounds in natural beauty, such as this peaceful creek.

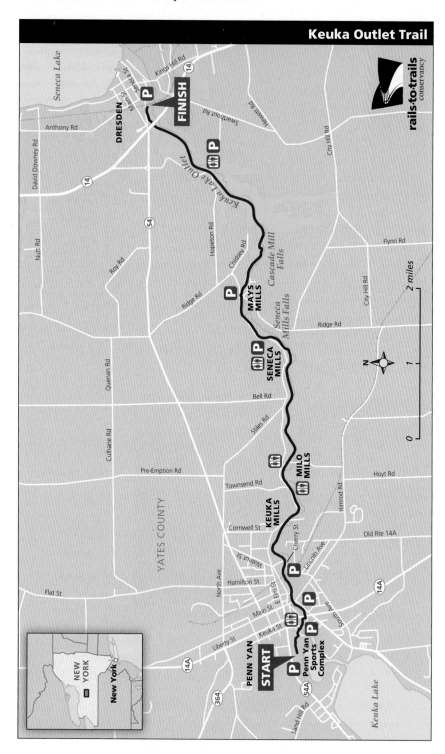

Keuka Outlet Trail

rails-to-trails
conservancy

becoming part of the Fall Brook Railway Company, it was acquired by New York Central, which stopped using the route after extensive damage from Tropical Storm Agnes in 1972.

From Penn Yan, the trail descends an easy grade to Dresden. Both towns are tourist destinations with plenty of services. The first 1.3 miles in Penn Yan is paved, and the remainder of the Keuka Outlet Trail is gravel, ballast, and dirt. The Friends of the Outlet have installed numerous interpretive signs along the route; you can also visit their website (**keukaoutlettrail.org**) to learn about trail events. Snowmobiling is allowed east of Penn Yan.

Penn Yan is named for its early transplants from Pennsylvania (PENN) and New England (YAN-kees). The trail begins at a sports complex at Keuka Lake's northern tip and joins the Keuka Outlet in 0.4 mile. Crossing under Main Street at 0.7 mile, one of the area's first mills—Birkett Mills—still operates across the stream. After Cherry Street, you'll soon be on the unpaved portion of the trail.

You'll pass nearly a dozen old lock sites along the canal, as well as seven former millsites, some deteriorated to crumbling brick walls or a set of rusty gears. At 3.5 miles, you'll likely hear the roar of Seneca Mills Falls before you see it, as it drops more than 40 feet in three cascades at the former paper mill site, now a popular picnic area. This is the only spot where you'll leave the old towpath and drop into the former canal channel as you pass through Lock 17.

The trail follows the creek through a narrow glacier-cut gorge for the next 3 miles. Cascade Mill Falls appears 1.3 miles past Seneca Mills Falls and is one of the few millsites on the eastern half of the trail. A covered picnic pavilion here features interpretive displays.

At 3.1 miles past Seneca Mills Falls, you'll cross under the NY 14 overpass on your way to the Dresden trailhead in another 0.2 mile. Seneca Lake is 0.5 mile east.

CONTACT: keukaoutlettrail.org

DIRECTIONS

To reach the trailhead in Penn Yan from I-90, take Exit 42, and turn right onto NY 14 after passing through the tollbooth. Go 0.7 mile, and turn right onto Cross Road. Then go 1.8 miles, and turn left onto Pre-Emption St. Go 18.4 miles, and turn right onto NY 54/Clinton St. Go 1.5 miles, turn left onto Main St., and then go 0.2 mile. Turn right onto NY 54A/Elm St. Go 0.5 mile, and look for Penn Yan Sports Complex on the left. The trail starts at the rear of the parking lot.

To reach the trailhead in Dresden from I-90, take Exit 42, and turn right onto NY 14 after passing through the tollbooth. Go 5.4 miles, and turn right onto NY 14/Seneca St. Then go 0.2 mile, and turn left onto NY 14/S. Main St. Go 13.2 miles, and turn left onto Main St. Then go about 200 feet, and turn right onto Seneca St. After 0.2 mile look for parking and the trail on the right.

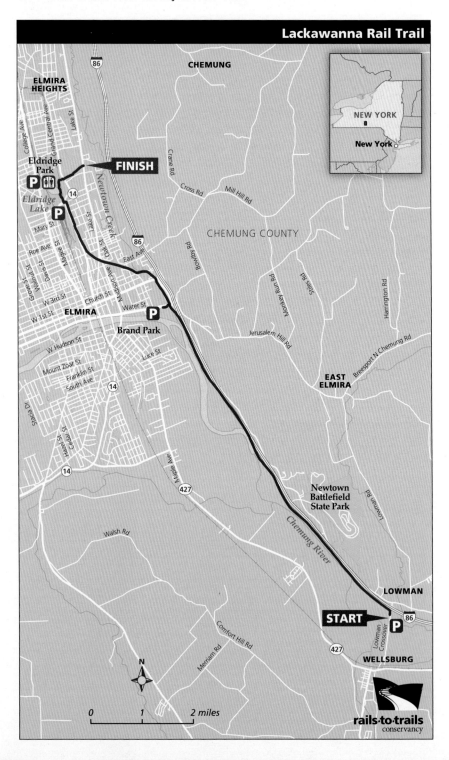

Lackawanna Rail Trail

The Lackawanna Rail Trail traces a short stretch of the old Delaware, Lackawanna & Western Railroad from Lowman to Elmira in southern New York. Much of it follows the meandering Chemung River, meaning "place of the big horn" in the local American Indian language. Originally confined within the city limits of Elmira, the trail now extends along the wooded river shoreline on an additional 5-mile segment completed in 2017.

The Delaware, Lackawanna & Western Railroad was completed through Elmira in 1882 as it connected Buffalo, New York, with Hoboken, New Jersey. The popular *Phoebe Snow* passenger train, advertised as burning cleaner coal than its competitors, traveled this route from 1949 to 1966. The line merged with its rival in 1960 to form the Erie Lackawanna Railroad, which later succumbed to flooding and declining economic conditions.

The first section of trail opened in 2013 in Elmira, a former transportation hub for trains and canalboats and the summer home of writer Mark Twain. City planners are

Much of the trail route follows the Chemung River.

County
Chemung

Endpoints
Lowman Crossover, just south of I-86 (Lowman), to Lake St., 0.1 mile north of Sullivan St. (Elmira)

Mileage
8.7

Type
Rail-Trail

Roughness Index
1

Surface
Asphalt

banking on the trail to help revitalize the local economy. The paved trail passes several local destinations, including Eldridge Park, a popular restored amusement park from the early 20th century.

The path starts at a small parking lot in the community of Lowman. It runs close to I-86 for the next 6 miles into Elmira but is screened from the expressway by woods most of the way.

About a mile from the trailhead, you'll encounter the Chemung River. A tributary of the Susquehanna River, it's used for canoeing and fishing for bass, trout, rock bass, and smaller sport fish. This section of trail is shaded in the summer and runs atop levees, where you'll find benches for resting and enjoying the scenery.

The area is rich in Colonial history. The Continental Army battled British forces and their Iroquois allies on a nearby hillside in 1779. The battle is commemorated at the Newtown Battlefield State Park on the other side of I-86, not directly accessible from the trail. After traveling 5.4 miles past the trailhead, you'll arrive at an old trestle spanning Newtown Creek; this was the location of gristmills in the 1700s.

Entering Elmira, the trail frequently uses old railroad underpasses or overpasses to cross streets. You'll have to cross four-lane NY 14 on a crosswalk, however, to reach Eldridge Park near the northern end of the trail. The last segment of the Lackawanna Rail Trail goes through the park, which has a vintage carousel, a skate park, a playground, paddleboats, a dog park, and restrooms, as well as the Mark Twain Mini Golf Course & Train Ride. You can also connect to the 1.1-mile Eldridge Park Loop around Eldridge Lake.

A 0.4-mile spur heads east out of the park but is not well marked. A northern extension is planned to bring the Lackawanna Rail Trail closer to the Catharine Valley Trail (see page 94). The City of Elmira is also working on spur trails to the river for improved fishing access.

CONTACT: cityofelmira.net/public-works/lackawanna

DIRECTIONS

To reach the southern endpoint from I-86, take Exit 57, and head south on Lowman Crossover toward Wellsburg. Go 0.1 mile, and look for parking on the right.

To reach the northern endpoint in Elmira from I-86, take Exit 56, and head west on NY 352/E. Church St. Go 0.3 mile, and turn right onto Judson St. Go 0.3 mile, and turn right onto Sullivan St. Go 1.5 miles, and turn left to stay on Sullivan St. Go 0.1 mile, and continue on Clemens Center Pkwy. Ext. Go 0.3 mile, and turn right onto NY 14 Truck, and then go 0.3 mile and turn left onto Eldridge Park Road. After 0.2 mile, look for parking. Heading south on the Lackawanna Rail Trail, go 0.2 mile, and turn left to follow the trail 0.4 mile to the endpoint on Lake St.

The Lancaster Heritage Trail begins in an eastern outer suburb of Buffalo and unwinds 4 paved miles into the delightful wooded countryside. Benches made of natural materials, including boulders, are placed at various locations along the way for resting and taking in the tranquil setting, and granite posts mark every 0.25 mile. Note, however, that there are no restrooms or drinking fountains along the way, so plan accordingly.

Begin your journey northeast of downtown Lancaster at Walter Winter Drive, where the trailhead offers a parking lot and a kiosk with information about the trail

Take a break on one of the many large rocks that line the Lancaster Heritage Trail.

County
Erie

Mileage
4.0

Endpoints
Walter Winter Dr., 0.1 mile south of Commerce Pkwy. (Lancaster), to Town Line Road, 0.4 mile north of Westwood Road (Dellwood)

Type
Rail-Trail

Roughness Index
1

Surface
Asphalt

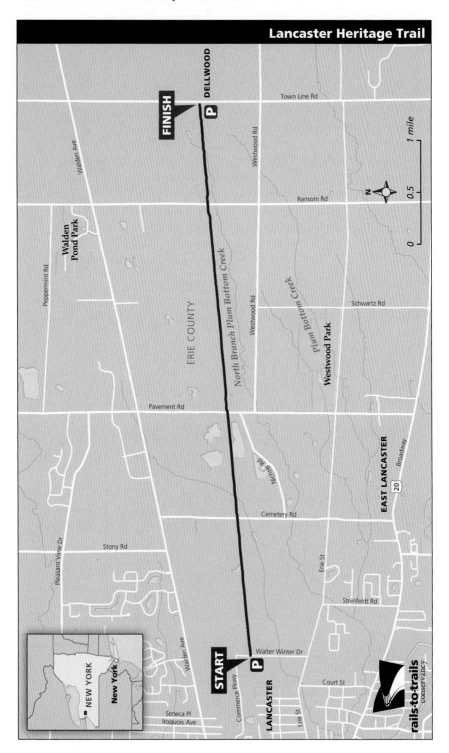

and its history. The rail-trail was developed on a portion of the former Delaware, Lackawanna & Western Railroad, built in 1882 to haul coal from Pennsylvania's Lackawanna Valley mines to Buffalo, as well as grain from Buffalo to the Port of New York. Trains ceased running in 1972, and the town purchased the corridor in 1984. The trail opened in 2010.

As you travel along, the leafy tree cover will occasionally open up to offer vistas of farm fields and ponds. Look for wildlife, such as deer, chipmunks, and birds. Over the course of the route, you'll encounter only three street crossings, which are well-marked and across low-volume roadways.

The trail ends at Town Line Road in the small hamlet of Dellwood, where a trailhead parking lot accommodates a handful of cars.

CONTACT: lancasterny.gov/departments/parks-recreation

DIRECTIONS

To reach the western terminus from I-90, take Exit 52E for Walden Ave. Turn right to head east on Walden Ave., and go 4.7 miles to Central Ave. Turn right and travel 0.2 mile to Commerce Pkwy. Turn left and travel 0.8 mile to Walter Winter Dr. Turn right; in 0.1 mile the trailhead parking lot will be on your left.

To reach the eastern terminus from I-90, take Exit 52E for Walden Ave. Turn right to head east on Walden Ave., and go 9.6 miles to Town Line Road. Take a right; in 1.0 mile the trailhead parking lot will be on your right.

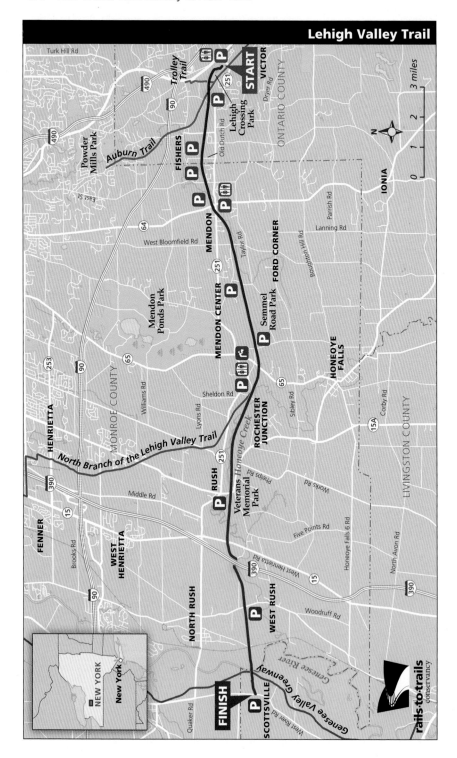

L ocated in the majestic Finger Lakes region, the Lehigh Valley Trail is a well-used gem with a sparkling future. Wandering 16.4 miles through beautiful landscapes and rich greenery, the trail connects to several other pathways and is part of an effort to create a larger trail system throughout the area. While doable on a road bike, the trail is better suited to hybrid or mountain bikes.

The path follows the former Route of the Black Diamond, a nickname given to the Lehigh Valley Railroad corridor for its role in transporting anthracite coal from Buffalo to New York City. Although the railroad discontinued operations in the mid-1970s, its nickname (the pathway is sometimes referred to as the Black Diamond Trail) and rail heritage are still part of the trail's identity today.

At its eastern end, the trail starts in the lovely Lehigh Crossing Park in Victor. The 54-acre park marks the confluence of the Lehigh Valley Trail, Auburn Trail (see page 80), and Trolley Trail and offers ample parking as well as a fishing pond, a playing field, a picnic area, and seasonal bathrooms. Helpful signs are placed around the park and along the remainder of the trail to steer visitors in the right direction.

Heading west, users will travel 0.8 mile on a stonedust path before reaching a railroad trestle bridge at a second intersection of the Auburn Trail. In 1.6 miles, you'll approach Old Dutch Road in Victor. For the next 1.4 miles to Mendon, horses are permitted on a parallel grass trail. In Mendon, the trail passes a cluster of youth baseball fields, restroom facilities, water fountains, a lightning protection shelter, and parking.

Continue under comfortable tree-lined shade to the Rochester Junction trailhead at Plains and Junction Roads in Honeoye Falls. Here the developing 14.5-mile North Branch of the Lehigh Valley Trail splits off and makes its way northwest, past the Rochester Institute of Technology campus. Ending at Genesee Valley Park, the North Branch connects with the Genesee Riverway Trail (see page 110),

Counties
Monroe, Ontario

Endpoints
Lehigh Crossing Park at Shallow Creek Trail and Victor Mendon Road (Victor) to W. River Road/County Road 84, 0.4 mile south of South Road/CR 141 (Scottsville)

Mileage
16.4

Type
Rail-Trail

Roughness Index
2

Surface
Crushed Stone

the expansive Erie Canalway Trail (see page 104), and the University of Rochester. In addition to its many connections, Rochester Junction also supplies visitors with parking areas, bathrooms, water fountains, and the opportunity to explore railway remnants and a replica freight house.

In 2.5 miles, you'll reach Veterans Memorial Park in the charming town of Rush. Along the way, slow down to enjoy breaks in the trail's surrounding foliage that permit views of nearby creeks and glimpses of golden agricultural lands. In town, you can find parking and several trailside eateries before crossing the fairly quiet West Henrietta Road to rejoin the last stretch of trail.

For the last 5 miles, travel over Honeoye Creek, under I-390, and through wetlands to an impressive railroad trestle bridge along the Genesee River. Immediately after crossing the river, you'll come face-to-face with large stone abutments. These railroad relics mark the intersection of the 68.8-mile Genesee Valley Greenway.

The final 0.5 mile includes a short but steep climb. Bicycle riders with narrow tires are encouraged to dismount to avoid injury. The trail ends alongside a designated parking area off West River Road/CR 84 in Scottsville.

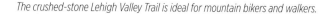

The crushed-stone Lehigh Valley Trail is ideal for mountain bikers and walkers.

CONTACT: monroecounty.gov/parks-lehighvalley.php

DIRECTIONS

From the vibrant downtown of Rochester, it's a short trip south to either end of the Lehigh Valley Trail. To reach the eastern trailhead in Lehigh Crossing Park from I-490, take Exit 29, and head south on NY 96 toward Victor; go 2.0 miles. Turn right onto NY 251 W/Victor Mendon Road, and go 0.2 mile. Turn right onto Shallow Creek Trail, then go approximately 0.1 mile to reach the parking area. The eastern trailhead is straight ahead.

To reach the Rochester Junction trailhead in Honeoye Falls, which connects to the developing North Branch of the Lehigh Valley Trail, take I-390 to Exit 11. From I-390 S, turn left onto NY 15, and go 0.3 mile; then turn left onto NY 251 E. From I-390 N, turn right onto NY 251 E. Travel 4.0 miles, then take a right onto Plains Road. Continue until you see the Freight House Lodge, which marks the intersection of the two trails. Parking for both trails is available on either side of Plains Road.

To reach the western trailhead in Scottsville from 1-390, take Exit 11 for NY 15 toward NY 251/Rush. From I-390 S, turn left onto NY 15, and go 0.3 mile; then turn right onto NY 251 W. From I-390 N, turn left onto NY 251 W. Travel 3.8 miles, and turn left onto NY 940H/River Road. Go 1.5 miles to reach a gravel parking area, which abuts the trail and sits directly across from an office park.

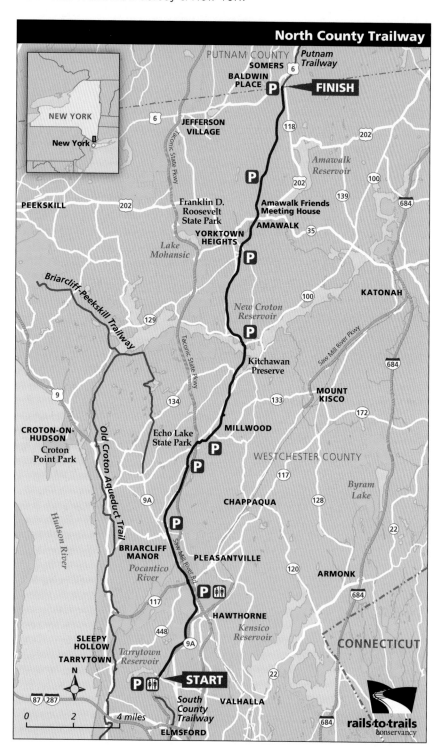

North County Trailway

The former "Old Put" commuter rail corridor that ran from the Bronx to northern bedroom communities in Westchester and Putnam Counties is popular once again, only this time it's for people riding bicycles, walking dogs, or pushing strollers. At just over 20 miles, the North County Trailway is the longest of four rail-trails created from the former New York Central Railroad's Putnam Division line. The others, combining for some 45 miles of trail travel, are the Old Putnam Trail, South County Trailway (see page 189), and Putnam Trailway (see page 179). All but the Old Putnam Trail are part of the 750-mile Empire State Trail, expected to be completed by 2020.

Several mid–19th-century railroad companies laid tracks that came under control of the New York and Putnam Railroad in 1894. Serving communities in Westchester and Putnam Counties, the primarily commuter rail service ran from the Bronx to Brewster. It became the Putnam Division of the New York Central after 1913, earning the nickname Old Put. Passenger service ended in 1958, and tracks began to be pulled in 1962.

County
Westchester

Endpoints
South County Trailway at Old Saw Mill River Road, 0.6 mile northwest of NY 9A (Elmsford), to Putnam Trailway at NY 118/Tomahawk St., 420 feet west of Miller Road (Baldwin Place)

Mileage
20.7

Type
Rail-Trail

Roughness Index
1

Surface
Asphalt

The trail crosses the New Croton Reservoir on a 384-foot steel-truss railroad bridge.

The paved trail starts as a continuation of South County Trailway as it rolls under Old Saw Mill River Road. (A trail to the left in 0.1 mile goes along the southern shore of Tarrytown Reservoir toward Sleepy Hollow and the Hudson River.) It trends slightly uphill to its junction with the Putnam Trailway in Somers. The trail is scheduled for repaving by the end of 2019. Vegetation screens sections that pass through residential and commercial areas or run next to roads. Two short sections (one spanning 0.5 mile and the other 0.8 mile) use the shoulder of Saw Mill River Road. Food and refreshments can be found in numerous towns along the route.

The pathway follows the Pocantico River and Saw Mill River Road north through Briarcliff Manor. You'll pass a short trail on the left at 5.2 miles that leads to the Briarcliff Manor Library, originally one of 23 railroad depots that served commuters in Westchester County. The first on-road section begins in a short distance. At mile 7.4, the other on-road section begins, passing Echo Lake State Park before ending in Millwood.

About 3.3 miles after regaining the trail in Millwood, you'll pass through the Kitchawan Preserve and cross the New Croton Reservoir on a railroad bridge. In another 3 miles, you'll enter the business district of Yorktown Heights, which has several Colonial and Revolutionary War landmarks, as well as a Putnam Division railroad depot. Plans call for a trail to head about 1 mile west from here to Franklin D. Roosevelt State Park.

One mile after Yorktown Heights, the trail comes within 0.5 mile of the 1830s Amawalk Friends Meeting House on Quaker Church Road. From the trail, you'll see pick-your-own orchards as you cross Granite Springs Road. Past the orchards, you'll soon arrive in Somers, which offers many snacking opportunities.

CONTACT: parks.westchestergov.com/parks-and-destinations/trailways

DIRECTIONS

To reach the Elmsford trailhead from I-87, take Exit 8 or 8A, and merge onto I-287 E/Cross Westchester Expy. Go 0.2 mile, and merge onto Saw Mill River Pkwy. N. Go 2.5 miles, and take Exit 23. Turn right, go 0.1 mile, and look for parking on your right. The trail at the rear of the parking lot goes left 300 feet to reach the North County Trailway. Alternatively, take Exit 23 and turn left onto NY 303/Old Saw Mill River Road. Go 0.1 mile, and look for parking on your right. Turn left onto a spur trail at the entrance to reach the North County Trailway in 0.2 mile.

To reach the Baldwin Place trailhead from I-684, take Exit 6; head west on NY 35. Go 1.6 miles, and turn right onto NY 100 N. Then go 0.6 mile, and turn left onto NY 139/Primrose Dr. Go 2.7 miles, and stay on the arterial to join US 202/Lincolndale Road. Go 1.8 miles, and turn right onto NY 118/Tomahawk St. Go 1.9 miles, and turn left to stay on NY 118/Tomahawk St. Go 0.1 mile, turn left into Somers Commons, and immediately look for parking on the left. Turn right onto the trail at the rear of the parking lot. (A left turn will take you to the Putnam Trailway.)

The O&W Rail Trail provides a glimpse into the area's history from the perspectives of both a historical canal and a railroad. The Delaware & Hudson (D&H) Canal carried coal from Honesdale, Pennsylvania, to Kingston, New York, for the New York City and Albany markets from 1828 to 1898. The canal was shut down in favor of the New York, Ontario and Western Railway, more commonly known as the O&W (and nicknamed the Old and Weary), which was in use until the mid-20th century. A major carrier of anthracite coal, the O&W was also an important carrier of milk and dairy products, as well as urban tourists seeking the fresh air of resorts and farmhouse boarding.

Today the trail is open in several disconnected sections, with 16.7 miles of trail open in Ulster County and

Counties
Sullivan, Ulster

Mileage
25.9

Endpoints
Ulster Co.: Northwest of Washington Ave. and Schwenk Dr. to Hurley Ave., 0.25 mile west of Snyder Ave. (Kingston); US 209, 1.4 miles south of NY 28 (Hurley), to County Road 1/Lucas Turnpike and Dejager Lane (Accord); Tobacco Road, west of CR 27 (Accord), to Main St., 0.3 mile east of 42nd St. (Kerhonkson).
Sullivan Co.: Railroad Ave., 0.1 mile northwest of Post Hill Road (Mountaindale), to Greenfield Road and Green Ave. Ext. (Woodridge); Roosevelt Ave. and Green Ave. to Joseph Road and Avon Lodge Road (Woodridge); Water St., north of Railroad Plaza (South Fallsburg), to Denman Road and Herner Road (Hurleyville)

Type
Rail-Trail

Roughness Index
1–3

Surfaces
Asphalt, Cinder, Crushed Stone, Dirt, Grass

A wooden bridge provides safe passage over Rest Plaus Road, as well as a view of the surrounding Ulster County countryside.

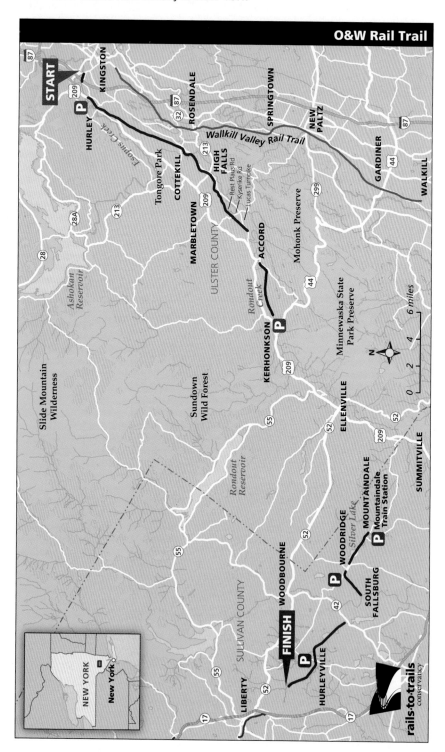

O&W Rail Trail

START

KINGSTON

ROSENDALE

SPRINGTOWN

HURLEY

Esopus Creek

Tongore Park

COTTEKILL

HIGH FALLS

Wallkill Valley Rail Trail

NEW PALTZ

GARDINER

WALKILL

MARBLETOWN

Rest Plaus Rd

Kyserike Rd

Lucas Turnpike

ACCORD

Mohonk Preserve

ULSTER COUNTY

Rondout Creek

Ashokan Reservoir

Slide Mountain Wilderness

KERHONKSON

Minnewaska State Park Preserve

N

6 miles

4

2

0

Sundown Wild Forest

ELLENVILLE

SUMMITVILLE

Rondout Reservoir

MOUNTAINDALE

Mountaindale Train Station

WOODRIDGE

Silver Lake

SOUTH FALLSBURG

WOODBOURNE

SULLIVAN COUNTY

FINISH

LIBERTY

HURLEYVILLE

NEW YORK

New York

rails-to-trails conservancy

another 9.2 miles available in Sullivan County. Note that the O&W Rail Trail does not connect across county lines.

Ulster County: 16.7 miles

In Ulster County, the rail-trail provides a scenic wooded path for recreational users. Generally it is rustic and unpaved. On its northern end, the O&W Rail Trail begins in Kingston, where it has a grassy surface best explored on a mountain bike or on foot. From this endpoint, note that the Wallkill Valley Rail Trail (see page 196) is only 2.2 miles away.

The O&W Rail Trail starts just west of the Washington Avenue and Taylor Street intersection and extends 0.5 mile before it peters out shortly after the I-87 underpass. You can pick up the trail again a mile farther southwest at a well-marked trailhead with parking located off US 209, south of Esopus Creek in the town of Hurley. From here down to Marbletown, the trail is sometimes referred to as the Hurley Rail Trail; from Marbletown south, it's sometimes called the Marbletown Rail Trail.

For 2 miles, the asphalt-surfaced trail runs adjacent to US 209. This portion is suitable for in-line skaters, road cyclists, and wheelchair users. It is particularly scenic as you continue south, as there is an American Indian planting field and a railroad tunnel in Hurley.

Traveling toward the community of Cottekill, roughly halfway from the start of this segment, the area becomes heavily wooded and grassy. Heading south from Cottekill Road, users will encounter steep grades and rougher terrain featuring mostly dirt and cinder.

As you continue south to cross NY 213, consider turning east for a view of the High Falls dam and access to the historical High Falls. This charming town features many businesses, restaurants, and the D&H Canal Museum. Several miles after High Falls, you'll cross Rest Plaus Road via an overpass that offers a great view of the surrounding countryside. Note that the overpass does not provide access to Rest Plaus Road itself.

As you approach the southern end of this segment, the trail will cross Kyserike Road. The trail jags west here and continues south to County Road 1/Lucas Turnpike, though there is no navigational signage. Here the area just north of the road traverses a private lumberyard. After the trail hits CR 1/Lucas Turnpike, there is a 1.5-mile gap to continue to the final trail segment. This gap is particularly difficult to navigate by bike, as it follows several heavily trafficked roads.

The southern portion of the trail is a 3.5-mile stretch from Accord to Kerhonkson. This picturesque wooded area follows Rondout Creek. The natural surface of the southern segment makes it perfect for horseback riding, walking, mountain biking, and winter sports.

Sullivan County: 9.2 miles

Three segments of the O&W Rail Trail are open within the town of Fallsburg: Mountaindale to Woodridge, 2.1 miles; Woodridge to South Fallsburg, 1.7 miles; and South Fallsburg to Hurleyville, 5.4 miles. When complete, the trail will stretch 25 miles through Sullivan County, from the D&H Linear Park in Summitville to downtown Liberty.

Begin your trail experience at the old Mountaindale Train Station, which is now a visitor center full of photographs and artifacts. There is also a local bike shop in case you need a tune-up or to rent a bike. The trail in this section is relatively flat on a dirt and crushed-stone path that runs alongside Silver Lake. The 2.1-mile segment ends in Woodridge, where you can find parking at the intersection of Green Avenue and Greenfield Road.

The next segment, which travels through the west side of Woodridge, is 0.6 mile away; you can connect to it with on-road riding on Broadway. This 1.7-mile trail is a similar ride through the dense tree canopy, with multiple picnic areas along the way for a short rest.

South Fallsburg, about 5 miles west of Woodridge, is a lovely small town that offers many food options to fuel up for your ride. This last section of the

The Sullivan County segment offers a beautiful wooded ride leading up to Hurleyville.

trail has a mixture of surfaces. Beginning at Water Street in South Fallsburg, you'll head northwest on the trail. Use caution in inclement weather, as this segment is mostly dirt and can get muddy in the rain. The relatively flat ride runs past Alta Lake and on to downtown Hurleyville, where you'll be greeted by a hand-painted HURLEYVILLE RAILS TO TRAILS sign. In Hurleyville, another parking lot is located next to a park and basketball court; from here you'll enjoy a newly paved pathway as you continue traveling northwest through tall mature trees to the trail's end at Denman Road.

CONTACT: **theoandwrailtrail.org;** Ulster County: **dandhcorridor.org;** Sullivan County: **owtrailssullivancounty.weebly.com**

DIRECTIONS

Ulster County: To reach the northern parking lot for the Hurley Rail Trail section, take I-87 to Exit 19, and merge onto NY 28 W. Go 0.5 mile, and use the right lane to merge onto US 209 S. Go 1.6 miles, crossing Esopus Creek; the parking lot and trailhead come up on the left just after you cross Esopus Creek.

To reach the southern endpoint in Kerhonkson, follow the directions above to US 209 S. Go 19.9 miles, and turn left onto 42nd St. (Clay Hill Road will be on your right). Cross Rondout Creek in 0.1 mile, then take an immediate left onto Main St. A parking area is on the right in 500 feet after the Kerhonkson Fire House. Proceed 0.1 mile east, with the creek on your left; the southern trailhead is located on Main St.

Sullivan County: To reach parking for the eastern section in Mountaindale from I-87, take Exit 4W to merge onto NY 17 W. Go 15.6 miles, and take the exit for Masten Lake Crossover. Turn left onto Masten Lake Crossover, then immediately turn left onto Wurtsboro Mountain Road. In 1.25 miles turn right onto Masten Lake Road, and follow it 7.5 miles. Turn right onto Main St./Mountaindale Road. In 0.4 mile turn left onto Old Post Hill Road, then turn left onto Railroad Ave. in 300 feet. Park by the old Mountaindale Train Station, now a visitor center with restrooms. To reach the trail, head past the parking lot and you'll come to a signboard for the MOUNTAINDALE O&W LINEAR PARK.

Parking is available for the western section in South Fallsburg. From I-87, take Exit 4W to merge onto NY 17 W. Go 22.5 miles, and take Exit 107. Continue onto Heiden-Thompsonville Road, and go 4.2 miles (it becomes Heiden Road). Turn right onto NY 42 N/Main St., and go 1.0 mile. Turn left onto Griff Court, and go 0.3 mile to 20 Water St.

Parking is also available in Hurleyville. From I-87, take Exit 4W to merge onto NY 17 W. Go 25.5 miles, and take Exit 105B. Turn right onto NY 42, and go 0.1 mile. Turn left onto Anawana Lake Road, go 4.2 miles, and then turn right onto Columbia Hill Road/Main St. Look for the HURLEYVILLE RAILS TO TRAILS sign in 0.3 mile on the left to reach the trail.

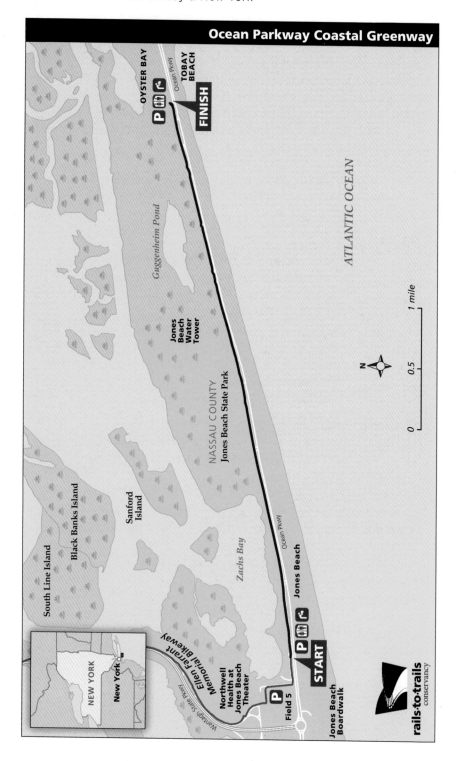

Ocean Parkway Coastal Greenway

Like Wantagh State Parkway, Ocean Parkway was built in the postwar 1930s to provide access to the crown jewel of the state park system, Jones Beach State Park. Unlike the former road, however, this one travels east–west and only recently added a pathway for nonmotorized traffic. The Ocean Parkway Coastal Greenway currently parallels its namesake roadway nearly 4 miles between the Northwell Health at Jones Beach Theater and the town of Oyster Bay, but there are plans to extend the trail farther east to Captree State Park for a possible total of 15 miles.

The trail begins where the Ellen Farrant Memorial Bikeway ends (see page 101), at Zachs Bay. The trail borders the northern side of the parkway, separated from the road by a grassy median and guardrail. The bay is to your left for about the first third of your journey. As you set off, you get a postcard-perfect panorama of the theater

Though its namesake road travels alongside the ocean, the Ocean Parkway Coastal Greenway skirts the bay side of the parkway.

County
Nassau

Endpoints
Southeast corner of Field 5 near Wantagh State Pkwy. and Ocean Pkwy. (Wantagh) to Tobay Beach, 0.8 mile west of Ocean Pkwy. and W. Gilgo Beach (Oyster Bay)

Mileage
3.6

Type
Greenway/Non-Rail-Trail

Roughness Index
1

Surface
Asphalt

sitting right on the edge of the water, but the vegetation soon rises high enough to form a screen.

As you ride on, the vegetation flattens out in places, opening up views of the marshland beyond. Mile markers painted on the asphalt help you keep track of how far you've gone. About midway, a Jones Beach State Park sign appears in the park's signature Art Deco style, a style that is echoed in many of the park's other structures, including the iconic Jones Beach Water Tower, looming to the west of the trail.

The trail ends at Tobay Beach in the town of Oyster Bay, where it loops around for a smooth transition back to the starting point. Bikes are prohibited on the beach, but there's plenty of bike parking outside the turnstile entryway. Tobay Beach features restaurants, a water park, and a marina. On weekends and holidays the beach is for town residents only, but nonresidents can access it for a fee on weekdays.

You can extend your ride by continuing on the Ellen Farrant Memorial Bikeway north from Field 5 in Jones Beach State Park to Cedar Creek Park in Seaport. Alternatively, you could choose to combine your ride with a beach day and use the tunnels near the western endpoint of the trail to cross underneath Ocean Parkway and reach the Jones Beach Boardwalk. Bicyclists must go slowly on the boardwalk, as it tends to be teeming with enthusiastic beachgoers.

CONTACT: www.dot.ny.gov/oppath

DIRECTIONS

To access the western end of the trail from I-495 E, take Exit 38 for Northern State Pkwy. Merge onto Northern State Pkwy., and travel 1.6 miles to Exit 31A for Jones Beach. You will now be traveling south on Meadowbrook State Pkwy. Continue 12.8 miles, then cross Jones Bay. Shortly after crossing the water, the road becomes Ocean Pkwy. Travel east on Ocean Pkwy. 2.4 miles to reach the entrance to Field 6 in Jones Beach State Park, which will be on your right. Note that there is an entrance fee for the park. Once parked, use the tunnel near the East Bathhouse to head under Ocean Pkwy. and access the trail on the other side. Turn right on the trail to travel on the Ocean Parkway Coastal Greenway (turning left will put you on the Jones Beach Bikeway going north).

For nonresidents, parking on the east end of the trail at Tobay Beach in Oyster Bay may be prohibitively expensive ($50), with limited availability (only weekdays) during the summer season. Therefore, visitors may prefer to park on the west end of the trail.

At first glance, there's no evidence that an aqueduct ever existed along the Old Croton Aqueduct Trail. The trail is often a singletrack dirt pathway that winds through communities and trees and provides an oasis of green just north of the Bronx. But take a closer look and the trail begins to hint at a history that spans more than 175 years.

Listed on the National Register of Historic Places, the Old Croton Aqueduct was completed in 1842, when water first flowed from the Croton River south into the Bronx, providing clean water to a city with a rising population that desperately needed it. The aqueduct quickly grew obsolete as New York City's population continued to boom, and a New Croton Aqueduct, three times the size, was built in 1890.

The Old Croton Aqueduct Trail gives visitors a lesson in New York history, starting from the north at the New Croton Dam. It begins to the right of the dam, and as you head south, you'll quickly pass the first of 21 remaining ventilators, 10- to 14-foot-high structures that were placed at roughly 1-mile intervals to allow fresh air to reach the water in the aqueduct.

After about 3 miles, you'll reach the town of Crotonville, one of several small towns along the trail. Another 2 miles farther is Ossining. This northern tip of the trail up to Ossining will be the most comfortable for horseback riders. The trail crosses many public streets along its 26 miles. Drivers tend to yield to trail users, but use caution at these crossings, which get more numerous as the trail continues south and enters urban areas.

Walkers can enjoy the trail's entire length; cyclists and other trail users may use the path as well but may find some sections difficult to traverse. Cyclists will need to be comfortable biking on the sidewalks and roadways of several streets of varying traffic volumes and speeds. Travelers should particularly use caution in the section of the trail following Albany Post Road, which has no sidewalks or shoulders, for about 0.3 mile south of Scarborough.

County
Westchester

Endpoints
Croton Dam Road at the New Croton Dam (Yorktown) to Lawton St., 150 feet northwest of Hancock Ave. (Yonkers)

Mileage
26.5

Type
Greenway/Non-Rail-Trail

Roughness Index
2–3

Surfaces
Crushed Stone, Dirt, Grass, Gravel

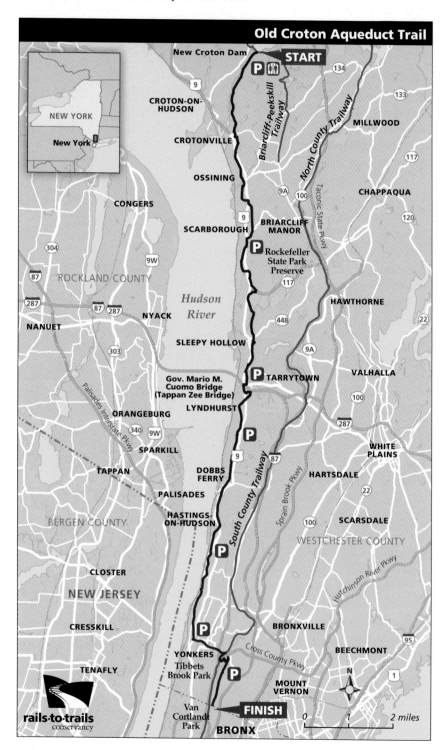

Old Croton Aqueduct Trail

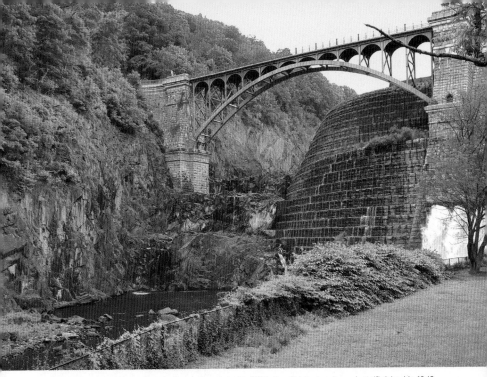

Though the New Croton Aqueduct was completed in 1890, the Old Croton Aqueduct (finished in 1842 and pictured here) continued to supply New York City with fresh drinking water until 1965.

Here walkers and casual cyclists will want to follow a 0.8-mile detour, which goes right on Scarborough Station Road, left on River Road, and left on Creighton Road back to the trail.

Follow the trail another 3 miles to the town of Sleepy Hollow, which is much quainter than its legend of the Headless Horseman suggests; this is another section of the trail that equestrians may enjoy. Rockefeller State Park Preserve, which offers a bridle path, is also nearby (though equestrians must have a permit).

Trail users get views of the newly constructed Gov. Mario M. Cuomo Bridge (formerly known as the Tappan Zee Bridge) about 2.5 miles south of Sleepy Hollow. A new shared-use path runs along the bridge and provides a nonmotorized crossing of the Hudson River. About 0.5 mile south of the bridge, the trail crosses through Lyndhurst, the site of a Gothic Revival mansion where cyclists are asked to dismount and walk through the park. Take the time to walk through Lyndhurst and enjoy its well-manicured landscaping.

Signage is infrequent on the Old Croton Aqueduct Trail, an intentional effort by the trail's developers to maintain its rural nature. Four miles south of Lyndhurst, trail users will find it easy to locate the historical Keeper's House and park headquarters, worth a stop to admire a piece of the trail's history. To stay on the trail, be on the lookout for the stones imprinted with OCA at many street crossings, as well as the wayfinding signs installed in summer 2018 at several areas that are difficult to navigate.

The remainder of the trail headed south is best suited for walkers, as the trail surface is occasionally rocky and winds through and around public streets in Yonkers. The southern end of the trail lies near the intersection of Lawton Street and Hancock Avenue in Yonkers, while the Old Croton Aqueduct continues south into the Bronx. There is no formal trailhead at the trail's southern terminus, and those reaching the trail by car can look for on-street parking nearby.

CONTACT: aqueduct.org and **parks.ny.gov/parks/96**

DIRECTIONS

To reach the southern terminus from I-87 S, take Exit 1 toward Hall Pl./McLean Ave. Merge onto Central Park Ave., go 0.5 mile, and turn right onto Forest Ave. Travel 0.2 mile, where Forest Ave. turns right and becomes Hancock Ave. Travel another 0.2 mile to the southern terminus near the intersection of Hancock Ave. and Lawton St.

To reach the southern terminus from I-87 N, take Exit 14 toward McLean Ave. Merge onto Jerome Ave., go 0.2 mile, and turn left onto McLean Ave. Make an immediate left onto Forest Ave. Travel 0.2 mile, where Forest Ave. turns right and becomes Hancock Ave. Travel another 0.2 mile to the southern terminus near the intersection of Hancock Ave. and Lawton St.

To reach the northern terminus from I-287 W, take Exit 6, and turn left onto Orchard St. Go 0.2 mile, and continue onto Cemetery Road. From I-287 E, take Exit 6, and turn left onto NY 22. Immediately turn left onto Cemetery Road. In 0.3 mile turn right onto Bronx River Pkwy., and go 1.7 miles. At Kensico Cir., take the second exit onto Taconic State Pkwy. Go 13.9 miles, and take Exit 13 for Underhill Ave./Croton-on-Hudson/Yorktown Heights. Head southwest on Underhill Ave. Travel 0.8 mile on Underhill Ave., and turn right onto NY 129 W/Croton Lake Road. After 3 miles, turn left onto Croton Dam Road. Parking is available at the New Croton Dam in 0.2 mile on the right.

The Old Erie Path reveals spectacular views of the Hudson River Valley as the rail-trail rolls along cliffs that border the river's western shore. Although fairly short, it joins two other rail-trails—Joseph B. Clarke Rail Trail (see page 138) and Raymond G. Esposito Memorial Trail (see page 182)—that combine for more than 8 miles of off-road travel in historic Rockland County.

The trail follows the original corridor of the Northern Railroad of New Jersey, which primarily ran passenger trains from Jersey City to Nyack and used tracks owned by the New York & Erie Railroad between Sparkill and Piermont. The Erie Railroad bought the line in 1942, after which it became Erie's Nyack and Piermont Branch. Passenger service ended in 1966.

The trail begins just east of the railroad Y-junction in Sparkill, where the Northern Railroad left the Erie

In Piermont, the trail arrives at a circa 1873 railroad depot, which houses a museum operated by the Piermont Historical Society.

County
Rockland

Endpoints
Joseph B. Clarke Rail Trail at Orangeburg Road and Highland Ave. (Piermont) to Raymond G. Esposito Memorial Trail at S. Broadway and Hawthorne Pl. (Grand View-on-Hudson)

Mileage
3.0

Type
Rail-Trail

Roughness Index
2

Surfaces
Dirt, Gravel

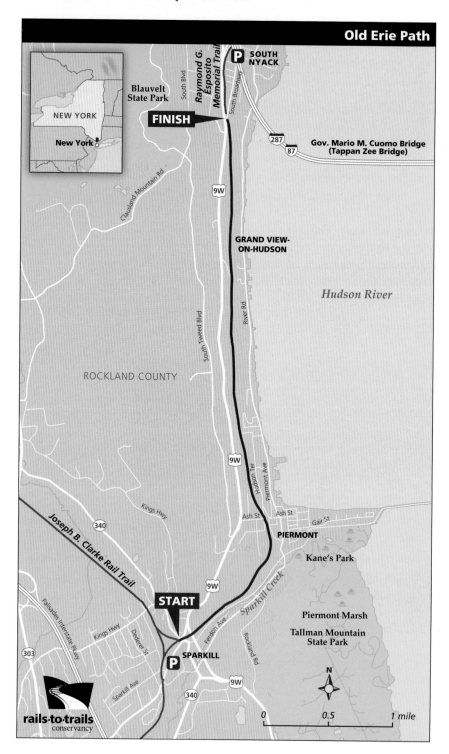

Old Erie Path

Railroad main line heading to Lake Erie. Called Depot Square, this is where today the Old Erie Path meets the 4.3-mile Joseph B. Clarke Rail Trail, which heads southwest to Tappan and northwest to Blauvelt.

You'll notice that the Old Erie Path has a rougher surface than the Clarke or Esposito trail; hybrid or mountain bikes are recommended over skinny-tire road bikes. The first mile goes through woodlands above Sparkill Creek, a tributary of the Hudson River, before it arrives in the village of Piermont at the circa 1873 railroad depot. Today the building on Ash Street is a museum operated by the Piermont Historical Society. A nearby marker—JC 25—tells the distance to Jersey City.

Piermont is noted for the mile-long pier built into the Hudson River in 1838 by the New York & Erie Railroad to pick up passengers and cargo. Plaques describe it as the site where more than a million servicemen embarked by ship to North Africa and Europe during World War II. You can reach the pier and Piermont's historical downtown and eateries by heading downhill on Hudson Terrace and then turning right onto Ash Street.

Leaving the old depot, a thick hardwood forest surrounds the trail through Grand View-on-Hudson, whose name is derived from its setting. The railroad company laid track about 200 feet up the cliffs that overlook the Hudson. The trees provide shade in the summer, while the leafless vegetation in the fall and winter allows for views of the Piermont pier, Westchester County across the Hudson, and the steel girders of the new Gov. Mario M. Cuomo Bridge (formerly known as the Tappan Zee Bridge). The new shared-use path on the bridge is expected to draw more traffic to local trails.

Homeowners, many of them above or below the corridor, access the trail by way of creative engineering: hillside stairways with handrails fashioned from the limbs of native trees, as well as decorative archways and gates on intricate pulley systems.

Crossing South Broadway, the pathway soon enters South Nyack and becomes the Raymond G. Esposito Memorial Trail, which ends in Franklin Street Park after a mile.

CONTACT: piermonthistorysociety.org

DIRECTIONS

To reach the endpoint in Sparkill from I-287, take Exit 13S to merge onto the Palisades Interstate Pkwy. Go 4.9 miles, and take Exit 5S onto US 303 S. Go 0.5 mile, and turn left onto Kings Hwy. Go 0.9 mile and turn right onto Orangeburg Road; then go 0.3 mile and turn right onto Main St. Go 0.1 mile, turn right onto Depot Sq., and look for on-street parking. Head northeast on the right trail fork 0.2 mile to reach the Old Erie Path.

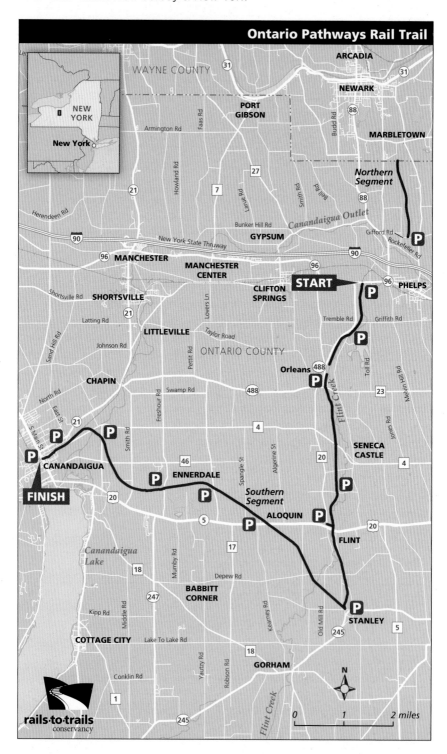

Ontario Pathways Rail Trail

The Ontario Pathways Rail Trail is the crown jewel of the trail system managed by the organization for whom it is named in Ontario County, New York. Comprising two disconnected segments, including a long V-shaped route, the trail runs through woodlands and picturesque farmland in rural communities dotting the northern fringes of New York's scenic Finger Lakes region. Although the trail was built on a former rail corridor and is open to a variety of nonmotorized uses, its rough surface of rocks and roots demands cyclists use mountain bikes or durable hybrids, and it may be better experienced on foot or horse.

The trail's beginning can be traced to two rail lines developed separately in the 19th century. Ultimately the railroads' successors were both acquired by the Northern Central Railroad, which in 1913 became part of the much larger Pennsylvania Railroad. An ill-conceived merger

An artistic gate separates a wooden bridge from the gravel path.

County
Ontario

Endpoints
Gifford Road, 0.2 mile east of Wilbur Road (Phelps), to 0.3 mile south of Silver Hill Road and Sweed Road (Arcadia); NY 96, 0.2 mile east of NY 488 (Phelps), to NY 332/S. Main St., between Ontario St. and Niagara St. (Canandaigua)

Mileage
24.3

Type
Rail-Trail/Rail-with-Trail

Roughness Index
3

Surfaces
Cinder, Dirt, Grass, Gravel

with the New York Central Railroad in 1968 led to the combined Penn Central's bankruptcy in 1970. Fortunately, with the help of a loan from Rails-to-Trails Conservancy, Ontario Pathways Inc. was able to purchase unsold portions of the rail corridor in 1994 to begin trail development.

Northern Segment (Phelps): 2.5 miles

If you are looking for a long and continuous experience, you can skip this segment, which is separated from the main, V-shaped trail by privately owned land and the New York State Thruway. But the stretch has its charms: its lack of road crossings promises a peaceful trip, and its green envelope of trees provides constant shade and the perfect perch for birds. Those who do visit this scenic section should be aware that the trail technically ends in the north without an outlet at the Wayne County line. Therefore, an out-and-back trip from the parking lot on Gifford Road in Phelps at the southern end of this segment may be best; from there, the trail heads north, unmarked, for 2.5 miles to Sweed Road.

Southern Segment (Phelps to Canandaigua): 21.8 miles

The main, V-shaped section of the Ontario Pathways Rail Trail begins on the opposite side of the New York State Thruway and spans nearly 21 miles. Start your trip at its eastern end in Phelps, where a large parking lot on NY 96 welcomes trail users. Like the northern segment, the trail proceeds through dense tree cover for its first several miles. Flint Creek is never far away, and a bridge offers trail users a close-up of the water below.

Travelers will find this charming mural, which depicts the 1916 Canandaigua train depot and was painted by Amy Colburn, on the west end of the trail.

Before long, a short detour onto NY 488 is required. (Follow the signs; you will reach a dead end if you continue beyond the detour access.) Exercise caution on the detour, as NY 488 sees fast-moving traffic. After nearly a mile, the trail resumes under tree cover before emerging into open farmland, where the sudden sunlight may be jarring. After alternating between the two environs and passing over US 20/NY 5 via a trail bridge, the trail eventually reaches its halfway point at a large trailhead park in Stanley.

From the park, you must turn sharply right, briefly paralleling the section of trail you just completed, to continue your journey. You soon may have a feeling of déjà vu as you pass over US 20/NY 5 again via a second trail bridge. The scenery along this stretch is primarily farmland, although a constant strand of trees on both sides blocks most of the direct sun. You'll feel more bumps and jolts from large tree roots and loose rocks (especially if you are on a bike) along this second half, so consider taking it slower until they clear up. There are also several road crossings along this stretch, many of which are offset; look for a green hiker sign at each intersection to locate your next move.

Eventually you'll cross Flint Creek a final time and immediately begin to closely parallel an active rail line (a rail-with-trail configuration) on the outskirts of Canandaigua. Shortly thereafter you'll emerge in the charming city's downtown, where numerous restaurants await hungry trail users. The community sits at the northern tip of Canandaigua Lake, so if you're not too tired from your trek, consider taking South Main Street south to reach the lake before beginning your return trip.

CONTACT: ontariopathways.org

DIRECTIONS

To reach the northern segment's Gifford Road trailhead from I-90/New York State Thwy., take Exit 43, and turn right onto NY 21. Take the first left onto NY 96, and travel 4.5 miles. Turn left onto County Road 25, and travel 3.5 miles until the road ends at a T-junction. Turn right onto NY 88, then take your first left onto CR 26. Immediately turn right onto Irvin Road and proceed to the road's end at a T-junction. Turn right onto Wilbur Road, and then immediately turn left onto Gifford Road. The trailhead and parking lot will be on your left in 0.3 mile.

To reach the V-shaped segment's eastern trailhead on NY 96 from I-90/New York State Thwy., take Exit 43, and turn right onto NY 21. Take the first left onto NY 96, and travel 7.3 miles. The trailhead and parking lot will be on your right shortly after NY 488.

To reach parking for the V-shaped segment's western end in Canandaigua from I-90/New York State Thwy., take Exit 44 and continue onto NY 332 for 8.6 miles. In downtown Canandaigua, turn left onto Niagara St. Ample public parking can be found on your left, across from Lafayette Ave.

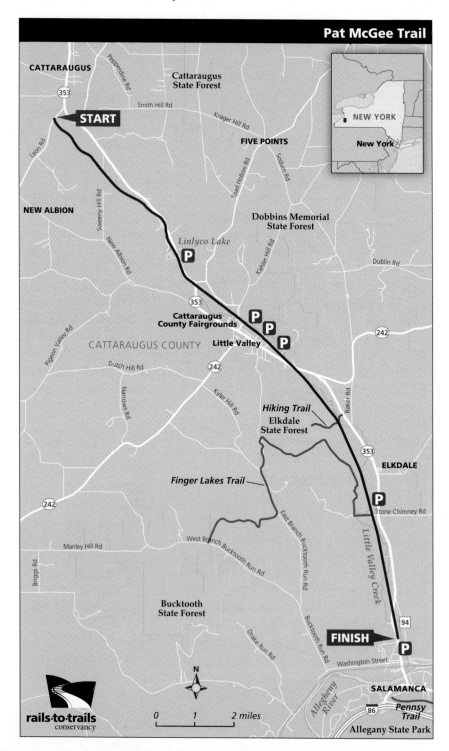

Pat McGee Trail

CATTARAUGUS

Pepperdine Rd

Cattaraugus
State Forest

Smith Hill Rd

353

Krager Hill Rd

FIVE POINTS

START

Leon Rd

Toad Hollow Rd

Sodam Rd

NEW YORK

New York

Sweeny Hill Rd

NEW ALBION

New Albion Rd

Dobbins Memorial
State Forest

Linlyco Lake

P

Kahler Hill Rd

Dublin Rd

353

Cattaraugus
County Fairgrounds

CATTARAUGUS COUNTY

Little Valley

P
P
P

242

Pigeon Valley Rd

Dutch Hill Rd

242

Narrows Rd

Kyler Hill Rd

Hiking Trail
Elkdale
State Forest

Baker Rd

353

ELKDALE

Finger Lakes Trail

P

Stone Chimney Rd

242

Manley Hill Rd

West Branch Bucktooth Run Rd

East Branch Bucktooth Run Rd

Little Valley Creek

Briggs Rd

Bucktooth
State Forest

Drake Run Rd

Bucktooth Run Rd

FINISH

94

P

Washington Street

N

SALAMANCA

rails·to·trails
conservancy

0   1   2 miles

86

Pennsy
Trail

Allegheny River

Allegany State Park

The key word in describing the Pat McGee Trail in western New York is *variety*. The rail-trail rolls for more than 12 miles across the Allegheny Plateau between Cattaraugus and Salamanca, passing through differences in climate, soil, and topography that give rise to 41 species of mammals, 150 types of birds, and 174 kinds of plants and trees.

Formally dedicated in 2005 to the memory of state senator and trail supporter Patricia McGee, the trail follows an Erie Railroad branch that ran between Salamanca and Dunkirk on Lake Erie. It later became part of the Erie Lackawanna Railroad and the New York & Lake Erie Railroad before it went out of service in 1990. The trail visits seven villages and hamlets along the route and crosses six bridges. Travelers face a gentle rise midway along the trail as it crosses the Eastern Continental Divide. Numerous interpretive signs along the route explain natural and historical features along the way.

Starting just south of Cattaraugus, the trail takes a steep dip across a bridge and begins a climb toward the

County
Cattaraugus

Endpoints
County Road 6/Leon Road, 0.3 mile southwest of NY 353/Cattaraugus Little Valley (Cattaraugus), to NY 353/Center St., 330 feet north of Forest Ave. (Salamanca)

Mileage
12.1

Type
Rail-Trail

Roughness Index
1–2

Surfaces
Asphalt, Crushed Stone, Grass

A journey on the Pat McGee Trail includes a multitude of views, including an agricultural valley.

Continental Divide. You'll find a lean-to here used by cross-country skiers and snowmobilers in the wintertime; it also serves as protection for sudden summer storms.

You'll cross over the Eastern Continental Divide about 3 miles after the start and pass the 11-acre Linlyco Lake between the villages of New Albion and Little Valley. In another 2 miles, you'll enter the county seat of Little Valley and pass the entrance to the Cattaraugus County Fairgrounds, which draws crowds to the fair in August and to stock car and demolition derbies throughout the summer. The town has a couple of diners for refreshments, or you can picnic at the community park in one of the gazebos or the picnic shelter. Paved for a short distance, the trail returns to crushed stone as you leave the village.

The final 6 miles to Salamanca runs alongside Little Valley Creek through a narrow agricultural valley. The open space across farm fields allows sweeping views of the surrounding hills. The Pat McGee Trail crosses a state hiking trail into Elkdale State Forest about 2 miles past the trailhead in Little Valley. Another 2 miles down the trail, it crosses another hiking path, the 950-mile Finger Lakes Trail. Just before that trail junction, you'll traverse a 123-foot-long railroad trestle, which is the longest on the rail-trail.

The trail ends as it enters Salamanca, once a busy railroad hub on the north bank of the Allegheny River. The city is within the Allegheny Reservation. The Seneca–Iroquois National Museum is located about a mile south at 814 Broad St., and the Salamanca Railroad Museum is housed in a restored passenger depot about 2.5 miles away at 170 Main St.

Cattaraugus County is studying potential connections between the Pat McGee Trail and several other trails in the county, such as the Allegheny River Valley Trail (see page 77) between Allegany and Olean.

CONTACT: enchantedmountains.com/trails/pat-mcgee-trail

DIRECTIONS

To reach the northern endpoint just south of Cattaraugus from I-90, take Exit 59 and turn left onto NY 60 S/Bennett Road. Go 3.3 miles, and turn left onto NY 83. Go 9.8 miles, and turn left to stay on NY 83. Go 2.3 miles, and stay straight onto NY 322 (NY 83 turns right). Go 4.7 miles, and turn right onto US 62/E. Plains Road; then go 4.8 miles, and turn left onto County Road 6/Leon New Albion Road. Go 11.6 miles, and look for a small parking lot on the left. The trail starts on the right.

To reach the southern endpoint in Salamanca from I-86, take Exit 20, and head northeast onto NY 417 E. Go 0.7 mile, and turn left onto NY 353/Center St. Go 0.9 mile, and look for parking on the right at the trailhead.

The old New York Central rail line that ran from the Bronx to northern bedroom communities in Westchester and Putnam Counties carried commuters during the workweek, but on the weekends tourists heading to resorts and vacation homes in northern Putnam County filled those passenger seats. Today, the Putnam Trailway follows nearly 12 miles of that rail-line route to popular lakes in the woodsy hills around Carmel and Brewster.

The trail follows a corridor created in the 1880s by several railroad companies that eventually became the New York and Putnam Railroad in 1894—soon known as the Old Put. By 1913, it had become the Putnam Division of the New York Central Railroad, providing passenger service until 1958. The railroad continued hauling freight into the 1980s. In the wake of the line's demise, four trails have opened along the 45-mile route. South to north they

The Putnam Trailway winds through the woodlands surrounding Middle Branch Reservoir.

County
Putnam

Endpoints
NY 118/Tomahawk St., 420 feet west of Miller Road, at North County Trailway (Baldwin Place) to Putnam Ave. between Eagle Ridge Road and Putnam Terr. (Brewster)

Mileage
11.9

Type
Rail-Trail

Roughness Index
1

Surface
Asphalt

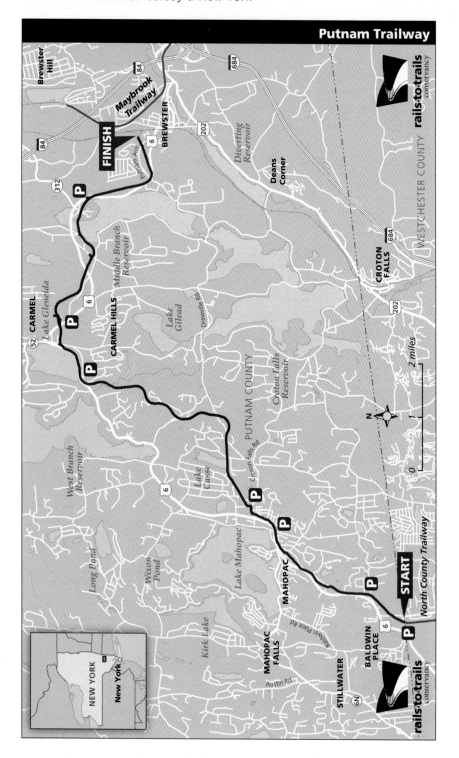

are Old Putnam Trail, South County Trailway (see page 189), North County Trailway (see page 154), and Putnam Trailway.

The paved trail—part of New York's developing 750-mile Empire State Trail—starts at the old passenger depot site in Baldwin Place. Although the Putnam Trailway slopes downhill toward Brewster from here, there are a few short, steep climbs in the wooded watersheds surrounding lakes and reservoirs in the north.

The trail follows US 6 through residential and commercial areas and arrives in Mahopac in about 2.2 miles at an old railway depot that's now an American Legion Hall. The hamlet encircles the 500-acre Lake Mahopac. Though the shoreline is privately owned, marinas rent boats for those who want to fish.

Crossing Croton Falls Road on the way out of Mahopac, the trail enters a hardwood forest that surrounds the path nearly to Brewster. In a mile, you'll pass the south shore of Lake Casse; a beach is at the lake's north end.

Traveling through the woods another 3 miles, you'll meet up again with US 6 on the shores of Lake Gleneida. These hills shelter numerous lakes and reservoirs chosen by New York City for its water supply. That's why swimming is prohibited in this lake, but boating, fishing, and ice fishing are allowed. Leaving the lake, the trail dips to cross a creek and in 2 miles crosses a 1,000-foot causeway across Middle Branch Reservoir.

The trail ends at Putnam Avenue in Brewster, but work is underway for a 0.5-mile, five-span pedestrian bridge across a road, rail yard, brook, and swampy area to join the Maybrook Trailway in late 2019. That will provide a trail connection to Poughkeepsie by the end of 2020.

CONTACT: putnamcountyny.com/parks-recreation/bike-path

DIRECTIONS

To reach the Baldwin Place trailhead from I-684, take Exit 6, and head west onto NY 35. Go 1.6 miles, and turn right onto NY 100 N; then go 0.6 mile, and turn left onto NY 139/Primrose Dr. Go 2.7 miles, and stay on the arterial to join US 202/Lincolndale Road; then go 1.8 miles, and turn right onto NY 118/Tomahawk St. Go 1.9 miles, and turn left to stay on NY 118/Tomahawk St.; then go 0.1 mile, turn left into Somers Commons, and immediately look for parking on the left. At the rear of the parking lot, take the trail to the left to join the Putnam Trailway.

To reach the Brewster trailhead from I-84, take Exit 19, and turn right onto NY 312 W/Dykeman Road. Go 1.3 miles (crossing US 6), and turn left onto Tilly Foster Road. Go 0.2 mile, and look for parking on the right. A short trail at the rear of the parking lot connects to the Putnam Trailway.

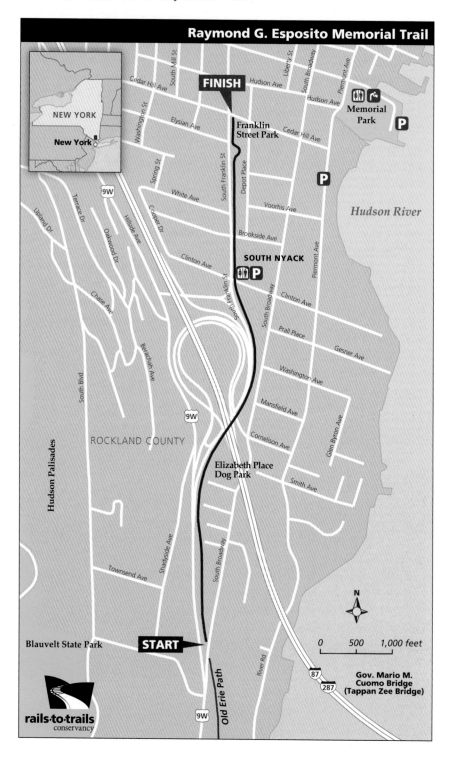

Raymond G. Esposito Memorial Trail

NEW YORK

New York

South Mill St

Cedar Hill Ave

Liberty St

South Broadway

Piermont Ave

FINISH

Hudson Ave

Washington St

Elysian Ave

Hudson Ave

Memorial Park

Franklin Street Park

Cedar Hill Ave

Spring St

White Ave

South Franklin St

Depot Place

Voorhis Ave

Hudson River

Cooper Dr

Hillside Ave

Oakwood Dr

Upland Dr

Terrace Dr

Brookside Ave

Clinton Ave

SOUTH NYACK

Piermont Ave

Chase Ave

South Franklin St

South Broadway

Clinton Ave

Prall Place

Berachah Ave

Gesner Ave

South Blvd

9W

Washington Ave

Mansfield Ave

ROCKLAND COUNTY

Glen Byron Ave

Cornelison Ave

Elizabeth Place Dog Park

Smith Ave

Hudson Palisades

Shadyside Ave

Townsend Ave

South Broadway

N

Blauvelt State Park

START

0   500   1,000 feet

Old Erie Path

River Rd

87

287

Gov. Mario M. Cuomo Bridge (Tappan Zee Bridge)

9W

rails·to·trails conservancy

The Raymond G. Esposito Memorial Trail travels from one end of the village of South Nyack to the other in 1 mile but greatly expands its reach by connecting with the Old Erie Path (see page 169) and a new shared-use path on the Gov. Mario M. Cuomo Bridge, formerly known as the Tappan Zee Bridge, which crosses the Hudson River from Westchester County.

The path follows the former route of the Northern Railroad of New Jersey, which began running trains from Nyack to Jersey City in the 1870s. The Northern was a business partner of the Erie Railroad, which acquired the Northern in 1942. It operated as Erie's Nyack and Piermont Branch until it ceased passenger service in 1966. The trail came into being about the same time that other Orangetown Township communities resuscitated another pair of disused Erie Railroad corridors into trails: the Old

The mile-long pathway offers a pleasant way to traverse the village of South Nyack.

County
Rockland

Endpoints
Old Erie Path at S. Broadway and Hawthorne Pl. to Cedar Hill Ave. and S. Franklin St. (South Nyack)

Mileage
1.0

Type
Rail-Trail

Roughness Index
2

Surface
Crushed Stone

Erie Path and the Joseph B. Clarke Rail Trail (see page 138). They connect to form more than 8 miles of pathway. The trail is named for former South Nyack Mayor Raymond G. Esposito.

Like the Old Erie Path, the Esposito Memorial Trail hugs the steep hillsides of the Hudson Palisades on the river's western shore and has scenic views of the river valley after the leaves have fallen. Starting at the Old Erie Path junction, the Esposito Memorial Trail has a firmer surface as it runs alongside US 9W. Just before it crosses I-87/I-287 on a bridge shared with US 9W, steep stairs on the right connect to the Elizabeth Place Dog Park.

After it crosses I-87/I-287, the Esposito Memorial Trail is accompanied by the new shared-use path built on the north side of the bridge spanning the Hudson River. Concerned that heavy bicycle traffic from the new path would overwhelm the Esposito Memorial Trail, local officials separated the two trails with a divider up to a new trailhead at Clinton Avenue. Both trails have access to a trail-only parking lot and restroom facility at Exit 10 on I-87/I-287.

After crossing Clinton Avenue, the Esposito Memorial Trail heads north 0.3 mile alongside residential South Franklin Street to its end at Franklin Street Park. In the park, a plaque marks the former site of the South Nyack depot, where commuter passengers would board for a trip to Jersey City and the ferry ride across to New York City.

While South Nyack is residential, the village of Nyack offers snacks, restaurants, and shops just a few blocks downhill on South Broadway.

CONTACT: southnyack.ny.gov

DIRECTIONS

To reach the northern endpoint in South Nyack from I-87/I-287 W, take Exit 11 and stay straight on High Ave. Go 0.5 mile, and turn right onto S. Franklin St.; then go 0.3 mile to Cedar Hill Ave. and Franklin Street Park. Look for on-street parking on S. Franklin St. or Cedar Hill Ave.

To reach the northern endpoint in South Nyack from I-87/I-287 E, take Exit 11 and turn left onto NY 59. Go 0.8 mile, and turn right on S. Franklin St. Go 0.2 mile to Cedar Hill Ave. and Franklin Street Park. Look for on-street parking on S. Franklin St. or Cedar Hill Ave.

The two diverse sections of the Shore Parkway Greenway Trail blend urban and scenic, offering views of sights ranging from the Statue of Liberty to wildlife refuges. Following the Belt/Shore Parkway, users can expect to witness takeoffs and landings at the nearby John F. Kennedy International Airport; cargo liners along Jamaica Bay; and a number of beaches, salt marshes, freshwater ponds, and maritime forests.

Howard Beach to Brooklyn: 7.9 miles

At nearly 8 miles, the longer eastern segment follows the Belt/Shore Parkway southwest from Howard Beach to Brooklyn. Although this section is paved, it contains steep slopes and bridges that make it unsuitable for wheelchair users. The shadeless concrete surface could be useful for

The western section of the trail provides impressive views of the Verrazzano-Narrows Bridge.

Counties
Kings, Queens

Endpoints
84th St. just north of 157th Ave. (Howard Beach) to Brigham St. and Emmons Ave. (Brooklyn); Bensonhurst Park at Bay Pkwy. and Shore Pkwy. to Owl's Head Park at 68th St. and Shore Road (Brooklyn)

Mileage
13.0

Type
Greenway/Non-Rail-Trail

Roughness Index
1

Surfaces
Asphalt, Concrete

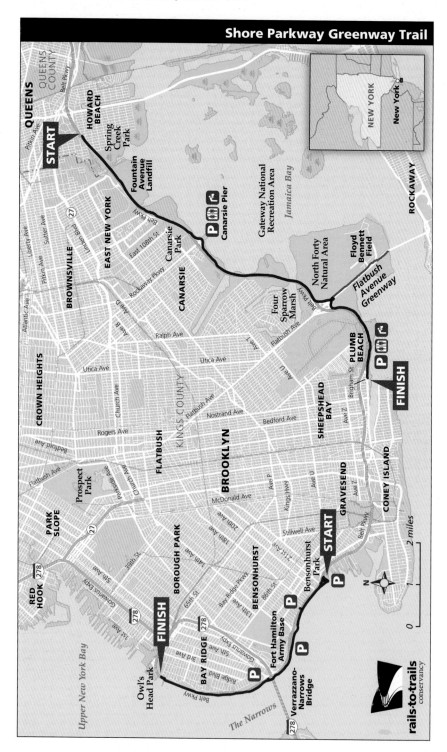

athletic training or commuting purposes. Note that the first parking area for this segment is located 3 miles into the trail, at Canarsie Pier.

From its beginning at 84th Street, the trail parallels the parkway, passing Spring Creek Park on the left in 0.4 mile. This stretch of trail can become quite noisy and unpleasant at times, as it closely follows the parkway. The water and greenery on the opposite side of the trail provide some relief, although smells from the Fountain Avenue Landfill natural restoration area can be overwhelming.

From Canarsie Pier, you can find parking, restrooms, and a drinking fountain. Continuing down the trail, you'll pass several parks and recreation areas around mile 5, including Four Sparrow Marsh and the North Forty Natural Area in Floyd Bennett Field. This historical (now deactivated) airfield provides users the exciting experience of biking along its runways. The field is located within the three-part Gateway National Recreation Area, where former landfills have been converted into wildlife habitat and recreation areas. The area makes up a significant part of the Atlantic Flyway for migratory birds.

Exiting this area, you'll reach a signaled crossing for the high-speed Flatbush Avenue, which can be dangerous. The crossing also intersects the 1.4-mile Flatbush Avenue Greenway. Toward the end of the eastern segment, the trail connects to Plumb Beach, where parking is available. In 0.5 mile the trail ends at Brigham Street, across from several hotels.

The paved pathway in Brooklyn offers separate lanes for cyclists and pedestrians.

Bensonhurst Park to Owl's Head Park: 5.1 miles

The shorter western section in Brooklyn begins at Bensonhurst Park and extends just over 5 miles north to Owl's Head Park. This segment along Upper New York Bay is the more scenic of the two, providing impressive views of Coney Island, the historical Fort Hamilton Army Base, the Verrazzano-Narrows Bridge, Staten Island's Fort Wadsworth and Battery Weed, the Statue of Liberty, and One World Trade Center.

The fully paved trail is wheelchair accessible, with separate sections for cyclists and pedestrians. There are several restrooms, benches, and parking areas along this stretch, which is heavily used by families, children, professional athletes, and everyone in between. The views and facilities make it worth the ride.

CONTACT: nycgovparks.org/parks/shore-road-park

DIRECTIONS

Eastern Segment: Several buses from Queens stop at 84th St. and 157th Ave., less than a block away from the easternmost terminus. For more information on bus routes, visit **mta.info.**

To access parking at Canarsie Pier from Belt/Shore Pkwy., take Exit 13 toward Rockaway Pkwy. If heading southbound, merge onto Shore Pkwy., and turn left onto Rockaway Pkwy. In 300 feet take the first exit at the traffic circle, and turn left in 0.1 mile. If heading northbound, take the first exit at the traffic circle, and turn left in several hundred feet. Head into the Canarsie Pier parking area.

Parking is also available at Plumb Beach. Located on Plumb Island, the beach is just off Belt/Shore Pkwy., east of Exit 9 or 9B toward Knapp St./Sheepshead Bay.

Western Segment: Subway riders can take the R train to the Bay Ridge Ave. station. The westernmost terminus is at the southwest corner of Owl's Head Park (53 68th St.), about four blocks away.

To access parking near the middle of the western trail segment from Belt/Shore Pkwy., head to where Belt/Shore Pkwy. travels beneath the Verrazzano-Narrows Bridge. Take Exit 2 to merge onto Fourth Ave. toward Fort Hamilton Pkwy. In 0.2 mile turn left onto Shore Road. Trail parking is located on the left at the Shore Road Park and Parkway.

The South County Trailway rolls 14.4 miles through one of the most densely populated parts of New York, but its route through pocket woodlots, parks, and golf courses and along riverbanks makes it seem more remote.

The trail runs through Westchester County between Yonkers and Greenburgh, connecting Van Cortlandt Park and Tarrytown Lakes Park. Much of the way is screened as it runs between Saw Mill River Parkway and the Saw Mill River. While all the trees provide shade in the summertime, the tree roots have created ridges in the asphalt that can make for bumpy travel for anyone on wheels.

The South County Trailway is part of a four-trail system that includes Old Putnam Trail to the south and the North County Trailway (see page 154) and Putnam Trailway (see page 179) to the north. They combine for 45 miles of mostly off-road travel along an old railroad corridor. Passenger and freight service began in the 1880s, and the corridor fell under control of the New York and Putnam Railroad in 1894. In 1913 it became the New York Central Railroad's Putnam Division, earning the nickname Old Put from commuters. Passenger service ended in 1958.

County
Westchester

Endpoints
Old Putnam Trail, 0.3 mile south of McLean Ave. near Tibbetts Road (Yonkers), to North County Trailway at Old Saw Mill River Road, 0.6 mile northwest of NY 9A (Elmsford)

Mileage
14.4

Type
Rail-Trail

Roughness Index
1

Surfaces
Asphalt, Concrete

The wide path feels remote despite its proximity to populated areas.

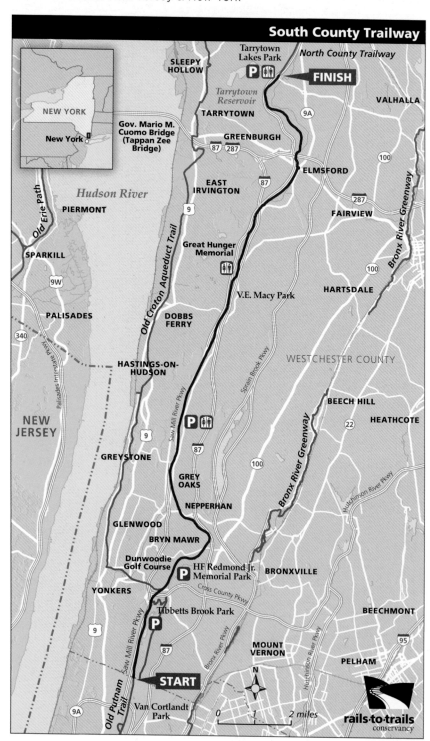

South County Trailway

Tarrytown Lakes Park

North County Trailway

SLEEPY HOLLOW

FINISH

VALHALLA

Tarrytown Reservoir

TARRYTOWN

9A

Gov. Mario M. Cuomo Bridge (Tappan Zee Bridge)

GREENBURGH

87 287

ELMSFORD

100

EAST IRVINGTON

87

Old Erie Path

Hudson River

PIERMONT

9

Old Croton Aqueduct Trail

FAIRVIEW

287

SPARKILL

9W

Great Hunger Memorial

Bronx River Greenway

V.E. Macy Park

HARTSDALE

100

PALISADES

340

Palisades Interstate Pkwy

DOBBS FERRY

WESTCHESTER COUNTY

HASTINGS-ON-HUDSON

Sprain Brook Pkwy

BEECH HILL

NEW JERSEY

9

Saw Mill River Pkwy

87

HEATHCOTE

22

GREYSTONE

100

Bronx River Greenway

GREY OAKS

NEPPERHAN

Hutchinson River Pkwy

GLENWOOD

BRYN MAWR

Dunwoodie Golf Course

HF Redmond Jr. Memorial Park

BRONXVILLE

YONKERS

Cross County Pkwy

BEECHMONT

Tibbetts Brook Park

Saw Mill River Pkwy

9

Bronx River Pkwy

87

MOUNT VERNON

95

Hutchinson River Pkwy

PELHAM

START

N

Old Putnam Trail

9A

Van Cortlandt Park

0   1   2 miles

rails·to·trails conservancy

NEW YORK

New York

The trail, part of the developing 750-mile Empire State Trail, starts at the north side of Van Cortlandt Park and begins an easy but steady climb north. In less than a mile, it reaches Tibbetts Brook Park, where you'll find a popular water park and the closest parking to the trailhead.

After crossing over Cross County Parkway and Yonkers Boulevard, the trail passes the 126-acre Dunwoodie Golf Course on the left and the HF Redmond Jr. Memorial Park on the right. In a mile, an observation point just north of the Palmer Road overpass reveals a view of north Yonkers from the trail's highest point.

The trail passes through the communities of Bryn Mawr, Nepperhan, and Grey Oaks, where you should expect traffic noise from Saw Mill River Parkway. You'll meet the Saw Mill River at a bridge about 6.2 miles from the start and soon pass the sprawling Mount Hope and Westchester Hills Cemeteries. In another 3 miles, the trail passes Woodlands Lake in V.E. Macy Park. The haunting Great Hunger Memorial across the lake memorializes the millions who died in the Irish potato famine.

Another 2.5 miles down the trail, you'll arrive in Elmsford, home of the only surviving railroad station from the "Old Put" days on the South County

Eamonn O'Doherty sculpted the Great Hunger Memorial *to remember those who were killed or displaced by the Irish potato famine of the mid-1800s.*

Trailway. It's a restaurant today, one of many places to eat in town. The final 2 miles to the junction with the North County Trailway pass through the wooded watershed of Tarrytown Reservoir. A spur trail travels the south shore of the lake toward Tarrytown and Sleepy Hollow.

CONTACT: parks.westchestergov.com/trailways

DIRECTIONS

To reach the Yonkers trailhead from I-87 N, take Exit 14 and merge onto Jerome Ave. Go 300 feet, and stay straight onto Central Park Ave. Go 0.2 mile, and turn left onto McLean Ave. Go 0.2 mile, and turn right to stay on McLean Ave., and then go 0.2 mile, and stay straight onto Midland Ave. Go 0.8 mile, and turn left onto Teresa Ave. and enter Tibbetts Brook Park. Go 0.2 mile, and turn left onto County Park Road. Then go 0.2 mile and look for parking on the left. From the parking lot, cross the street, turn left, and then turn right onto the first trail. Go a short distance and take the next trail left, and then go 0.3 mile and bear right. Go 0.1 mile, turn left onto another trail, and follow this to the junction with the South County Trailway. Turn left to reach the southern endpoint in 0.7 mile. From I-87 S, take Exit 1 toward Hall Pl./McLean Ave. Merge onto Central Park Ave., and immediately make a sharp right turn onto Bajart Pl. In 0.2 mile turn left onto Wendover Road, and go 0.2 mile. Turn right onto Midland Ave., and follow the directions above from there.

To reach the Elmsford trailhead from I-87, take Exit 8 or 8A, and merge onto I-287 E/Cross Westchester Expy. Go 0.2 mile, and merge onto Saw Mill River Pkwy. N. Go 2.5 miles, and take Exit 23. Turn right, go 0.1 mile, and look for parking on your right. (The trail at the rear of the parking lot goes left 300 feet to reach the North County Trailway.) Alternatively, take Exit 23 and turn left onto NY 303/Old Saw Mill River Road. Go 0.1 mile, and look for parking on your right.

The Walkway Over the Hudson State Historic Park—the longest pedestrian bridge in the world at just over 1.6 miles—emerges from the trees and over the rooftops of the old riverfront town of Poughkeepsie, crosses the vast Hudson River, and touches down in the hamlet of Highland on the west side of the river.

The walkway opened in 2009 in commemoration of the 400th anniversary of Henry Hudson's historic 1609 journey up the river. From the bridge, the views of the lush Hudson Valley and the river, 212 feet below, are simply breathtaking. Visitors are greeted by walkway volunteers and staff at welcome centers, which opened to the public in 2018 and are located at either end of the trail.

When it first opened in 1889, the Poughkeepsie-Highland Railroad Bridge that is now the walkway was hailed as the Great Connector, as it offered a vital link

This astonishing former railroad bridge crosses the Hudson River, which lies 212 feet below.

Counties
Dutchess, Ulster

Mileage
1.6

Endpoints
William R. Steinhaus Dutchess Rail Trail at 61 Parker Ave. (Poughkeepsie) to Hudson Valley Rail Trail at 87 Haviland Road (Highland)

Type
Rail-Trail

Roughness Index
1

Surface
Concrete

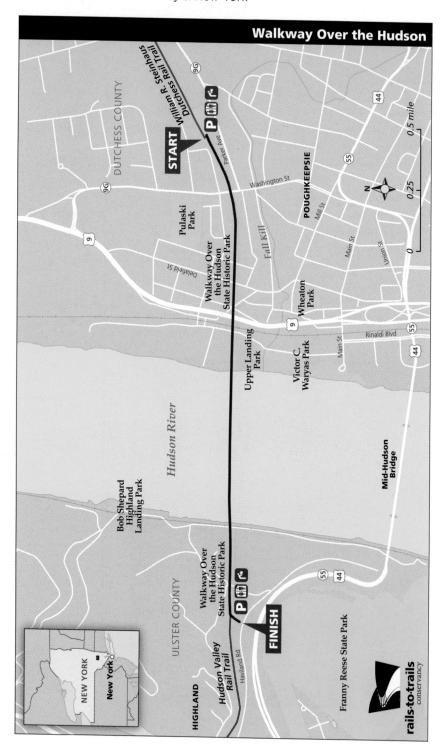

Walkway Over the Hudson

DUTCHESS COUNTY

William R. Steinhaus
Dutchess Rail Trail

9G

START

P

Parker Ave

Washington St

POUGHKEEPSIE

44

55

Pulaski
Park

9G

9

Delafield St

Walkway Over
the Hudson
State Historic Park

Fall Kill

Mill St

Main St

Union St

N

0   0.25   0.5 mile

Wheaton
Park

9

Upper Landing
Park

Victor C.
Waryas Park

Main St

Rinaldi Blvd

55

44

Hudson River

Mid-Hudson
Bridge

Bob Shepard
Highland
Landing Park

ULSTER COUNTY

Walkway Over
the Hudson
State Historic Park

P

FINISH

55   44

Franny Reese State Park

HIGHLAND

Hudson Valley
Rail Trail

Haviland Rd

NEW YORK

New York

rails-to-trails
conservancy

between New England cities and supplies from Pennsylvania, the Midwest, and farther afield. Today, the bridge serves as a linchpin in a 20-mile expanse of connected pathway. Two rail-trails join the walkway and spin out into the hillsides in either direction: the Hudson Valley Rail Trail (see page 131) on the west bank and William R. Steinhaus Dutchess Rail Trail (see page 202) to the east.

Together, the three rail-trails were welcomed into Rails-to-Trails Conservancy's Rail-Trail Hall of Fame in 2016. They are also part of the Empire State Trail, a developing 750-mile trail network spanning the state from New York City to Canada and Buffalo to Albany.

CONTACT: walkway.org

DIRECTIONS

Trailhead parking lots are available on either side of the Walkway Over the Hudson bridge: at 61 Parker Ave. in Poughkeepsie and at 87 Haviland Road in Highland.

To reach the parking lot in Poughkeepsie from I-84, take Exit 13, and head north on US 9. Continue on US 9 N for 14.4 miles to NY 9G in Poughkeepsie; you will travel under the Walkway Over the Hudson on the way to this exit. Look for brown WALKWAY OVER THE HUDSON directional signs as you approach your exit. Turn right onto NY 9G, which becomes Washington St., for 0.6 mile. Turn left onto Parker Ave. In 0.3 mile, a large parking lot will appear on your left.

To reach the parking lot in Highland from I-87, take Exit 18 for NY 299 E. Turn right onto NY 299, go 5.1 miles, and then turn right onto US 9W S. Continue on US 9W for 2.1 miles, then turn left onto Haviland Road. Parking will appear on your left in 0.5 mile.

The Walkway Over the Hudson can also be reached by train; take an Amtrak train (**amtrak.com**) or Metro-North Railroad's Hudson Line (**mta.info/mnr**) from Grand Central Station in Manhattan to Poughkeepsie. The Poughkeepsie Station (41 Main St.) is 0.7 mile from the Walkway Over the Hudson entrance at Washington St.

Note: An ADA-compliant elevator, located in Poughkeepsie's Upper Landing Park (83 N. Water St.) near the Hudson River waterfront, goes up to the Walkway Over the Hudson bridge. However, the elevator operates seasonally and is weather dependent, so check the trail website before a visit.

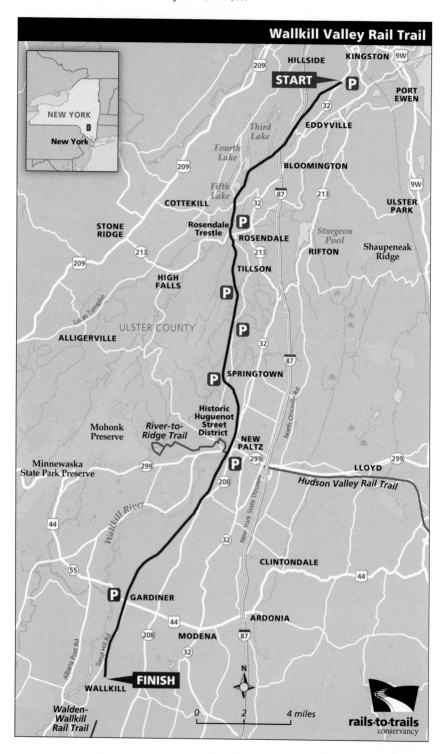

Wallkill Valley Rail Trail

NEW YORK

New York

HILLSIDE
KINGSTON   9W
209
START   P
PORT
EWEN
32
EDDYVILLE

Third
Lake

Fourth
Lake   BLOOMINGTON
209
9W
Fifth
Lake   87   213
COTTEKILL   ULSTER
PARK
32
STONE   Rosendale   P
RIDGE   Trestle   ROSENDALE   Sturgeon
213   213   Pool   Shaupeneak
209   RIFTON   Ridge
TILLSON
HIGH   P
FALLS

Lucas Turnpike
ULSTER COUNTY   P
ALLIGERVILLE   32
87
P   SPRINGTOWN

Historic
Huguenot
Mohonk   River-to-   Street
Preserve   Ridge Trail   District   NEW
PALTZ
Minnewaska   299   P   299   LLOYD   299
State Park Preserve   208   Hudson Valley Rail Trail

Wallkill River
44   32
CLINTONDALE
55   44

P   GARDINER
Albany Post Rd
Sand Hill Rd   44   ARDONIA
208   MODENA   87
32
FINISH   N
WALLKILL
Walden-   0   2   4 miles
Wallkill
Rail Trail   **rails·to·trails**
conservancy

While the Wallkill Valley Railroad no longer carries fruits and vegetables from Ulster County to New York City, trail users can still discover small, family-owned farms and farmers markets serving up fresh produce, meats, and locally made products and beverages along this route. Today the Wallkill Valley Rail Trail is popular among locals for walking, biking, horseback riding, and cross-country skiing, and it highlights the diversity that embodies America's rich history.

The corridor's current incarnation as a linear park welcomes all nonmotorized trail users, and the path is well maintained and easy to navigate. The Wallkill Valley Rail Trail is mostly unpaved except when entering the various towns to which it connects. Even so, the unpaved sections are easy to traverse with a hybrid bike, even after inclement weather. Parking is plentiful along the trail, which provides an excellent tree canopy and scenic views of mountains, water features, and prairies. This trail has excellent wayfinding signage and allows many opportunities to enjoy the cafés and other amenities of the several small towns it unites.

As you head south from Kingston to Rosendale, enjoy vistas of Third, Fourth, and Fifth Lakes, as well as the historical cement-mining facilities visible from the trail. Around

County
Ulster

Endpoints
Just north of NY 32 and Rockwell Lane (Kingston) to Denniston Road, 0.2 mile east of County Road 19/Sand Hill Road (Gardiner)

Mileage
21.3

Type
Rail-Trail

Roughness Index
1

Surfaces
Asphalt, Cinder, Dirt, Gravel

The trail connects several charming communities and offers diverse scenery, including woodlands, lakes and streams, farmland, and prairies.

mile 8, one of the best features of the trail is the Rosendale Trestle, about 150 feet tall and 900 feet long, offering great views of the surrounding Hudson Valley.

From Rosendale, the rail-trail travels beside orchards, organic farms, lakes, streams, and the Wallkill River and provides access to the towns of New Paltz and Gardiner. The National Park Service has designated this multiuse trail as a National Recreation Trail, and it's no wonder. Just west of New Paltz are Mohonk Preserve and Minnewaska State Park Preserve, which provide access to more than 30,000 acres of woodlands, cliffs, trails, and lakes. Fishing opportunities are also available along the Wallkill River.

At 15 miles, the trail meets the Historic Huguenot Street District in New Paltz, which was once home to American Indians and European settlers. Today the district includes a visitor center and local history archive, archaeological sites, historical stone houses, a reconstructed 1717 Huguenot church, a replica Munsee wigwam, and a burial ground that dates to the town's first European settlers.

From New Paltz, the trail intersects several others, including the new River-to-Ridge Trail, which extends 4.9 miles west to connect the Wallkill River and Shawangunk Ridge. Looking east, the western terminus of the 3.6-mile Hudson Valley Rail Trail is less than 3 miles away.

Continue another 7 miles south from New Paltz to finish your journey at the southern terminus in Wallkill. This spot is only 2.5 miles from the northern terminus of the 4.3-mile Walden–Wallkill Rail Trail traveling down to Walden and then Wallkill. Note that although no parking is available at the Wallkill end-point, you may find parking 2.5 miles north in Gardiner.

CONTACT: wallkillvalleylt.org

DIRECTIONS

To reach parking at the northern terminus from I-87, take Exit 18, and turn left to merge onto NY 299 W. In 1.0 mile, turn right onto New Paltz Bypass/N. Putt Corners Road. In 1.4 miles, turn left onto Shivertown Road, and go 1.1 miles; then turn right onto NY 32 N, and go 11.2 miles. Turn left off the highway onto Rockwell Terr., and go 0.1 mile to Rockwell Lane. Continue straight into a new gravel parking lot. Head to the far end of the parking lot and turn left to begin your journey south.

There is no designated parking area at the southern terminus, but trail users can find a parking lot 2.5 miles north in Gardiner. To reach this parking lot from I-87, take Exit 17 and continue straight toward NY 300. Turn left onto NY 300 N., and go 2.7 miles. Continue straight onto NY 32 N, and go 9.2 miles. Turn left onto US 44/Main St. in Gardiner. In 2.5 miles, turn right onto Second St. Parking is found immediately on the left, opposite the trail. From this trailhead, as you face the trail from the parking lot, you may either turn left and head 2.5 miles to the southern terminus or turn right to pick up the trail heading north.

Visitors can expect a couple of easy climbs as they travel on the Warren County Bikeway through the southern Adirondacks for 10 miles between Glens Falls and Lake George. It's well worth the effort, as visitors are rewarded with scenic views, ice cream stands, and the opportunity for a dip at a Lake George beach. Note that dogs are prohibited on the trail, and snowmobiles are allowed December–March between Bloody Pond Road and Fort George Road.

The area's combative early history is reflected in names like Old Military Road, Bloody Pond Road, and Lake George Battlefield Park. In fact, a cave on the Hudson River in Glens Falls inspired James Fenimore Cooper to write *The Last of the Mohicans,* a historical novel about the French and Indian War, in 1826.

The trail is among the earliest rail-trail conversions, with the project beginning in 1978. It follows a branch

Mid-trail, travelers will encounter the idyllic setting of Glen Lake.

County
Warren

Endpoints
Platt St. between Katherine St. and NY 32/Warren St. (Glens Falls) to W. Brook Road and Beach Road (Lake George)

Mileage
10.0

Type
Rail-Trail

Roughness Index
1

Surface
Asphalt

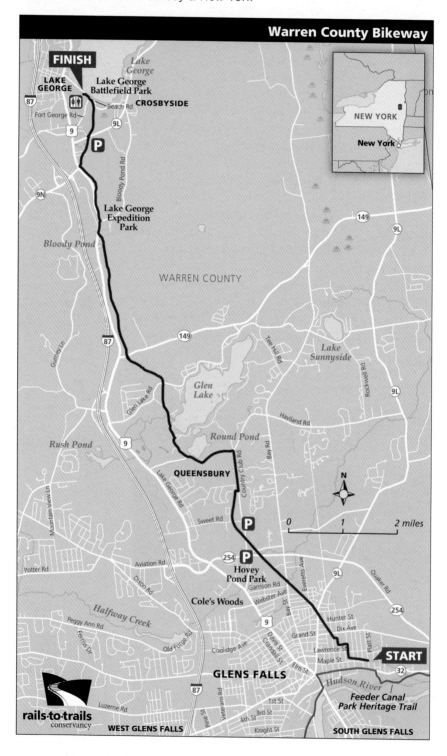

Warren County Bikeway

FINISH

LAKE GEORGE

Lake George Battlefield Park

CROSBYSIDE

Beach Rd

Fort George Rd

87

9

9L

9N

Lake George Expedition Park

Bloody Pond Rd

Lake George

Bloody Pond

WARREN COUNTY

87

Gurney Ln

149

Lake Sunnyside

Tee Hill Rd

Rockwell Rd

9L

149

9L

NEW YORK

New York

Glen Lake

Glen Lake Rd

Haviland Rd

Round Pond

Bay Rd

9

Rush Pond

Lake George Rd

QUEENSBURY

Country Club Rd

N

Sweet Rd

0   1   2 miles

Mountain View Ln

Potter Rd

Aviation Rd

Dixon Rd

254

P

P

Hovey Pond Park

Garrison Rd

Webster Ave

Everetts Ave

9L

Quaker Rd

254

Cole's Woods

Halfway Creek

Peggy Ann Rd

Ferris Dr

Old Forge Rd

9

Bay Rd

Davis St

Crandall St

Grand St

Hunter St

Dix Ave

Platt St

START

32

Coolidge Ave

Elm St

Lawrence St

Maple St

GLENS FALLS

Hudson River

Feeder Canal Park Heritage Trail

rails·to·trails
conservancy

Luzerne Rd

87

Veterans Rd

Pine St

1st St

3rd St

4th St

Knight St

WEST GLENS FALLS

SOUTH GLENS FALLS

of the Delaware & Hudson Railroad, which carried vacationers from the main branch to resorts and steamboat connections on the 32-mile-long Lake George. The trail's terminus in Glens Falls is about 0.1 mile north of the Feeder Canal Park Heritage Trail, which connects to the Champlain Canalway Trail. The latter pathway is part of New York's developing Empire State Trail system, which will span 750 miles.

Starting in Glens Falls, the trail climbs steadily about 8 miles before dropping 2 miles to Lake George. The trail begins on Platt Street, although trail parking is 0.5 mile ahead via trail and quiet residential streets.

The path leaves Glens Falls behind as it crosses NY 254 on a pedestrian bridge and enters Queensbury, an area originally settled by Quakers, who left during local fighting in the Revolutionary War. One mile past the bridge, take a left onto Country Club Road to follow a marked, 1.2-mile on-road segment. The trail resumes just west of Glen Lake, locally popular among anglers.

The trail enters a hardwood forest for the next 5 miles to Lake George, although tourist-oriented snack and refreshment stops are located at major road crossings such as NY 149 (6.2 miles from the start), Bloody Pond Road (8.1 miles), and NY 9L (9.3 miles). The trail's high point comes at mile 8.1, where it crosses Bloody Pond Road; this is also the site of the Lake George Expedition Park, which features dinosaur-themed kiddie rides.

From here it's a 2-mile downhill jaunt to the town of Lake George, where you'll find such tourist attractions as a sandy beach, a steamboat dock, restaurants, taverns, ice cream shops, and a Spanish mission–style train station. The trail ends at Lake George Battlefield Park, which commemorates vicious fighting here during the French and Indian War.

Long-range plans call for extending the trail 7 miles north to Warrensburg.

CONTACT: warrencountydpw.com/parks_rec07/bikeway.htm

DIRECTIONS

To reach the Glens Falls trailhead from I-87, take Exit 18, and head east toward Glens Falls on Main St./County Road 18. Go 0.8 mile, and continue straight onto Broad St.; then go 0.4 mile, and bear right onto Hudson Ave. Go 0.8 mile, and take the second exit on the traffic circle onto NY 32/Warren St. Go 0.2 mile, and turn left onto Center St. Then go 0.1 mile, and turn right onto Maple St. Go 0.3 mile, and turn left onto Leonard St. Go 0.2 mile, and look for parking on the left. To reach the eastern endpoint, backtrack on Leonard St. 0.2 mile and turn left onto the trail. The endpoint is 0.3 mile ahead at Platt St.

To reach the Lake George village trailhead from I-87, take Exit 21, and head northeast onto NY 9N. Go about 0.2 mile, and turn left onto US 9. Go 0.9 mile, and turn right onto W. Brook Road/CR 69. You'll find on-street parking on W. Brook Road.

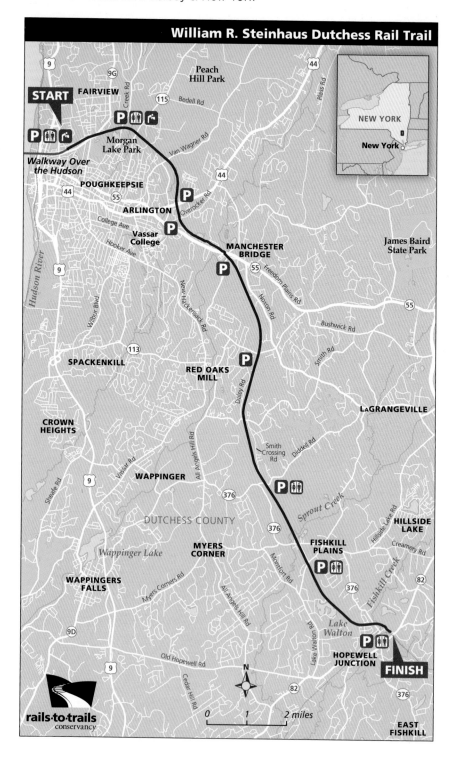

William R. Steinhaus Dutchess Rail Trail

The William R. Steinhaus Dutchess Rail Trail—named for the county executive who championed it—is a local treasure in the Hudson Valley region of New York. The 13.1-mile trail runs through what seems like a perpetually green landscape of dense tree cover, linking Poughkeepsie at the Hudson River with smaller towns to the southeast.

At its Poughkeepsie end, the Dutchess Rail Trail begins at a shared parking lot with the Walkway Over the Hudson State Historic Park (see page 193). The stunning converted railroad bridge takes trail users over the Hudson River and leads directly to the Hudson Valley Rail Trail (see page 131) in Ulster County. Together, the three rail-trails were welcomed into Rails-to-Trails Conservancy's Rail-Trail Hall of Fame in 2016 and offer a seamless, combined route of just over 20 miles. They are also part of the Empire State Trail, a developing 750-mile trail network spanning the state from New York City to Canada and Buffalo to Albany.

At the southern end of the trail is Hopewell Depot, built in 1873; take time to explore the historical museum inside.

County
Dutchess

Mileage
13.1

Endpoints
Walkway Over the Hudson trailhead at 61 Parker Ave. (Poughkeepsie) to Martin Road and NY 82 (Hopewell Junction)

Type
Rail-Trail

Roughness Index
1

Surface
Asphalt

Traveling east from Poughkeepsie, the route passes a large golf course and Morgan Lake Park, a popular spot for fishing. After Morgan Lake, the trail begins to turn south, running through the communities of Arlington and LaGrangeville and skirting the eastern edge of Red Oaks Mill. This section includes an expansive bridge over NY 55, and the entire length of the trail features a mixture of new bridges and converted railroad bridges and tunnels.

In Wappinger, trail users travel along a section called Veterans Memorial Mile, which features signage honoring each of the five branches of the military. Traversing a wooded corridor, this segment offers a quiet place to reflect and remember those who have served their country.

The path continues through the town of East Fishkill and ends in Hopewell Junction. Approaching the terminus, you'll pass the Hopewell Depot. Built in 1873, this former hub on the Maybrook Line of the New York, New Haven and Hartford Railroad now offers a museum and historical photo gallery inside. Across from the depot, visitors will also find a replica switching tower.

CONTACT: co.dutchess.ny.us/CountyGov/Departments/DPW-Parks/17055.htm

DIRECTIONS

On its northern end, the Dutchess Rail Trail shares a trailhead with the Walkway Over the Hudson at 61 Parker Ave. in Poughkeepsie. To reach this parking lot from I-84, take Exit 13, and head north on US 9. Continue on US 9 N for 14.4 miles to NY 9G in Poughkeepsie; you will travel under the Walkway Over the Hudson on the way to this exit. Look for brown WALKWAY OVER THE HUDSON directional signs as you approach your exit. Turn right onto NY 9G, which becomes Washington St., for 0.6 mile. Turn left onto Parker Ave. In 0.3 mile, a large parking lot will appear on your left.

To reach the trailhead parking lot in Hopewell Junction from I-84, take Exit 16N for the Taconic State Pkwy. Take the parkway 3.9 miles to Exit 41 for Beekman Road/County Road 9. Take a left onto Beekman Road, and continue 2.2 miles, when the road merges with NY 82. Take your next right after the merger; this will be Turner St. A parking lot will appear on your right almost immediately after the turn onto Turner St.

Additional parking lots are available along the trail's route at nearly every major road intersection.

Popular with residents of Saratoga County who commute under their own power or love to exercise outdoors, the nearly 9-mile Zim Smith Mid-County Trail is considered the backbone of a growing trail system, with connections to major tech companies and hiking trails. Near-term plans call for extending the trail east to Mechanicville by late 2019 or early 2020 for an eventual connection to the future Champlain Canalway Trail. Longer-term plans propose a northern route through Saratoga Spa State Park to Railroad Run in Saratoga Springs. The trail, named for local historic preservationist Zimri Smith, has been honored as a National Recreation Trail by the U.S. Department of the Interior.

The trail follows an old railroad corridor completed as the Rensselaer and Saratoga Railroad between Ballston

Sections of the Zim Smith Mid-County Trail offer a remote wooded feel.

County
Saratoga

Endpoints
Oak St., 0.3 mile south of
E. High St. (Ballston Spa),
to Coons Crossing Road
between Ushers Road
and NY 67 (Halfmoon)

Mileage
8.9

Type
Rail-Trail/Rail-with-Trail

Roughness Index
1–2

Surfaces
Asphalt, Crushed Stone

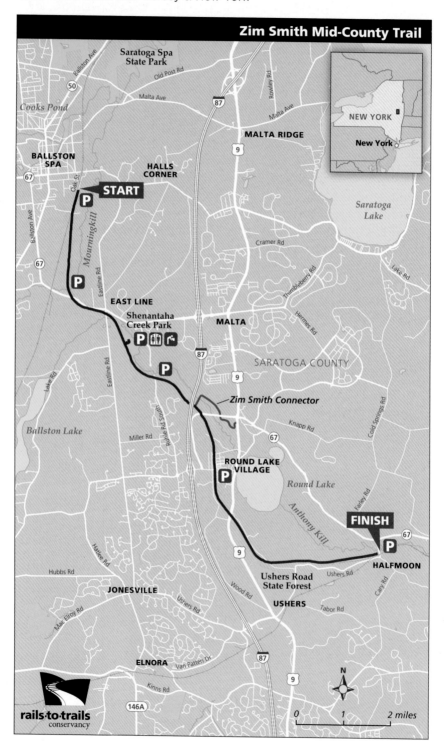

Zim Smith Mid-County Trail

Spa and Troy in 1836. Leased by the Delaware & Hudson (D&H) Railroad beginning in 1871, it was acquired by D&H in 1945.

Ballston Spa marks the northern trailhead. At one time, four railroads passed through the village, founded near a mineral spring known for its curative powers. The paved trail starts out along an active railroad for a short distance, a configuration known as rail-with-trail, before veering into the woods, passing an industrial park, and arriving at Shenantaha Creek Park. The name means "deer water" in Iroquois, and you can find flax mill ruins there. The park also has restrooms and a drinking fountain, as well as other recreational amenities.

The path rolls through remote woodland another 1.5 miles until it passes beneath I-87 and beside a dirt trail on the left known as the Zim Smith Connector. The connector goes 1.2 miles east to US 9 in Malta, where it connects to a paved trail system serving the Luther Forest Technology Campus, home of chip makers and other tech companies.

In another mile, a handsome white-frame church and other period buildings signal your arrival in Round Lake Village, which is listed on the National Register of Historic Places. The Victorian village, with quiet streets and gingerbread cottages featuring long porches, recalls a time when it served as a Methodist camp meeting site with thousands of visitors every summer. The Round Lake Auditorium, dating from the late 1800s on Wesley Avenue, is home to a working 1,900-pipe organ that was named a National Historic Landmark in 2017.

Leaving Round Lake, the trail crosses US 9 in 0.7 mile. The crushed-stone surface on these last 3 miles will be paved with asphalt as part of the Mechanicville extension project. The trail passes bird-viewing spots in the wetlands and currently ends at Coons Crossing Road in Halfmoon. The extension will travel about 3 miles along the south side of the railroad yard to Elizabeth Street Extension in Mechanicville.

CONTACT: saratogaplan.org/explore/public-preserves-trails/zim-smith-trail

DIRECTIONS

To reach the Ballston Spa trailhead from I-87, take Exit 13S toward US 9 S. Go 0.6 mile on US 9 S, and turn right onto Malta Ave./County Road 63. Go 2.9 miles, and turn left onto Hyde Blvd.; then go 0.6 mile, and turn left onto E. High St. Go 0.2 mile, and turn right onto Oak St. Go 0.3 mile, and look for parking at the end of the street.

To reach the Coons Crossing trailhead from I-87, take Exit 10 to Ushers Road. Head northeast on Ushers Road 0.7 mile, and veer left to stay on Ushers Road; then go 0.6 mile, and bear right to stay on Ushers Road. Go 1.3 miles, and turn left onto Cary Road/Coons Crossing Road. Go about 300 feet and look for parking on the left or right.

Summer wildflowers decorate New York's Wallkill Valley Rail Trail (see page 196).

Page iii: TrailLink user slipsoup; *page vi:* Brian Housh; *page ix:* Ryan Cree; *page x:* courtesy of Cattaraugus County Tourism; *page 7:* Torsha Bhattacharya; *page 9:* courtesy of the Atlantic County Parks and Recreation; *page 11:* TrailLink user measure55; *pages 15 and 16:* TrailLink user rcpat; *page 19:* Anthony Le; *pages 21 and 23:* Kevin Mills; *page 27:* TrailLink user magseg; *page 29:* TrailLink user rcpat; *pages 31 and 33:* Avery Harmon; *pages 35 and 38:* Leeann Sinpatanasakul; *page 41:* TrailLink user c8user; *page 43:* Yvonne Mwangi; *page 47:* TrailLink user rcpat; *page 49:* TrailLink user slipsoup; *page 51:* TrailLink user realhoff; *page 55:* Leah Gerber; *page 57:* Kevin Belanger; *page 61:* Leah Gerber; *page 63:* Anthony Le; *page 65:* Torsha Bhattacharya; *page 69:* Leeann Sinpatanasakul; *page 73:* Kevin Belanger; *page 75:* TrailLink user 2mules; *page 77:* courtesy of Cattaraugus County Tourism; *page 81:* TrailLink user davewright; *page 83:* Kevin Belanger; *page 87:* Andrew Dupuy; *pages 91 and 92:* Torsha Bhattacharya; *page 96:* Brian Housh; *page 97:* TrailLink user powerkatie; *page 101:* Yvonne Mwangi; *page 105:* TrailLink user eglerb; *page 106:* TrailLink user npevans; *page 108:* TrailLink user irishrunner; *pages 112 and 115:* Eli Griffen; *page 117:* Andrew Dupuy; *page 119:* Brandi Horton; *page 121:* Katie Guerin; *page 125:* Scott Stark; *page 129:* Torsha Bhattacharya; *page 131:* Fred Schaeffer; *pages 135 and 136:* Anthony Le; *page 139:* TrailLink user kocka10; *page 141:* TrailLink user willbike; *page 145:* Brian Housh; *page 147:* TrailLink user loluvlinkinpark; *page 152:* Eli Griffen; *page 155:* TrailLink user apps224; *page 157:* Patrick Wojahn; *page 160:* Anthony Le; *pages 163 and 167:* Yvonne Mwangi; *page 169:* Betsy Franco Feeney; *page 173:* Suzanne Matyas; *page 174:* Anthony Le; *page 177:* courtesy of Cattaraugus County Tourism; *page 179:* TrailLink user crbrown87; *page 183:* Andrew Goodwillie; *page 185:* Torsha Bhattacharya; *page 187:* Yvonne Mwangi; *page 189:* TrailLink user linda.payson; *page 191:* TrailLink user fd8838; *page 193:* Aaron Schmidt; *page 197:* Brian Housh; *page 199:* TrailLink user markemarks; *page 203:* Brandi Horton; *page 205:* TrailLink user slipsoup; *page 210:* Brandi Horton.

The nation's leader in helping communities transform unused rail lines and connecting corridors into multiuse trails, Rails-to-Trails Conservancy (RTC) depends on the support of its members and donors to create access to healthy outdoor experiences.

Your donation will help support programs and services that have helped put more than 23,000 rail-trail miles on the ground. Every day, RTC provides vital assistance to communities to develop and maintain trails throughout the country. In addition, RTC advocates for trail-friendly policies, promotes the benefits of rail-trails, and defends rail-trail laws in the courts.

Join online at **railstotrails.org,** or mail your donation to Rails-to-Trails Conservancy, 2121 Ward Court NW, Fifth Floor, Washington, D.C. 20037.

Rails-to-Trails Conservancy is a 501(c)(3) nonprofit organization, and contributions are tax deductible.

SHARE THE TRAIL

Be nice.
Trails are for everyone.

Calling all trail users! Rails-to-Trails Conservancy
challenges YOU to be the best you can be on America's pathways!
Remember—safe + fun = a great time for everyone!

#sharethetrail

Visit **railstotrails.org/sharethetrail** for more.